# Shooting Leave
### SPYING OUT CENTRAL ASIA
### IN THE GREAT GAME

## John Ure

*Illustrations by Toby Ward*

CONSTABLE · LONDON

For my grandson,
Thomas Alexander Burns Ure,
born on the day this book was completed

Constable & Robinson Ltd
3 The Lanchesters
162 Fulham Palace Road
London W6 9ER
www.constablerobinson.com

First published in the UK in hardback by Constable,
an imprint of Constable & Robinson Ltd, 2009.
This paperback edition published in 2010

A copy of the British Library Cataloguing in Publication Data
is available from the British Library

ISBN: 978-1-84901-469-4

Printed and bound in the EU

'For Allah created the English mad – the maddest of all mankind.'

– Rudyard Kipling (1865–1936), in *Kitchener's School*

# CENTRAL ASIA
## IN THE
## GREAT GAME

SIA

CHINA

*Lake Balkhash*

*Issyk Kul*

*Tien Shan Mountains*

■ Osh

■ Kashgar

*Taklamakan
Desert*

*Baroghil
Pass*   *Darkot Pass*
■ Kunduz   *Ishkoman Pass*   *Khunjerab Pass*
■ Hunza
Gilgit ■   *Mustagh Pass*

*Hindu Kush*

KASHMIR

■ Kabul   *Khyber Pass*   Attock
■ Peshawar        ■

PUNJAB

TIBET

■ Lahore
■ Simla

*Himalayas*

■ Lhasa

*Indus River*

INDIA

SINDH

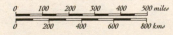

0   100   200   300   400   500 miles

0   200   400   600   800 kms

# Contents

# Acknowledgements

A travel book owes much to those who have helped one along the way, but a work about the travels of others over a century ago is a more solitary affair. Nevertheless I am grateful to those who first aroused my interest in Central Asia and encouraged me to travel there and develop a curiosity about my remarkable predecessors. Chief among those who inspired me in this way were the late Sir Fitzroy Maclean and my ambassador in Moscow in the 1950s – the late Sir Patrick Reilly, who had a family connection (explained in this book) with the Great Game. My enthusiasm for the region and for the subject was also greatly enhanced by earlier writers, ranging from John Buchan through Peter Hopkirk and John Keay to Colin Thubron.

As always, I am indebted to the staff of the London Library, and also of the British Library (India Office records) and the Royal Geographical Society for their help in tracking down source material.

I am particularly grateful to my diplomatic colleague and friend Sir Nicholas Fenn (a former High Commissioner to India) for finding time to read the typescript of this book and offer valuable comments, at a moment when he had many other more pressing preoccupations.

I would also like to thank Toby Ward, the distinguished

artist-in-residence at St Martin's-in-the-Fields, for having taken the trouble to read this book carefully and provide all the line drawings in the text.

# A Personal Preface

The region that James Elroy Flecker's called the 'last blue mountain barred with snow' has an enduring appeal. Ever since making a first expedition to Central Asia – then largely under Soviet jurisdiction – and Afghanistan from my post at the British embassy in Moscow in the late 1950s, I have been intrigued with the whole area. This is indeed, as Robert Byron said, 'where Asia loses her inferiority complex', where boys behave as men, and where men accept you on their own terms and not on yours. During my first night in Kabul, I was invited on a five-day shooting trip in the Hindu Kush by an Afghan prince and warlord whose reputation was terrifying; but I never felt safer than as his guest in the mountains.

Subsequent trips from Moscow took me overland into Iran (or Persia, as the land of the Shahs still seemed to be). Sometimes I travelled alone, jumping train on one occasion in Erevan (the capital of Armenia) and giving the slip to my KGB minders. Sometimes I took what Flecker described as the 'golden road to Samarkand . . . for lust of knowing what should not be known'. This was a period so long before glasnost that the outer reaches of the Soviet Union were opaque to the point of impenetrability. Any information became intelligence; any trip an adventure. At other times I explored the Caucasus with my ambassador or – more excitingly – Uzbekistan with Sir Fitzroy Maclean, who had held my job at the embassy just 20 years before and who had memorably recorded his own early travels to Bokhara in his book *Eastern Approaches*. I could have had no more entertaining and instructive travelling companion.

I was to revisit the region in the 1970s when retracing Tamerlane's great fifteenth-century campaign from Samarkand to the Bosphorus; researching later books on the Cossacks and on nomads also drew me back to the area in the 1980s; and in the 1990s I was to lead groups of travellers on the silk road across Asia and on a tour – specially devised with the help of Peter Hopkirk – entitled 'The Great Game', which began at the Khyber Pass and penetrated, via Gilgit and Hunza, into the Pamir and Tien Shan mountains before ending at Khiva, Bokhara and Samarkand.

The more ground I covered, the more I felt I was treading in the footsteps of my compatriots of a century before. Young army officers (as I had been a year or two before) and young political officers (as I was as a junior diplomatic secretary at the embassy) were dispatched or encouraged to go on shooting leave – very much as I had been in Afghanistan and elsewhere – to find out about closed areas and to make contact with local chiefs: in their case khans and emirs, in my case commissars and apparatchiks.

All my compatriots of a century earlier had been involved in the Great Game – the century-long confrontation between the British Raj in Simla and the court of the Tsars in St Petersburg – which was similar to the game I was involved in during the Cold War. As I began to identify particular nineteenth-century officers and political agents, I soon discovered they were all very different from each other: some were arrogant imperialists; some were almost missionary-like in their Christian zeal; some were chancers and bounders; some were committed sportsmen to whom the shooting was more important than the leave; most described themselves as English (though often, in fact, they were Scottish) and some were not compatriots at all, but Russians; all were enterprising and brave; and most had faced much greater danger and shown much more daring than I had ever been called upon to do. In writing about them I have tried to establish their personalities as well as their achievements, their place in society as well as their place in the mountain passes and deserts of Central Asia.

Inevitably, my selection of candidates has been somewhat arbitrary. There are no common denominators – in terms of nationality, profession, age, or even shooting enthusiasm – that apply to all of them. The criteria for selection have been their dash and daring, their desire to mix sport and duty, their operation as individuals rather than as part of organized military units or diplomatic missions and their patriotic commitment to the cause in hand.

And that cause was a common cause. Whether they came north from India or south from Russia, they were part of the Great Game's struggle for mastery of Central Asia. I have tried to indicate where their adventures fitted into the pattern of the struggle between the Raj and the Tsars, and to fill in enough of the context of that confrontation – be it the briefly perceived threat of a Franco-Russian alliance, the Afghan Wars, the Crimean War or the Indian Mutiny. What I have not tried to do is to write another comprehensive history of the Great Game itself; this has been done already – notably by Peter Hopkirk to whom all students of this period and this part of the world are indebted. Mine is a series of vignettes or snapshots, not a panoramic view.

As with the characters, so also with the geography: it is selective. It could be argued that Tibet and the Sinkiang province of China caused the same sort of anxieties to the British authorities in India as did Persia, Afghanistan and the khanates of Central Asia, but with a few exceptions, the shooting-leave adventures of the young officers largely took place in the mountain ranges of the Pamirs and Hindu Kush or the steppes around the Caspian and Aral Seas. Those other eastern terrains were more the province of experienced explorers, commercially orientated traders and fully equipped armies, rather than young 'blades' intent on mixing sport and spying.

Turning to more recent times, those who explored the remote parts of Central Asia and particularly Afghanistan in the 1950s, 1960s and 1970s tended to think of this region as a private world which one shared with the heroes of John Buchan novels, with Eric Newby or with those who had been bold enough – like Sandy Gall – to report on the ground about the Russian–Afghan running hostilities of the 1980s. Then, after the assault on the twin towers in New York in September 2001, the whole world quite suddenly became aware of the terrain of Afghanistan and her neighbours. Regular troops, journalists, special forces and others converged on this strange stage: the Hindu Kush, Panjshir Valley and Helmand Province became household names; the dust and rocks, the Kalashnikovs and funny hats, the handsome bearded faces and angry eyes of Pathan tribesmen all filled our television screens.

Perhaps the stories of my nineteenth-century heroes are now more relevant than they would have been a few years ago. It will be easier to identify with those Victorian characters who risked their lives in this region, as have so many in the opening years of the twentieth-first century. Be that as it may, their stories stand for themselves and in their own right.

# Introduction to the Frontier

'The legend's writ, the frontier-grave is far away.'
– Sir Henry Newbolt (1862–1938), in *Clifton Chapel*

Although the expression 'the jewel in the crown' was not applied to India until Victorian times, its value had been apparent to the British from the start. But a jewel of value attracts predators and must be protected.

The British first consolidated their mastery of the subcontinent in the late eighteenth century, but in the opening years of the nineteenth century two such predators appeared on the horizon. The first and most obvious was the northern empire of tsarist Russia; ever since the days of Peter the Great, successive tsars had cast covetous eyes in the direction of the riches of India – a land, as they saw it, of rajahs and rubies, golden temples, wide rivers and lush paddy fields.

The other and more recent menace was Britain's inveterate foe: Napoleon Bonaparte. Although primarily a threat to his European neighbours, Napoleon had also shown an alarming interest in destinations further east. In 1798 he had invaded Egypt with an army of 40,000 troops and he had engaged in correspondence first with Tsar Paul I and later – more seriously – with Tsar Alexander I about the possibility of a joint invasion of British India and a carve-up of the spoils. There had been periods, notably after the peace talks at Tilsit in 1807 and before the French invasion of Russia in 1812, when there seemed a real possibility of such a wild venture being embarked upon.

Any invasion route would have had to pass through Persia and Afghanistan, and fears about French and Russian intentions were heightened by the discovery that both countries were courting the Shah of Persia and the King of Afghanistan, and trying to establish a diplomatic and quasi-military presence in those countries.

There was not long to wait before the French threat was removed: with Napoleon in full retreat from Moscow across the frozen terrain of Russia, the prospect of his venturing further into Asia evaporated for good. However, the Russian threat increased throughout the nineteenth century. Alexander and his successors were to pick up and run with the ambition of Peter the Great. As the decades passed, there was a steady Russian expansion into the Caucasus, with its access to Persia, and into Central Asia, with its access into Afghanistan and the mountain ranges – the Hindu Kush, the Pamirs and the western Himalayas – which formed the natural boundary and defences of British India.

During the same period, particularly during the first half of the nineteenth century, the British had also been expanding the bounds of empire. Lord Clive, having won the battle of Plassey in 1757 and established control over most of central India, declared that 'to stop is dangerous, to recede is ruin', and his successors had continued to press forward. On the one hand, this expansion widened the buffer zone between the vulnerable heartland of India and any aggressors from the north. On the other hand, an ever-shifting frontier meant that the fringes of empire were always virtually unknown territory to the imperial power. Vast tracts of mostly mountain and desert territory were a hidden hinterland as far as the governor-general in Calcutta was concerned and an even greater mystery to the British government in London. Someone, somehow, had to reconnoitre this hinterland to determine how easy it would be for an enemy to penetrate it, and to see how practicable it would be for the British Raj to defend it.

Until the reforms following the Indian Mutiny of 1857, the British military presence in India had not been predominantly the British army but the army of the Honourable East India Company – colloquially known as 'John Company'. This was divided into three 'presidencies': Bombay, Bengal and Madras. The commander-in-chief and, indeed, the governor-general himself, who were based in Calcutta and moved to the hill station of Simla in the hot and monsoon seasons, reported ultimately to the directors of the East India Company in London. Although the rank and file, the NCOs and the junior (or 'native') officers of the East India Company army were Indians – 'sepoys' – they were under the command of British officers holding commissions from the Company.

These officers had usually been trained at one or other of the Company's schools in England: East India Company College (founded by the Company in 1806 and still a flourishing English public school called Haileybury College) or Addiscombe College (founded in 1809 and no longer in existence). The latter in particular produced many of the men who feature in this book, and the college was the subject of a self-congratulatory book by a

Colonel Vibart in 1894 which is packed with merry tales of the pranks of the young cadets – a sort of cross between *Tom Brown's Schooldays* and Rudyard Kipling's *Stalky & Co*. Vibart even persuaded General Sir Frederick 'Bobs' Roberts VC (himself an old Addiscombe boy) to write an introduction to the book in which he refers to it as a 'rough and ready sort of school' and goes on to 'wonder whether the greater refinement – indeed luxuries – to be found in some schools of the present day is as beneficial to boys as the less softening influences of Addiscombe [where cadets were] prepared to uphold the honour of their country and to fight for its interests in a land [India] where every-thing – public safety, national honour, personal reputation – rests on the force of individual character'. No wonder that by the time they reached India these officers had developed a degree of camaraderie. Their units were reinforced by regiments of the regular British army whose officers held the King's or Queen's commission and would mostly have been trained at the Royal Military Academy at Sandhurst (established there in 1812).

It was this corps of young officers who were to be charged with the challenging, exciting but arduous task of spying out the unknown hinterland – the deserts of Baluchistan in southern Persia, the steppes of Kazakhstan and the emirates of Central Asia, and the mountain passes of the Hindu Kush, the Pamirs and the Karakorams. The task was as much political as military, and frequently they were seconded to the Political Service of the Raj. They were an elite band who needed ingenuity as well as courage, robust physique as well as intelligence, patience as well as daring. Sometimes they travelled in humble disguises: Lieutenant Henry Pottinger, travelling across Baluchistan in 1810, started off in the guise of a Tartar horse dealer and switched to that of a Muslim pilgrim, which landed him in difficulty with inquiring mullahs. Sometimes they paraded the glories of their regimental uniforms to impress local emirs or tribal chiefs. Either way, things could – and frequently did – go badly wrong.

However, there were compensations: usually these young subalterns were ambitious as well as brave and knew that reconnaissance achievements on the frontier would be likely to draw them to the attention not only of senior officers but also of the governor-general or viceroy himself. Many of them went on to achieve distinguished careers in their own right, some being rewarded with knighthoods in the Order of the Indian Empire or in the more prestigious Order of the Star of India.

Sometimes the political content of their brief was greater than the military or geographical: the objective of a long journey through fearsome terrain infested by hostile tribesmen might be to make discreet contact with some mysterious, despotic but influential emir or chieftain. Along with ammunition and camping equipment, they would carry desirable gifts such as duelling pistols or ivory-handled daggers.

But whatever their specific task, one factor remained common to all these young officers sent out on covert and exploratory missions: they were expendable. Disappearance without trace was a risk they knowingly accepted. They may have been encouraged by the knowledge that their potential enemy – the tsarist government in St Petersburg – was dispatching its own young officers on similar missions; and in the same way that well-born English officers served alongside Indian troops, Russian aristocrats (including Count Tolstoy and the poet Mikhail Lermontov) served alongside the roughest Cossack units.

These young officers – usually still subalterns – were not the only instrument in the hands of the nervous frontier authorities. There were qualified cartographers and engineers from the various Indian Survey teams. There were also – from about 1860 onwards – a body of native espionage agents known as 'pundits' who often disguised themselves as holy men and measured distances with abacuses hidden in rosaries, log books and compasses concealed in prayer wheels, and thermometers (for calculating altitude) inside pilgrim staves. Their contribution to the mapping of the frontier was impressive and has been chronicled elsewhere.

Sometimes the frontiers and the forbidden regions beyond them were revealed by the brutal expedient of sending in columns of troops or armies without adequate reconnaissance. The Afghan Wars, the Sikh Wars and Sir Charles Napier's campaign to conquer Sindh in 1842 were all examples of this more heavy-handed approach: occupation rather than exploration. These campaigns, too, have been recorded extensively elsewhere.

The young British officers with whom this book is concerned have often only had walk-on roles in other memorable books about the Great Game; they will be centre-stage in this one.

Some were fiercely imperialistic; some were ardently Christian; some were embarrassingly vainglorious; others were modest and self-deprecating; all were distinctive characters in their own right who had remarkable tales to tell and a ready – but long-forgotten – audience in Victorian England. While their superiors – the colonels and generals – have generally usurped the limelight, there were good reasons why these exploratory missions had to be assigned to young officers. Foremost among these reasons was the health factor. Indian army life, with its many months of every year spent sweltering on the plains or enduring the rains, was not conducive to long life and fitness. William Hodson (who raised Hodson's Horse – later to become the 10th Bengal Lancers) wrote home to his father: 'At the age at which officers become colonels and majors, not one in fifty is able to stand the wear and tear of Indian service. They become still more worn in mind than in body. All elasticity has gone; all energy and enterprise worn out.' And he went on to recount how, in the Second Sikh War of 1848–9, one cavalry brigade commander needed two men to help him mount his horse, and one infantry brigadier was so blind that he could not tell which way his men were facing on the battlefield.

The officers who are the subject of this book tended to be not only young but also good horsemen, good swordsmen and first-class shots. Indeed, shooting wildlife was one of the lures to venturing into the mountains: deer and wolves, ibex and mouflon, panthers and snow leopards . . . all were sought after as trophies and for entries in the game book. Hunters were as yet untroubled by considerations of conservation.

In recent times, it has become fashionable to query whether the Russian threat to India was ever as great as it was perceived. Even during the nineteenth century, British governments of different persuasions took different views: Conservative governments and ministers – notably Lord Curzon – tended to be hawkish and see the threat as real and requiring a forward policy to halt it; Liberal governments – notably those of Mr Gladstone – tended to discount the threat and prefer a policy of masterly inactivity.

Those who favoured a forward policy were encouraged by the relentless advance of Russia into Central Asia. The khanates and emirates fell like ninepins: Samarkand in 1868, Bokhara effectively in the same year, Khiva in 1873, Khokand in 1875, Geok Tepe in 1881 and Merv (now known as Mary) in 1882. Also, there was never any shortage of Russian leaders and army officers making aggressive and provocative statements about their intentions. One of the most explicit was Captain Terentyeff who, in his book *Russia and England in the East* (published in the 1870s), touched on a particularly raw nerve as far as the British were concerned: the possibility of another Indian Mutiny coinciding with an invasion attempt by Russia. Many British officers considered that if the Russians had not been still reeling from their loss of the Crimean War at the time of the Indian Mutiny in 1857, they might have taken massive advantage of the situation. In a passage quoted by Captain Fred Burnaby, Terentyeff wrote: 'Sick to death, the natives [of India] are now waiting for a physician from the North. Some time will naturally elapse before they care to repeat the experiment of 1857 . . . but it cannot be said with any certainty that small sparks of rebellion may not, if supported by an impetus from without, produce a general conflagration throughout the length and breadth of India.'

On the other hand, the doves in British politics were quick to point out that the Russian performance in the Crimean War had not been very impressive, particularly when it was considered that they were operating on their own territory with open lines of communication and supply. India presented vastly greater logistical problems, as the Tsar's abortive attempts on Khiva earlier in the nineteenth century had shown. In the closing era of the Great Game, there was also the disappointing performance of Russia in the Russo-Japanese War of 1904–5 to cast doubt on the effectiveness of a far-flung Russian campaign.

While all this debate was going on, it was not only on the frontiers of India that young British officers took time off to explore. Wherever the tentacles of the British empire extended, and even in regions where they did not, intrepid military travellers made explorations. As I recounted in *Cucumber Sandwiches in the Andes* (1973), Lieutenant Charles Brand (of the Royal Navy) and Captain Francis Head (an army officer with an interest in geology) set out to cross the Andes in the mid-1820s and had innumerable adventures with raging torrents, rickety bridges, frost-bitten and frozen companions (some of whom did not survive), and recalcitrant mules. There was a tradition of finding time for enterprising and daring exploits.

However, the practice was most evident and most productive in India. Young officers spent their local leave (as opposed to their 'furlough' or home leave every few years) on shooting expeditions in the foothills of the Himalayas, and their longer treks – instigated and authorized by the authorities to spy out the mountain passes – were to become euphemistically known as 'shooting leave'. It was ironic that what was described as 'leave' should in fact constitute the most dangerous and demanding tasks they would ever undertake in their whole lives.

# Chapter 1

## Henry Pottinger:
## The Make-Believe Holy Man

'We have just enough religion to make us hate, but not enough
to make us love one another.'
    – Jonathan Swift (1667–1745), in *Thoughts on Various Subjects*

Late in the evening of 2 January 1810, two young British officers from the Honourable East India Company – Captain Charles
Christie and Lieutenant Henry Pottinger, both of the Bombay
Native Infantry regiment – embarked furtively on a small boat
in Bombay harbour and set sail westward up the coast towards
Gujarat and Baluchistan. They were disguised as Muslim horse-
dealers and accompanied by an agent of their supposed employer
and a couple of Hindustani servants who were sworn to secrecy.
Also on board were a number of genuine Afghan horse-dealers
who had no reason to doubt their story and whose presence lent
some credibility to the whole enterprise.

The expedition was a unique one which had its origins in the
power politics of Europe. Ever since General Bonaparte (shortly
to become the Emperor Napoleon I) had invaded Egypt with his
formidable French army, he was known to have had ambitions
in the East. And the ultimate objective of such ambitions was
inevitably the rich prize of India, currently – but not irrevocably

as far as he was concerned – under the rule of his bitterest enemy: Britain. The French had been preparing the way for an overland advance towards India: they had not only accredited an ambassador to the court of the Shah of Persia, but this envoy and his staff were known to be assiduous in collecting intelligence about the surrounding countryside over which their army would have to march.

Both the governor-general in India – Lord Minto – and the British government in London viewed these developments with concern, if not alarm. Each of them had sent a representative to the Persian court and the governor-general's envoy, Brigadier General Sir John Malcolm, had been authorized to employ 'political assistants or surveyors' who could make their own assessment of the terrain between Persia and India, essentially the vast tract of unknown land called Baluchistan. This was the mission on which Christie and Pottinger embarked that dark winter evening in Bombay.

It was a dangerous mission for a number of reasons: the land was uncharted; it consisted largely of desert, poorly punctuated with wells; the natives of Baluchistan were known to be deeply suspicious and hostile towards European intruders (who were assumed – not without reason – to be the forerunners of conquering armies); and, as if all these were not sufficient hazards, the whole region was riddled with bands of brigands who could ambush anyone unwise enough to travel through their territory.

Christie and Pottinger were both from a stable of typically brave young officers, but Pottinger – whose separate exploits and whose own published account we are to follow closely – had demonstrated from a very early age an exceptional talent for adventure. He was born in Ireland in 1789 and sent to school at Belfast Academy, but at the age of 12 he ran away to sea. Soon afterwards, in 1803, he managed to get a passage to India to join the marine service there. At this juncture, his career was radically changed by intervention from an unexpected quarter: Lord Castlereagh, a fellow Irishman who was later to become one of the most celebrated of all British foreign secretaries, had been appointed the previous year as president of the East India Company's board of control, and he now decided to secure a cadetship for the young Henry Pottinger in the Company's army. This was a more promising prospect than any that had previously been open to him, and it involved a prolonged period of studying Indian customs and languages in Bombay. Pottinger showed a flair for this and by the end of 1806 – at the age of 17 – he was gazetted as an ensign in the Bombay Native Infantry. Four years later, as he set out with Christie to sail along the coast towards Baluchistan, he was already a lieutenant with some campaigning experience in Sindh behind him.

Once Christie and Pottinger landed on the coast of Baluchistan they realized they would have to take their disguises even more seriously: 'we completely metamorphosed ourselves, by having our heads shaved and adopting the entire native costume', Pottinger wrote. They took advice from a local merchant about the acceptability of the present they had brought from Bombay to ease their path; they were told that some Scottish tartan rugs would not be well received as they were too like the local blankets (but that advice proved to be quite mistaken). They also had help in procuring suitable camels for the journey and took on the services of an Afghan guide who had genuine experience of horse-dealing. Other merchants tried in a kindly way to warn them not to take the trail to Kalat (the capital of Baluchistan) as the local Bezunja tribe 'care not for the king, the khan, God, or the Prophet, but murder and plunder every person and thing they can lay their hands on'.

To start with, the terrain was not too dire but the flat countryside was uncultivated with patches of impenetrable jungle. The villagers were busy tending their flocks and herds. They had one nasty shock early on when – by an extraordinary stroke of bad luck – a water-carrier recognized them both from a chance encounter the previous year when the two officers had been on the military campaign into Sindh. They talked their way out of it by explaining that they had changed their occupation since then and that they were now itinerant horse-traders. They moved on quickly, with their confidence in the disguise badly shaken.

At Bela, the next settlement they reached, they had another narrow squeak. The chief had received a letter from a local merchant warning him that Christie and Pottinger were agents of the East India Company exploring the country with a view to its occupation by the British, and that they should – at best – be promptly sent back to the coast and put on a boat to Bombay. This time they survived by persuading the chief that his correspondent was telling a pack of lies as he feared that they might be diverting commerce away from his own trade route. Captain Christie added greater credibility to their pretended role by delivering a dissertation on the finer points of the Indian market; Pottinger found it hard not to collapse in laughter at this virtuoso performance.

Nevertheless, they were getting jumpier all the time: sooner or later accusations would stick and being sent home was the least of the risks they ran. For the moment, however, they had not only got away with their story, but the local chief even procured safe-conduct for them through the dreaded Bezunja country, while the chief's brother regaled them with hunting tales of the wild game he had shot in the mountains. They must have wished they were on genuine shooting leave and could have joined him. Instead, they busied themselves, assiduously noting down the details of the 'tolerably good mud wall' that, together with the river, provided the settlement's only defence from attack.

Moving on from Bela, they eventually encountered the Bezunja chief who told them that if they had entered his territory without his consent 'he would have annihilated our whole party', but as they had arrived with an introduction he would be happy for them to stay as his honoured guests for a week.

However, Christie and Pottinger were mindful of the need to press on and cover the ground they had been sent to reconnoitre. Sometimes they travelled as much as 35 or 50 miles a day, always arousing conjecture due to their appearance in these barren wastes, and on 9 February they reached Kalat. Here again they ran into somebody who claimed to have seen them a year before with the British army in Sindh; this time they escaped being discovered by their host's assumption that they were embarrassed by their 'reduced circumstances and station in life' (to traders rather than officers) and that there was nothing more sinister to their changed appearance than that. So they pressed on with their surreptitious reconnaissance of the defences of Kalat, noting the height of the fortifications, the number of bastions, the loop-holed walls and the fact that the mud structures were not only devoid of cannon but probably not strong enough to support them anyway. Only the residence of the khan of Kalat was 'more capable of defence'. However, Pottinger assessed that the Baluchi soldiers were formidable warriors and 'all capital marksmen' who in close combat would throw away their firearms and resort to swords and daggers.

Suspicion still followed their every move. Messengers had

preceded them to Kalat, warning against them as dangerous intruders and 'it therefore seemed highly advisable for us to quit Kalat with the least possible delay'. They invented some instructions from their supposed employer urging them to press on to Kandahar and Herat, but before they had time to leave two Afghans denounced them as spies and their own Hindustani servants were demanding bribes to keep the secrecy to which they had been sworn.

Despite all this embarrassment, they had a brief respite when their baggage caught up with them and the local population all rallied round, complaining of different ailments and demanding cures from their medicine chest. Being 'anxious to acquire friends by obliging . . . [they] dispensed the medicines with a liberal hand according to the best of our judgements'. Their efforts nearly backfired when many of their patients disregarded their instructions and swallowed a week's worth of pills in one go or drank the medicines intended for external application. There were other problems, too: one young girl who had eye trouble was so heavily veiled that they could not see – let alone inspect – her eyes. Other young women wanted potions for fertility or to enhance their attractions. One man whom they treated died four days later from a slow poison 'that one of his five step-mothers had administered to him', but happily Christie and Pottinger were not blamed.

Getting away from Kalat proved difficult; in particular, they had great problems securing bills of exchange and were charged excessive commission because the Hindu traders 'saw our impatience and took care to profit by it'. They found it necessary to pretend that they intended to return to Kalat, and went so far as to leave a packet of valuables (in fact 'a bundle of old clothes not worth five shillings') to consolidate

the impression.[1] They did well to get away before any of their increasingly numerous subterfuges caught up with them.

The party now consisted of Christie and Pottinger, two Hindustani servants and four local camel drivers. There were five camels in all, some of them with double saddles. The route lay north between bare hills with more distant mountains and at times narrowed to a path only 2 feet wide with 'on the left hand side an abyss at least a quarter of a mile deep'. Despite these conditions and the cold and rain, they continued to cover some 30 miles a day.

---

1. The author employed a similar gambit when travelling through the Caucasus in the late 1950s. He left a suitcase full of old and unwanted clothes on a train and his KGB minders stayed with the case rather than following him as he left and failed to return to the train – leaving him free to explore on his own and not followed for several days.

They were greatly cheered by finding the most difficult defile that they had ever seen anywhere, which, if properly defended, would prove an 'insurmountable barrier' to an invading army. Pottinger recorded that at this juncture they congratulated themselves on the accomplishment of the objective for which they had quitted India. Napoleon would have a hard time if he attempted to invade by this route.

At their next halt – Nooshky – they were advised that they should try to overtake another caravan, but that they should not press on alone or they risked being 'murdered and plundered'. But when they objected to the fee that a local guide demanded the Baluchis who crowded round 'began to be rude and troublesome'. The visitors faced speculation about whether they were Sunni or Shia Muslims, but managed to persuade their interlocutors – by reciting the Sunni creed – that they were the former and therefore acceptable.

While they were in Nooshky letters arrived for them from Kalat reporting that two agents of the ruler of Sindh had arrived there with the purpose of seizing Christie and Pottinger and carrying them off to Hyderabad where the soles of their feet would be beaten until they confessed to being spies. Obviously, their activities and route were more widely known than they realized.

Partly for this reason, and partly to cover more territory, Christie decided that he and Pottinger should split up at Nooshky and go separate ways: Christie would head for Herat in Afghanistan, and Pottinger for Kerman in Persia, where Christie hoped to join him later. This was deviating from their instructions but they felt that they would attract less attention separately and would also be able to survey more of the unknown terrain, and so better fulfil their objectives.

However they had one more narrow squeak before they parted. Although they had agreed that they would only speak in Hindustani when anyone else was in earshot, in their urgency to make plans before the split they became careless and were overheard talking in English. When challenged about what language they were speaking, Pottinger took a gamble and declared it was Telinga (an obscure dialogue spoken in Telingana in faraway southern India) on the assumption that no one in those parts would be familiar with the dialect. But luck was against him. His enquirer came back with a fakir who allegedly spoke Talinga and wanted to practise it. Pottinger bombarded him with a barrage of English and, when the fakir was obviously baffled by this, declared that clearly the fakir could not speak Talinga after all – which happily turned out to be the case.

When Christie finally set off, Pottinger was consoled by the Sidir (or ruler) of Nooshky, who had been told that Christie and Pottinger were brothers (yet another of their subterfuges) and 'strove to cheer me, by declaring he would take every care of me for the sake of my brother'. Pottinger, true to form, took advantage of his friendliness to learn much useful local intelligence.

It was with huge relief that Pottinger, after a stay of 16 days, finally quit Nooshky on 25 March with a party of five attendants 'none of whom were well armed, so that we had to trust more to our good fortune in not meeting people inclined to plunder us, than to our means of repelling them'. He was still in Baluchistan but heading northwestwards towards Persia.

It is clear from Pottinger's account of his mission that he enjoyed the thrill of being on his own and having a wholly independent command (he was still only 20). Despite a fever he pressed on into the mountains where the track was 'not more than two yards wide, the rocks rising like walls for many hundreds of feet on each side'. In such steep gullies the risk of flash floods was very real, and when storms broke at night Pottinger feared that the rivers would overflow 'and sweep us all off'. Once out of the mountains the conditions changed dramatically. The desert was arid and the single well they passed was 'either dried up, or so deep we could not reach it [the water] with the rope'. Flat barren desert gave way to sand dunes of such steepness that it was necessary to make diversions in order to find a surface the camels could climb without backsliding. Loose particles of sand penetrated eyes, mouths and nostrils; thirst became the main problem when only a few days before flash floods had been the threat. When the winds got up, they positively flayed both men and camels. This was dire terrain for a small party: it would be lethal for an army, Pottinger noted with satisfaction.

In these circumstances, night travel often seemed the best option but navigation by the stars was not always possible. Pottinger had recourse to surreptitiously consulting his compass – which his companions took to be some sort of mysterious device for establishing the direction of Mecca.

When he reached the village of Kullugan, Pottinger became obliged to adopt an even deeper level of subterfuge. One of his companions, who had gone ahead to announce their arrival and try to ensure a friendly reception, returned from the village to tell Pottinger that the local headman had said he would only be safe there if he presented himself not only as a Muslim (which he was assumed to be) but also as a Holy Man, learned in Islamic law, on a pilgrimage to Meshed (Mashhad) – in fact, virtually as a mullah. 'We are now in Mukran,' he was told, 'where every individual is a robber by caste.' A merchant or horse-dealer would be fair prey but a Holy Man would be protected by his sanctity.

Pottinger 'immediately assumed a religious air and mien'. He even managed to participate in religious discussions, impressing his listeners with his theological skills and resolving various questions under dispute. The following day he was obliged to attend prayers at the mosque but managed to model his behaviour on that of the headman and others around him. Once more he had got away with it. However, even outside the mosque his new role as a Holy Man dogged him: the women, who would have been too shy to confide in a layman, felt free to pour out accounts of their physical and mental frailties to a dedicated pilgrim. As usual, fertility potions were the most frequent requests.

Pottinger soon realized that the reputation for violence and danger which hung over Kullugan was not unfounded. Every house had a refuge on an upper floor to which the inhabitants would retreat at night, pulling the ladder up behind them, in case the house was attacked by robbers. Soon after he left the village, his party was overtaken by a group of 18 armed men who had been following them at a distance for most of the day with the intention of attacking them at twilight. On hearing that Pottinger was a Holy Man on pilgrimage, they abandoned any idea of molesting his party and he 'had to undergo the ceremony of embracing them all round'.

On the next day a genuine mullah at a village called Gull invited Pottinger and his companions to a meal and sprang on him a request to say some prayers; Pottinger 'stroked down his beard' and murmured some appropriate phrases which turned out to be acceptable. On another occasion, when he was pressed to join in prayers at a mosque, he excused himself on the ingenious grounds that 'having worn cloaths [sic] on our backs upwards of a month . . . every good Moolsulman was bound to cleanse his person . . . prior to making his petition to heaven'.

The mullah guise was proving both tricky and indispensable.

The close observation of strategic terrain continued. On 10 April he passed through a defile in the mountains which he estimated would be tenable by a few men against any force: in fact, a good spot to halt an invader as 'stones hurled down would be attended with inevitable death to anyone coming up'.

Once out on the desert steppes again there were other hazards. Wolves, hyenas and jackals could be heard howling, but the local villagers were more concerned about droves of wild boar ravaging their crops. Pottinger saw such boar as suitable game for shooting expeditions and deplored the villagers' apparent reluctance to hunt them on the grounds that they were unclean animals and therefore unsuitable quarry for a Muslim. If Arabs hunted them and shot them, why should 'ignorant Indians' not do so? Pottinger's comments probably reflect the sentiments of a frustrated marksman rather than an aficionado of pig-sticking – a sport which was only to become really popular among British officers in India rather later in the century, and then chiefly among cavalry officers rather than infantrymen such as Pottinger.

When he reached the settlement of Huftur 'on a shrubby plain' on 13 April, he had a new embarrassment. The chief called on him and explained in impeccable Persian that he thought Pottinger was not what he purported to be (an alarming statement!) but that he was in fact 'a prince in disguise'. Pottinger gave him a handsome pistol which the chief accepted with alacrity and he stopped asking embarrassing questions.

However, Pottinger was running out of gifts for local chiefs and headmen. At Bunpoor (Bampur) an acquisitive khan insisted that he give him a pair of pistols, and when Pottinger reluctantly offered one of the pair and explained that he had to be able to defend himself in the bandit-infested region he was about to enter, the khan declined to give him a guide and effectively detained him until he surrendered the coveted second pistol. Money, food, gifts and credibility were all running out fast.

To make matters worse, his eyes were beginning to suffer from exposure to the glare of the sun; at times they were so weakened that he could barely see five yards. He therefore muffled himself up to keep out the light, and rode with 'an old black silk handkerchief tied over my turban'. He ruefully recorded that, being so wrapped up, he was unable to make his usual observations and notes about the territory.

When his eyes had somewhat recovered, Pottinger decided that he was tired of being suspected of being a European: it laid him open not only to danger but also to exploitation (all Europeans were assumed to be rich) and tiresome public attention in every village or settlement he passed through. He was convinced his new guide spread it around everywhere they went that Pottinger was a European and so he promptly dismissed him, to the consternation of his camel drivers. From then on he had to find and bribe local shepherds to take him on to the next habitations, and he was never quite sure that they were not leading him into an ambush. However, his greatest anxiety during the next few days was not about attack but thirst: the party had virtually run out of water and they were tormented by incredibly realistic mirages – 'in hollows where water might be expected to lodge, I have seen bushes and trees reflected'. The camels became so thin and ill-nourished that Pottinger and his attendants had to walk to ease their load.

Pottinger was now – by 24 April – leaving Baluchistan and entering the Persian-speaking region of Nurmansheer. Here he found the settlements more strongly fortified and better guarded than in Baluchistan, reflecting the fact that the residents lived in terror of Baluchi attacks. This would be a more formidable region to conquer, he concluded, as he noted down the details of bastions and walls. He and his party were made to sleep outside the walls; no chances were being taken here with dubious strangers.

Although as he neared the Persian frontier the risks of hostility and attack were less than in Baluchistan, the atmosphere was still far from friendly. After so many weeks of arduous travel, Pottinger was losing his patience with local obstruction. When he approached a very small circular fort called Booja, he reported, 'I had scarcely alighted from my camel, when an ill-looking dirty scrub, who afterwards turned out to be the chief of the place' demanded in a very truculent way to know who he was and why he was there. Pottinger reacted angrily, asking 'by what right he had presumed to make this inquiry'. The exchange became ever more acerbic, with the chief threatening to send Pottinger under escort to be interrogated by the local khan, while Pottinger for his part declared that he was 'an English merchant, and he had better beware how he interfered with him'. In the end Pottinger moved on at first light the next day before anyone else had a chance to hold him up.

Pottinger's impatience again came to the surface at his next halting place – the town of Bumm. He found himself 'waiting full two hours under the gate-way among a pack of unmannered and boisterous matchlockmen, who . . . annoyed me very much by their inquisitive impertinence'. His temper was not improved by being accosted by a 'bigoted Syynd . . . or descendant of the Prophet' who strutted around trying to convince Pottinger of the impropriety of the Christian religion. Whereas a few weeks earlier Pottinger had been only too pleased to pass himself off as a Muslim pilgrim and Holy Man for the sake of his own safety, now that the threat was largely over he resented Muslims attempting to win him over to the faith. When Pottinger refused to be browbeaten, the Syynd started abusing him for wearing Islamic dress while consuming hog's flesh, wine and other prohibited items of diet. Pottinger almost lost his temper completely and would have struck the man had he not reckoned that 'I should most likely, and my people also, have been murdered in the scuffle that would have ensued'. In the event, Pottinger thought it more prudent to try to outwit the tiresome cleric: when his interlocutor 'sneeringly asked if I knew where the Almighty was', he asked the cleric in return to tell him 'where the Almighty was not present'. This was considered a wise answer and allowed the cantankerous exchange to end without recourse to violence.

In the end Pottinger left Bumm, well provided with a mounted guide, some bags of flour and other provisions for the next stage of the journey on to Kerman, and favourably impressed with the 'polished and elegant' manners of the Persian ruling class. He made his usual detailed notes about the fortifications of Bumm, which he described as 'beyond any comparison the most defensible in Persia'. This was a place which would stand a better chance than others he had visited of resisting a French – or Russian – advance.

On 3 May, after three months of incessant and risky travel, Pottinger eventually reached Kerman where he slept an untroubled night for the first time since leaving the coast of Baluchistan. His clothes were too dirty and torn for an audience with the local prince, so he borrowed an outfit from an Indian merchant and reckoned that even then he had lost considerable face by not being properly attired. The prince asked him 'in a very loud voice . . . where I had been and what could have induced me to undertake the journey'. Pottinger replied with yet another fabricated story, this time about having been sent to approve the horses for the Indian army and having had to travel overland as the sea was too rough at this season. He concluded that 'this was plausible enough to pass with the prince'. He explained he was hoping to report to Brigadier General Malcolm (the governor-general of India's ambassador to the Shah) and added for good measure – but quite untruthfully – that he was Malcolm's nephew. This last invention he hoped would win him greater respect, and it did. Pottinger had become adept at inventing and modifying his story as he went along.

At Kerman he expected to meet up with Captain Christie who, he hoped, would have arrived from Herat. So he stayed on for more than three weeks, studying the local scene and drawing some unflattering conclusions about the Persians: 'With their equals, the Persians are affable and polite; to their superiors, servile and obsequious; and towards their inferiors, haughty and domineering . . . all ranks are equally avaricious, sordid and dishonest . . . in debauchery none can exceed them.' It seems that his earlier favourable impression of the politeness of the Persian ruling classes had been somewhat modified. He commented wryly that some of his readers would think him too severe, but he felt confirmed in his harsh verdicts by witnessing the brutal punishments doled out by the prince: those condemned of a variety of crimes were blinded or had their noses cut off along with 'their manhood'. Pottinger might have survived the hazards of crossing Baluchistan, but he was still living in a nightmare world.

Nor was there yet an end to the attempts to lure him into dangerous indiscretion. While at Kerman an agent provocateur was sent to try to inveigle him into admitting that he was the precursor of a British army of occupation; the bait was that his interlocutor wanted to convert to Christianity and had 6,000 local inhabitants ready to come to the aid of any British invaders. Pottinger was too wary and experienced to fall into this sort of trap.

By the end of May, Pottinger despaired of Christie arriving and left Kerman for Shiraz and Isfahan. He was so soured with what he had seen of the prince, and the latter's lack of attention to him, that he unwisely declined to pay a farewell courtesy visit. The prince won the last trick, however, by sending a messenger to say – in effect – that since Pottinger declined to behave like a guest he was being charged for his accommodation and taxed for his camels as if he were a stranger. Pottinger paid up with a bad grace.

Although having now completed his mission and reached a region which was – at least to some extent – known to others, Pottinger could not drop the practice of noting down everything of strategic interest. Even a remote settlement between Kerman and Yazd was recorded as having been 'considered a strong place, and had made a stout resistance' against the first Qajar shah's army in 1794. The arid nature of the 1,500-mile journey since he landed on the coast of Baluchistan was vividly illustrated by the fact that only now did he cross a stream 'sufficiently deep to have taken a horse above the knee': neither Napoleon's hussars nor the Tsar's Cossacks would find it easy to water their horses in the region. Nor had the dangers of the passage altogether evaporated: the mountains and plains near Yazd were 'a famous rendez-vous for highwaymen' and they rode 'with our pieces loaded, and the matches ready lighted'.

At Shiraz he was received by the Persian governor 'dressed in a vest entirely covered with pearls and precious stones' and made contact with a fellow British lieutenant in the Madras Native Infantry (an assistant to General Malcolm who had been left there in his commander's absence). It was then that he felt that his ordeal was over 'and I once more began to fancy myself a British officer'.

But even at Shiraz there was still no sign of Christie. So Pottinger pressed on – a further two days' march – to Isfahan, now accompanied by a medic from General Malcolm's staff. When installed at Isfahan he had a visit one evening from a man who at first failed to recognize him and whom he did not recognize either. It was Captain Christie. Both officers were so weather-tanned, so habitually and convincingly dressed in Persian attire, and so fluent in the local language, that – despite being close friends, fellow officers and supposed 'brothers' – they had both bamboozled each other as successfully as they had the suspicious and inquisitive natives along their route. It was quite a tribute to their skills of deception.

Their mission was recognized as a valuable and successful one by General Malcolm, who invited – or more likely ordered – Christie to stay on in Persia 'to fulfil that part of the treaty relative to organizing the Persian troops'. It was to prove an unfortunate appointment for Christie: two years later, when the Russians invaded Persia, he was among the first to fall. He was arguably the first fatal casualty of the Great Game.

Pottinger was more fortunate. He made his way back to India via Baghdad and Basra. His reputation had been greatly enhanced by his Baluchistan adventure. After a period of service in the Mahratta War, he was appointed to a more political role in Sindh and created a baronet. He went on to diplomatic posts in China and became the first governor of Hong Kong. This was followed by a spell as governor of the Cape of Good Hope in South Africa and –

eventually – a return to India as governor of Madras in 1847.

Pottinger's strength was his daring in the face of danger, and his nerve – some would say cheek – in taking on assumed personalities. To pose as a Holy Man among a community of dedicated and fervent Muslims was no easy feat of deception. Even to pose convincingly as a native merchant – a 'box wallah' – when he was in fact a British commissioned officer was to assume a significantly more modest role which did not come easily to proud officers of the Raj. All this he accomplished with adroit aplomb. What he was less good at was reacting sensitively to local chiefs, headmen, clerics, sentries ('matchlockmen') and court henchmen; he frequently made enemies of them and thus complicated his own progress. This trait of his personality was to endure and, as he rose through the ranks of the army to become a senior administrator, it was to become a handicap. As governor of Madras these shortcomings came to the surface: Pottinger – by now the Rt Hon. Sir Henry Pottinger Bart, GCB – was found to be out of sympathy with the natives of Madras and insensitive to problems that needed urgent attention or reform. He retired somewhat under a cloud in 1854 and died in England two years later. It is tempting to speculate how he might have fared in the Indian Mutiny had he still been there when it broke out the year after his death. One thing is certain: he would have been resolute and courageous in restoring the authority of the Raj he had loved and served so bravely.

# Chapter 2

## Alexander Burnes: A Star in the East

'We should be like stars now that it's dark;
Use ourselves up to the last bright dregs
And vanish in the morning.'
— Christopher Fry (1907–2005),
in *The Lady's Not for Burning*

Alexander 'Bokhara' Burnes was a heavyweight player in the Great Game and was a legend in his own time, but is now principally remembered for campaigns and activities which were far removed from 'shooting leave'. His admirers and critics alike have tended to concentrate on the first and last chapters of his professional life: both were dramatic. But what went between is no less sensational.

Burnes (distantly related to the poet Robert Burns, who spelt his name without the 'e') was born in Montrose in Scotland in 1805, a few months before the Battle of Trafalgar secured Britain against an invasion by Napoleon. His father had been provost of his home town and was well placed to secure a cadetship for his fourth son with the East India Company. Alexander Burnes sailed for India aged 16 – by no means unusually young at that period – and on arrival was classified as a 'Griffin' (a raw recruit) and lodged in a 'chummery' with other new arrivals to learn Hindustani.

Burnes excelled at languages and by the age of 19 was an adjutant of the 21st Bombay Native Infantry. He showed an interest in exploring and took the trouble to write up his reports and submit them to his seniors. So, in 1830, when it was decided to chart the Indus river, under the pretext of shipping four enormous dray horses upriver to Lahore as a gift from King William IV of England to the Maharaja Ranjit Singh, ruler of the Punjab, Burnes was selected to lead the expedition. His skilful handling of this task has been much recounted and established his reputation.

Burnes is also well remembered, but more controversially so, for his involvement with the Army of the Indus, the invasion force which entered Afghanistan in 1839 and placed a supposedly pro-British ruler on the throne of Kabul. His heart was not really in the enterprise, as he had been a firm supporter of Dost Mohammed (the deposed ruler) until the lack of British support had driven the latter into accepting overtures from the Russians. However, the ambitious Burnes had hoped to end up as the British envoy to Afghanistan and he failed to foresee how the tide of opinion was turning against the British in Kabul. His own murder (at the age of 36), outside his house and away from the military compound, was the starting pistol for the fatal retreat from Kabul and the total destruction of a British army of some 16,000 men and followers in the mountain passes of Afghanistan. Burnes was held by some to be in part responsible for that disastrous phase of the First Afghan War.

However, between the glorious success of the Indus expedition of 1831 and the appalling failure of the campaign to Kabul of 1839–41, Burnes had in fact undertaken one of the most ambitious and memorable of all 'shooting leave' excursions: he had travelled from India through the Punjab and Afghanistan to

Kabul, over the Hindu Kush and across the Turkoman-infested deserts to the mysterious and reputedly sinister city of Bokhara. He had returned to tell the tale – to tell it, in fact, in the stately homes and fashionable drawing rooms of England – and to earn the sobriquet of 'Bokhara Burnes'. This is the story of that often overlooked chapter of his life.

If there were any doubts about the political motivation of this supposedly private trip, they were resolved in Burnes's preface to his subsequently published account of his journey. He wrote: 'The design [for the trip] received the most liberal encouragement from the governor-general of India, Lord William Bentinck . . . His lordship was of opinion that a knowledge of the general condition of the countries through which I was to travel, would be useful to the British government.' Burnes goes on to say that it would have been objectionable and highly imprudent to have crossed the countries lying between India and Europe 'as I had voyaged on the Indus – an accredited agent; and I was directed to appear (which I myself had suggested) as a private individual'. The public motivation and the private camouflage amounted almost to a definition of shooting leave.

Burnes recruited a more junior officer from his own regiment to accompany him, but the latter was not given permission to be away for long. In the end he took with him a surgeon from the Bengal army called James Gerard, as well as a surveyor and a Hindu boy called Mohun Lal. Initially, Burnes decided not to conceal that he was a European, but at the same time he travelled in native dress and adopted native habits and customs to avoid drawing attention to himself. It followed from this decision to keep a low profile that they would eat local food and so be able to cut down the number of pack animals they took with them. Despite these precautions, most of his British friends in

India foretold a disastrous outcome: they reminded him of how William Moorcroft (the explorer and horse-trader) and his companions had perished in these parts only six years before.

The journey started safely enough. When he reached Lahore, Ranjit Singh received him cordially and offered to take him tiger-hunting, sending four elephants to transport his guests to his magnificent camp, with tents made of scarlet and yellow cloth and the ground covered with Kashmir carpets. The maharaja himself wore a green hunting coat lined with fur, and carried a diamond-studded dagger. Hounds and falconers followed on. However, they failed to flush out any tigers and had to be content with wild boar, some of which were cut down with scimitars while others were trapped and later baited by dogs. The whole process, Burnes declared, 'might not be duly appreciated by a European sportsman' as the prey had little chance of escape and there was much cruelty. At least it was a hunting expedition on a grand scale and there was to be little enough shooting in the course of Burnes's so-called leave. Nor would there be such comforts again.

On leaving Lahore, they threw away their European clothes and started travelling in as native a manner as possible: 'we gave away our tents, beds and boxes, and broke our tables and chairs'. They even shaved their heads and donned 'ponderous turbans', and they jettisoned their knives and forks and ate with their fingers like the locals. A single pony or mule was all that was necessary to carry each man and his gear. While pressing forward in this modest and inconspicuous manner, Burnes occupied himself with two subjects which showed the range of his interests: the first was to try to trace Alexander the Great's progress over this terrain, and the second was to study how salt was mined. He also collected ancient coins. This was an officer with a keenly inquiring mind.

When he reached the Indus, Burnes decided to 'make the attempt of fording the great river', even though it 'gushed with amazing violence'. There were three separate branches of the river to be forded and Burnes mounted an elephant and 'dashed into it'. His satisfaction at safely reaching an island in mid-river was soon blighted by the fact that some stragglers who had joined up with his party were swept downstream: one man and two horses were drowned. When Burnes suggested that they should turn back to the near-side bank without completing their crossing, the chief who had produced the elephants would not hear of it: 'What is the use of a Sikh if he cannot pass the Attock [Indus]?' was his hard-hearted comment.

Although they had forded the Indus at this point to prove that it could be done, they recrossed the river and proceeded to the normal ferry-crossing point at the fort of Attock. Here they encountered another problem. The garrison of the fort had mutinied and seized control of the ferry boats; they complained that Ranjit Singh owed them arrears of pay and were impervious to the letters from the maharaja which Burnes produced. This setback brought out the diplomat in Burnes: he did not press to enter the fort, but slept in a dilapidated mosque nearby, where he persuaded the inhabitants that there was nothing improper in a couple of infidels seeking such shelter. He also refrained from provoking or irritating the mutinous garrison of the fort, and after a few days of patient waiting the mutineers gave them a boat in which to make the crossing.

They were now in Afghanistan which then stretched as far east as Peshawar (now in Pakistan). Burnes's Sikh escort – provided by Ranjit Singh – could not continue into Afghanistan, but a party of Afghans had been dispatched from Peshawar to meet him. Neither escort would approach the other but 'drew up at a distance of three hundred yards from each other'; Burnes and his party then crossed from the protection of one to the other. However, they were not to be escorted for long and Burnes realized that life would be more dangerous now that they were outside the reach of his friend Ranjit Singh. He made appropriate dispositions: he disguised his letters of credit as an amulet on one wrist and his 'polyglot passport' similarly on the other wrist. He distributed his cash – in ducats – between other members of the party. He had to trust them not to steal the money, just as he had to trust them later not to give away his own and Gerard's true identity. Burnes's party also took it in turns to keep watch at night; although the first Afghan chief they met assured them they should consider themselves 'as secure as eggs under a hen', they were taking no chances.

At Peshawar they were also well received by the chief – the Emir Dost Mohammed – who let them stay in his seraglio 'which he had prepared and, I need not add, emptied, for our reception'. (He normally had 30 wives and some 60 children there.) Burnes managed to get through a banquet, not only eating with his hands but cheerfully accepting pieces of meat torn off by his host for his consumption, but he did find he 'almost lost the use of my legs from the irksome position of constraint in which I had so long sat'. He was always prepared to go the extra mile to comply with local customs, though, and this was rewarded by Afghans dropping in unannounced at his quarters for a gossip at all times of day and night. He was at pains not to be caught writing or taking notes, which he knew would be viewed as suspicious. Nor did he express his shock and horror at seeing, lying on a dung heap, the murdered corpses of a man and a woman who had been caught in adultery; the chief expressed approval of their killing, telling the murderer, 'You have acted the part of a good Mohammedan'. The following day a 12-year-old boy cheerfully told Burnes how he had salvaged his father's severed head after a tribal encounter. Life in Peshawar required a strong stomach.

Before he left Peshawar he was advised by a holy man, who thought Burnes was an Armenian, to be careful not to be mistaken for a European – particularly not an Englishman, 'for the natives of these countries believe the English to be political intriguers, and to possess boundless wealth'. They were also advised that Dr Gerard should not dispense medicines, as that both drew attention to their presence and gave the impression they were rich. By the time they left on 19 April they reckoned that they 'need not much longer fear the snows of Cabool and the Hindoo Koosh'.

They were now in a land where they felt they could trust nobody. One of the hill chiefs they encountered advised them to go through the Khyber Pass, but he was himself from the Khyber region and as 'no-one trusts a Kyberee, it was deemed not prudent'. Instead, the route they chose involved crossing the Kabul river on a raft of inflated skins, and the current was so strong that on the 250-yard crossing they were carried more than a mile downstream. Burnes noted that this river provided a potential line of supply all the way to the Indian Ocean. On a different crossing their rafts were whirled around in the smaller eddies and they were warned that if they got into a big whirlpool they 'might revolve in hunger and giddiness for a whole day'.

Camping on the far side, they were overlooked by 'a truly cut-throat band' who had perched themselves on some overhanging rocks. One local chief who approached them and invited them to join him on a hawking trip was later discovered to have murdered his sister and two nephews to achieve his position; they declined the invitation. On another occasion, a Persian who was accompanying them and riding ahead suddenly started firing his carbine, although they had already passed the point of known danger of ambush; when they caught up with him, he told them he had bravely fought off an assault while 'his antagonist's ball had whistled past his ear!'. Burnes was inclined to think the Persian had dreamt up the whole incident to illustrate his courage, but there was no doubt Afghanistan was living up to its reputation.

On 1 May, Burnes reached Kabul for the first time in his life. He found the approaches unimpressive, but once under the shade of its fine bazaar he 'believed myself in the capital of an empire'. The city was to exert a great attraction for him. He was slightly disconcerted that at the customs house they insisted on searching his baggage, but concluded it was 'more prudent to exhibit our poverty than to allow the good people to form designs against our supposed wealth'; his sextant and other paraphernalia were laid out for all to see, but instead of worrying about this surveying and spying equipment, the customs officials 'set us down without doubt as conjurers, after a display of such unintelligible apparatus'. This slight embarrassment behind him, Burnes went on to stay with the brother of 'the governor of Kabul' (whom most people dubbed variously as king or chief); this brother was invariably hospitable to Europeans and was described by Burnes as 'the patriarch of Cabool'.

Three days later the patriarch arranged for Burnes to dine with the governor. As Dr Gerard was ill (ironically the doctor spent much more time sick than the other members of the party), Burnes took with him a strange character called Reverend Joseph Wolff, a Jew who had adopted Christianity in a very extreme missionary form and had already travelled extensively in Central

Asia. (Wolff is the principal subject of Fitzroy Maclean's book *A Person from England*.) Burnes was well received and the conversation ranged widely over the usual topics: How did European countries get on with each other? How were taxes collected? Did England purloin the riches of India? If she did not, did this fact account for our peaceful subjugation of the country? Did England have designs on Afghanistan? And finally, had Burnes ever seen a rhinoceros? The governor also asked Burnes a certain amount about himself and applauded his decision to travel in local attire. When it came to the Rev. Joseph Wolff's turn to face the questioning, the eccentric cleric would have got into an acrimonious theological argument if Burnes had not used his role as interpreter to divert the argument: his diplomatic skills were once again put to the test.

Burnes had already charmed the rulers of the Punjab and Peshawar; he now repeated these successes with the ruler of Kabul. The latter invited him to come back for further talks and gave him letters to the chiefs of the Oxus and the emir of Bokhara. He even offered him command of his army (Burnes had not concealed that he was an officer) with its 12,000 horse and 20 guns, but Burnes was not interested in seeking other employment. And the charm worked the other way round too: Burnes came away from this first visit to Kabul having 'imbibed a very favourable impression of their national character'. He seemed blind to the latently more treacherous aspects of Afghan behaviour – 'no people are more incapable of managing an intrigue' – a fatal misconception that was to cost him his life ten years later.

On exploring Kabul, Burnes came across some evidence of Russian trade and influence, including the distinctive blue paper and other products sold in the covered bazaar. He found he was able to make these sorties 'without observation, and even without an attendant'. He noted that the Bala Hissar (a palace and prison in one) had 'poor, irregular and dilapidated fortification, and could never stand an escalade'. The prison part was occupied by the younger branches of the royal family, in which they were confined for life for no reason except their potential rivalry. Most gratifying was the fact that Burnes could cash letters of credit for gold, which he saw as evidence of the high standing of the British for reliability and honesty. To the last, he observed local practices: he left the city after noon-time prayers at the mosque on a Friday – the approved hour of departure.

Burnes had taken the precaution of hiring a professional caravan conductor for the next dangerous stage of the journey. This official quickly justified his salary by securing accommodation – 'by bribing a mullah to leave it' – and by chasing off unauthorized customs officers, mostly searching for valuable copies of the Koran being illegally smuggled out of the country. When they reached the Oonna Pass in the Hindu Kush they found it under snow and guarded by three forts. Sometimes they had to cross the same stream as many as 20 times as they followed riverbeds deep into the mountains. This was the country of the Hazaras – the tribe despised by the Pathans. They were living in extreme poverty and 'prevented by snow from stirring out of their houses for six months of the year'. So they were well able to tend Burnes for an attack of snow-blindness.

After various falls and tumbles in the snow while crossing the passes, they progressed out of Hazara territory and into that of the Uzbeks, who had an unsavoury reputation for man-stealing. This was a no-man's-land between the domains of the rulers of Kabul and Kunduz; no love was lost between the two. Burnes observed that taxes had to be paid to Kabul in horses and to

Kunduz in slaves – a fact which said something about their relative values. However, the Uzbeks were fanatically religious – justifying stealing Jewish women from caravans on the grounds that their children would be Muslims – and it was here that Burnes first learnt the importance of not sleeping with his feet pointing towards Mecca: 'I ever after observed the bearings of the compass indoors as attentively as I had hitherto done outside.'

Even here Burnes was disturbed to find evidence of Russian influence and intrigues. Russian liquor and card games – and their 36-card packs – had penetrated as far as Bokhara, as had accounts of the parade-ground drill of Russian soldiers: the concept of marching off always with the same foot first, filled the Uzbeks with astonishment and amusement. In general, the locals had the impression that Russia was a land of wine and women, a veritable paradise if not a strictly Islamic one.

At one pass – known as the Black Pass – Burnes encountered a party of robbers who were rapidly reinforced by fellow brigands who had been lying in ambush. Fortunately, his caravan conductor had anticipated trouble and hired an additional escort; both sides formed up for a fight and sent forward two horsemen to parley with each other from a range of a hundred yards. In view of the number and strength of the escort they were allowed to pass through, but two camels which had loitered behind were seized with their drivers 'who would now become slaves for life'. Burnes was convinced that had the caravan conductor not taken on an escort, the rest of them would have shared this fate 'and found ourselves next day tending herds and flocks among the mountains'. When the conductor 'stroked down his beard and thanked God', Burnes silently did the same. He also busied himself on the long rides by taking instruction in different forms of formal Islamic address; he was not one to waste time.

When they reached Kulum, the frontier town of Murad Beg's widespread domain based around Kunduz, they were able to relax in a caravanserai (a fortified overnight stopping place) and change their clothes for the first time for many days. And here Burnes – the darling of the British generals and the assiduous student of Islam – allowed himself some slightly smug reflections: all their hardships were 'but the petty inconveniences of a traveller, which sink into insignificance when compared with the pleasure of seeing new men and countries, strange manners and customs, and being able to temper the prejudices of one's own country by observing those of others'. Burnes might have been feeling justifiably pleased with himself, but this was probably because he did not realize he was about to face the most alarming dangers of his whole trip.

Until now, the various rulers on whom he had called had all been friendly; the danger to Burnes and his party had been mostly from bandits in the hills and his apparent poverty had been some protection against them. At Kunduz he risked being faced for the first time by a cruel and despotic ruler in the person of Murad Beg who was known to hate Europeans and likely to murder them. (He had previously tried to kidnap William Moorcroft when the latter had travelled through the region in 1824; Moorcroft had only escaped by fleeing, disguised as a native, with the help of a local holy man.) It was therefore essential that Burnes both kept as far away from Murad Beg as possible, and that he converted his comfortable Asiatic clothing to the role of serious disguise.

From the start things started to go wrong. Burnes had been nervous about going to any of the settlements in Kunduz, but their companion and guide, who was a trader known as the Nazir, had insisted that they should go through the frontier town of Kulum. To their horror, they now found that the customs-house official there had dispatched a messenger to Murad Beg asking what he should do with the visitors and was determined to detain them there until he got an answer. Burnes also feared that the customs man – who was a Hindu from India – might have seen through his disguise. Burnes considered doing a runner and even persuaded the caravan conductor that this would be the safest plan, but the Nazir was determined that they should wait. He claimed to have good connections in Kunduz and that the reply would be favourable. However, when the reply came it confirmed Burnes's worst fears: it was a summons to Murad Beg's capital at Kunduz. Burnes insisted that the Nazir should accompany them, although the Nazir himself showed a disconcerting tendency to slip away on his own. Burnes also set about establishing his character as an Armenian from India since 'the name of Englishman, which had carried us in safety in all other places, was here replete with danger . . . it conveyed notions of great wealth'.

As well as the caravan conductor and the Nazir, the Indian customs official came with them to Kunduz; Burnes calculated that 'an impression might be made on such a person by persuasion and gold'. So he turned all his charms on this man, establishing supposedly common ground between them; he told him he knew his home town; he displayed his knowledge of Hindu gods and spoke warmly of them; he offered to help him in any way he could in India (without implying that he was a person of influence there); and finally Burnes offered him a monetary reward if all went well in Kunduz. He ended up feeling confident that, come what might, the customs officer – whatever his private suspicions – would not give him away.

However, Burnes was still very nervous about going to Kunduz and meeting the fearsome Murad Beg. When they stopped to feed their horses, it occurred to him that he would never have a better chance to escape: they had no guard set over them (as they had done at Kulum). They could ride well clear of Murad Beg's domains before the next morning. Only one consideration held him back: Dr Gerard was still at Kulum and, if Burnes escaped, he would be in even worse trouble. So Burnes did the honourable thing and pressed on to Kunduz.

He must have regretted that honour had obliged him to go on when, after a 45-mile stretch with no water, they were confronted with what appeared to be a line of lighted matchlock guns across their route, 'which we could not but conclude were robbers, since this country is infested with banditti'. A tea merchant travelling with Burnes thought that the best plan was to give the impression that they too had lots of matchlock guns: 'he busied himself in tearing up rags, rubbing them with gunpowder, and lighting them' to demonstrate that they were an armed body of men when, in fact, they only had one gun between them. When one of their party called out in Persian, he was instantly silenced since Persian – being the language of commerce – suggested that they were rich merchants and so valuable prey. The two parties veered off in separate directions and a clash of arms was avoided. Burnes later discovered that the other group were peaceable traders, too, playing the same game of matchlocks.

When they reached Kunduz it was apparent that the Nazir's claim to have good connections there had some justification: they were well received by Murad Beg's vizier. Burnes thought the safest course was to adopt the style and manner of being the Nazir's servant 'and evinced on every occasion as much humility as possible' (not many British officers would have been prepared to do this). He elaborated his Armenian guise, agreeing with the others that he should be presented as a watch-maker from Lucknow on a visit to a relative in Bokhara. Dr Gerard was to be described as a sick relative left behind in Kulum. All this amounted to 'as much evasion as my ingenuity could invent'. When the caravan conductor queried the ethics of so much lying, Burnes quoted an Islamic saying to the effect that 'an untruth that preserves peace is better than a truth that stirs up troubles'.

With this web of subterfuge in place, they were dispatched to meet Murad Beg himself who was on tour in a nearby village. While they were kept waiting outside a fort, admiring the Uzbeks riding to and fro with their gold-mounted long knives stuck into their girdles, Burnes thought it best to pull up some long boots to 'hide my provokingly white ankles'. His face had 'long been burnt into an Asiatic hue'. When ushered into Murad Beg's presence, the Nazir and the others offered appropriate presents, but Burnes was portrayed as too humble to be expected to do this and merely obsequiously kissed the chief's hands in a manner which implied familiarity with the correct procedure.

Murad Beg, who was sitting on a tiger skin, glared at them with his small piggy eyes and harsh Tartar features and questioned the Nazir and the customs official. The latter then said his spiel: 'Your slave has examined the baggage of the two Armenians, and found them to be poor travellers. It is in every person's mouth that they are Europeans, and it would have placed me under your displeasure had I let them depart; I have therefore brought one of them to know your orders.'

This was the crucial moment – possibly the most crucial of Burnes's life so far. Any of the three people with him might have betrayed him and none of them had any particular reason not to do so. Murad Beg stared at Burnes and said to the customs officer: 'Are you sure he is an Armenian?' The officer assured him he was and the notoriously anti-European chief issued an order for their safe-conduct over the frontier to Bokhara. A scribe prepared and sealed the document, and Burnes commented later, 'I could have embraced him when he pronounced it finished.'

He was not quite out of the woods yet. Murad Beg's son sent for Burnes and asked him various probing questions about the Armenian faith; Burnes was equal to the challenge and explained that Christians were 'people of the Book' and could not be blamed for not being followers of Mohammed when 'the New Testament had been written before that personage (on who be peace) had appeared on earth'. His explanation was accepted and the son declared that Burnes was at least better than a Hindu.

Burnes's charm had once again saved the day. On the journey back to Kulum, the Indian customs officer (whose statement had been so vital to their safety) hinted that the whole Hindu community realized that Burnes was a European, but as the Uzbeks were bad people they did not deserve to be told the truth: 'Whoever you be, therefore, you are now safe.' But Burnes was taking no chances: he rode through the night – 70 miles and 20 hours in the saddle – straight back to Kulum and Dr Gerard. Safe he might be, but Burnes was totally exhausted by the experience and found he 'could not revive myself by sleep for the fatigue which I had undergone'.

When Burnes decided to give the customs officer a reward of 20 gold ducats, and thought it would be more discreet to pass the money via the Nazir, he was disconcerted to find that the Nazir had pocketed 15 of them for himself. He paid the money a second time, and left Kulum in the company of 'our avaricious friend the Nazir' who exasperated Burnes by his exaggerated and ostentatious Islamic practices, which were at odds with the dishonesty of the man. However, Burnes was too canny to make an issue of these things: he had needed to rely on his companion's goodwill in the past and might well have to again.

Having finally got safely clear of the clutches of the ruler of Kunduz, Burnes's next stop was Balkh. This 'mother of cities' was reduced to a population of 2,000 and was largely derelict – 'a mine of bricks for the surrounding country'. Burnes went in search of Moorcroft's grave, but otherwise did not find much to detain him. They left as part of a caravan of 20 camels, with a man hunched in each side of a pannier bag on the back of a camel.

Their next hazard was to be the Turkoman raiders, into whose territory they now passed. The best plan seemed to be to hire a Turkoman escort armed with swords and spears to protect them, though Burnes admitted it might not have seemed altogether prudent to commit themselves to one band of Turkomans to

defend them against another. However, the escort delivered them safely and appeared to be an equal match of light dragoons.

They were held up on the banks of the Oxus for two days, waiting to be ferried across its half-mile width by bridled horses swimming ahead of their rafts. Burnes was intrigued: 'I have never before seen the horse converted to such a use.' Although he did not go into details in his published book, he did not waste the two days, but busied himself with measuring and estimating the potential of the Oxus for troop transportation. Once on the road again, he found the social life as part of a caravan was full of good fellowship: 'it levels out distinction between master and servant . . . both share everything'.

Now Burnes's anxieties were fastened on the nature of his reception at Bokhara. Although the horrifying experiences of fellow British officers Charles Stoddart and Arthur Conolly (who endured dire imprisonment followed by death in Bokhara in 1842) lay in the future, the Emir Nasrullah already had an unsavoury reputation. Burnes was upset when rumours reached them 'that the king [emir] had heard of our approach, and not only had prohibited our entering the city of Bokhara, but objected to our prosecuting the journey'. Their worries were intensified when officials from the court intercepted them and three times searched their baggage; their imminent arrest was also rumoured.

Burnes responded in a typically effective way. He sat down and wrote an obsequious letter to the emir's vizier employing all the terms he had been taught: the vizier was successively addressed as 'the Tower of Islam, the Gem of the Faith, the Star of Religion, the Dispenser of Justice, and the Pillar of the State'. The emir was referred to as 'the Commander of the Faithful' and Bokhara as 'the Citadel of Islam'. He was confident his letter would do the trick and sure enough a messenger came back by return to say they would be welcome. Burnes's long hours of tuition on his ride between Kabul and Kulum had not been wasted.

But was it a trap? On arrival – through one of the 12 gates in the 20-foot-high and 8-mile-long walls surrounding the city – Burnes lost no time in adapting his dress to conform to local practices: 'our turbans were exchanged for shabby sheep-skin caps, our kummerbunds were thrown aside, for a rude piece of rope'. They were also careful to dismount before entering the city as 'none but a Mohammedan might ride within the walls' (a point which Colonel Stoddart was later to overlook at his peril).

They did not have to wait long for a summons to the vizier; Burnes went alone as, once again, Dr Gerard was unwell. His presents of a silver watch and a cashmere shawl were declined by the vizier, who said 'he was but the slave of the king'. (This did not prevent him later accepting a different present which had greater appeal to him: a patent compass which 'would enable him to point to the holy city of Mecca'.) Burnes then faced a two-hour interrogation on the usual subjects: his profession, his religion and the reasons for his journey. Burnes gave honest answers, stressing – in his usual endearing manner – the lofty reputation of Bokhara as a main incentive for the journey. The only regulation the vizier imposed on Burnes was that 'he must prohibit our using pen and ink, since it might lead to our being misrepresented to the king'. He obviously was scared as to how the emir might react to European visitors and kept Burnes well away from him, which was just as well when the subsequent fate of his next English visitors, Stoddart and Conolly, is recalled.

Burnes had to be content with viewing the emir from afar on his way to prayers and did not like the look of him when he did. As Burnes stood dutifully by the roadside to watch the emir pass, and stroked his beard respectfully as the citizens were doing, he reflected that the emir's lot was not altogether a happy one. Because 'poison is common, and the rise of his majesty himself to the throne is not without strong suspicion of a free distribution of such draughts', the emir never tasted or drank anything that had not been tried out first on his courtiers, so – Burnes concluded – he could never 'enjoy a hot meal or a fresh cooked dinner'. Burnes himself was advised never to eat anything he had been given without inviting the donor to eat some first himself.

Burnes not only charmed the vizier and viewed the emir, he also sat gossiping in the Registran (the bazaar square) with Persians, Turkomans, Tartars, Cossacks, Chinese, Russians, Afghans, Armenians and Bokharan Jews (he particularly admired the looks of the last group whom he found 'remarkably handsome . . . more than one Rebecca'). He collected news; he noted the foreign slaves had mostly adopted – or purported to adopt – the Islamic faith; he studied the minaret from which criminals were hurled to their death; he heard stories of the rigours of Islamic law including tales of stoning to death; and he remembered to turn his head and gaze away when members of the emir's harem passed on horseback, thus avoiding 'a blow to the head' from their minders. He also recorded the sources of the goods on sale – tea from China, spices from Manila, cotton from Europe, sugar from India – realizing that 'no people could be more liberal encouragers of commerce than the rulers of Bokhara' and he noticed the policing in the streets that enabled bales of cotton to be left out overnight. In fact, Burnes was the perfect reporter, always tactful, always observant. He summed up his experience by commenting: 'Simple people! They believe a spy must measure their forts and walls; they have no idea of the value of conversation.' But one thing Burnes was warned not to do was to produce any maps or papers while talking to acquaintances: 'there are innumerable spies about the king, and it might be productive of very serious consequences'.

Burnes met some Russian slaves who were well treated but forced to profess Islamic beliefs and who longed to return to their native land, from the fringes of which they had been kidnapped as children. The Bokharan answer to any criticism of this practice was that the Russians often fared far worse in their own country, especially if they suffered 'cruel banishment to Siberia'.

At a later interview with the vizier he was pressed very hard about religious subjects: he was at his most diplomatic, baring his chest to show he did not wear a crucifix – 'an idol', equivocating about eating pork (he quickly moved on to professing he liked horse flesh, which he didn't) and explaining how liberal the British were in India towards Islam. The vizier concluded that Burnes's beliefs were at least 'better than the Russians', just as in Kunduz he had been found 'better than a Hindu'.

After a month in Bokhara, Burnes realized it was time to move on, but 'there were difficulties on every side'. No caravan could safely pass to the Caspian owing to local blood feuds. Everyone advised against going via Khiva where the khan was 'inimical towards Europeans'. Eventually, the vizier of Bokhara arranged for Burnes to join a caravan heading for Meshed and Persia. The vizier summoned the conductor of the caravan and a Turkoman chief who was accompanying them, and he made it clear that 'if any accident befell them [Burnes and Gerard] your wives and families are in my power and I will root them from the face of the earth'. He further advised Burnes to travel 'without show' and to keep clear of involvements. Perhaps the vizier's greatest service was warning them off joining a Russian caravan at Bokhara which (he later learnt) was plundered by the Kirghiz: 'we should have met with catastrophe . . . I had to congratulate myself on having attended to the [vizier's] advice'.

Burnes was relieved to have got away and to be able once more to ride and write; throughout their time in Bokhara he had only 'used the pen at night with leaden eyes; but, even then, with fear'. Even now their troubles and dangers were not over. They had to pass uncomfortably close to the camp of the hostile khan of Khiva, and wait – for almost a month – until they got a (rather unconvincing) permit from the khan's camp. The rigours of the desert lay ahead, with the usual hazards of dried-up wells and Turkoman slaving raiders. When their caravan reached a recognized trading station, there were demands for tax payments and awkward questions from the Turkomans about who Burnes and Gerard were. This time – rather than being presented as Afghans, Uzbeks, Armenians or Jews – they were described as Hindu pilgrims.

When they reached Sarakhs they waited again, this time until a Turkoman raiding party had returned (which they did with 115 captured slaves) as they feared that if they encountered them in the desert rather than as 'guests' they might be viewed as fair prey. But Sarakhs was not a safe haven: one Turkoman chief had received a tip-off (presumably from an informer within their own caravan) that Burnes and Gerard were wealthy traders in disguise and would have to be reported to the khan and detained when the caravan moved on. This was deeply worrying; but fortunately the chief was bought off with a gift of precious tea. It was only when they reached Meshed in Persia that they were really safe at last.

From there they went to Astrabad (now called Gorgan) near

to the southern point of the Caspian Sea, and on to Tehran. There Burnes stayed with the British minister and had an audience with the Shah before returning to India by sea through the Persian Gulf and the Indian Ocean, while Gerard went home separately. Burnes had been away for just over a year.

Burnes's triumphant survival of what must be reckoned as the ultimate shooting-leave expedition was due to many factors. He blended naturally into Central Asia, speaking the languages and keeping a consistently low profile while remaining attentive to local gossip and advice. As well as being a brave and resourceful traveller, he was also a skilful courtier: to him, oriental flattery came naturally. One after another, the men on whom his fate depended – the rulers of Lahore, Peshawar, Kabul, Kunduz and Bokhara among them – succumbed to his charm and attentions. Even when his fate did not depend on securing the goodwill of his royal interrogators, Burnes could not resist laying on his flattery with a trowel, as Benjamin Disraeli would have said. In his audience with the Shah of Persia in Tehran, the Shah asked him what was the most remarkable phenomenon he had seen in all his travels. Without a moment's hesitation, Burnes replied: 'Centre of the universe, what sight has equalled that which I now behold, the light of Your Majesty's countenance, Oh Attraction of the World!' This was a young officer who knew how to please.

# Chapter 3

## James Abbott: The Knight Errant

'An Englishman whose heart is in a matter is not easily baffled.'
  – Walter Bagehot (1826–77), in *The English Constitution*

On Christmas Eve, 1839, Lieutenant James Abbott of the Bengal Artillery set out from Herat in western Afghanistan on one of the most dangerous, demanding and diverse missions that it was possible for the East India Company to devise. He was to return to duty in India two years later, minus two fingers, hacked off in a sabre attack which had nearly cost him his life. The tale of his mission filled 800 pages and two fat volumes of Victorian prose.

The officer who sent him on this mission was Major Elliot D'Arcy Todd, the British resident envoy at Herat, who had a watching brief to try to forestall threats to British India from the region to the north – the khanate of Khiva and the steppes between the Caspian and Aral seas. These formed the southern extremities of the Russian empire of Tsar Nicholas I and were the domain of roving bands of Turkoman and Kazakh raiders and slave traders. It was not a hospitable terrain.

Abbott's brief was both extensive and somewhat vague. He was to travel north to the desert town of Merv and then on to Khiva, where he was to present himself to the khan – the absolute ruler of that arid kingdom. He needed to secure the friendship of the khan and to ascertain the truth of whether the Russians were in the process of invading the territory and absorbing it into Russian Central Asia. At the same time he was to explain that the British could not send the artillery support that the khan had requested; so his leverage was limited. Despite that, he was to go on to suggest that if the khan freed his Russian slaves this would remove the pretext for an invasion. Also, he was to note the nature of the terrain (over which there had been no previous survey) and to assess the defensive potential of the various towns and forts that he passed through. The East India Company – and by extension the British government – wanted to gain a clearer picture of the problems that would confront an invader or defender of the region, including the threat posed by the roving bands of tribesmen who ranged over the surrounding steppe.

It would have been a tall order for the most experienced and well-equipped officer, but Abbott was neither. His father had been a merchant in Calcutta so he had always been destined for a career in India. After a traditional education in England, first at a private school in Blackheath – where one of his fellow pupils was Benjamin Disraeli – and then at Addiscombe College, he had arrived in India in 1822, aged 16. He had become a Second Lieutenant in the Bengal Artillery and later served in the Army of the Indus with the East India Company, where he was attached as a political assistant to Major Todd in Herat. Although he was a good linguist and had some working knowledge of French, Latin and Hindustani, his Persian was fairly rudimentary and he spoke no Russian or any of the Kazakh or Turkoman tongues.

Abbott was seriously ambitious. He undertook his mission 'in the hope of making a name for himself' and – as he explicitly explains – of winning honours from the Queen, from the government and from 'a public whose opinion is of the utmost consequence to an Englishman'. When things went wrong, he was well aware that 'my fame, as well as my life, was staked upon the venture'.

Although his background and qualifications for service may have been typical of many young officers, his character had its complexities. He was fiercely and, at times, arrogantly patriotic. There are regular references in his book to his being 'superior to all around me' and to the fact that 'an Englishman had but one way of proceeding in all cases – and that was to advance'. He reminded the khan of Khiva that he represented 'the greatest and most powerful country in the world' and as such deserved to be received by 'the highest officer ever employed in ceremonial'. He demanded 'one of the largest apartments for the reception of nobles and chiefs' in Khiva, and when the khan's vizier invited him to call, rather than calling on him, he recorded that, 'none perhaps but an European resident of India can comprehend the sacrifice which this concession cost me'. On another occasion he confessed that his high-handed remarks to the vizier had made a personal enemy of him. His national pride spilled over dangerously into an exaggerated sense of his own importance when he declared to his readers that 'the destinies of nations were dependent on my steps'. However, there is no denying that – even if he made enemies in the process and appears pompous in retrospect – it is this sense of national superiority and of high destiny that spurred him on when others would have given up in despair.

Abbott was also proud of his Christian faith and saw it as being self-evidently superior to other faiths; he was inclined to see the hand of the Almighty hovering over him at all moments of special danger. Possibly because of puritanical tendencies, he was a teetotaller and disapproved of drinking. His hosts – despite their Muslim faith – were often disappointed at his inability to provide them with 'warm medicine' (spirits) or to join in their drinking on festive occasions.

The converse of this sense of national and religious superiority was an unfortunate tendency to denigrate other races and nationalities. He found Asians greedy for gifts and 'avarice – the universal demon of Asia', while also disliking both their table-manners and the physical appearance of Islamic women. Above all, he distrusted Asians, believing them to lie 'from the sheer love of deceiving'. It is with this deeply held bundle of prejudices that he set out on his mission.

Abbott left Herat with a small retinue of escorts, guides and servants. From the beginning he was bedevilled by the fact that he did not trust them. The chief among his retainers was an Afghan called Peer Muhummud Khaun, a relative of the vizier of Herat (who was no friend to the British). Abbott decided this man was too senior a person to be charged with such a humble task and so he must have had some other more sinister purpose: probably to undermine Abbott's standing with the khan of Khiva by suggesting that he was in reality a Russian agent. Therefore, as soon as Abbott crossed from the territory of Herat to that of Khiva he dismissed and sent home Peer Muhummud, even though this weakened the effectiveness of his armed escort just at the moment when he was entering the 'very stronghold of robbers'. He also missed the companionship of one of the few members of the party whose Persian he could understand. Abbott then entertained grave misgivings about one of his servants whom he threatened to horse-whip on account of his insolence. The servant later failed to put Abbott's pistol by his bedside and Abbott subsequently found it cocked and ready to fire: he concluded that the offended servant 'had the intention of shooting me'. He too – not surprisingly – was dismissed.

The start of the route to Khiva, via Merv, followed a modest mountain chain through the steppes; the grassy plains were infested with snakes and the hillsides were alive with antelope. Black-tented nomad camps – consisting of felt circular yurts – were scattered over the valleys. When a local chief sent a messenger to conduct Abbott and his party to their camp, Abbott concluded that 'this was extremely discourteous for the chief should have come himself to meet me'. However, he was none the less glad of the shelter provided. The wealth of the local nomads consisted of flocks of sheep and herds of horses, but in this case they had been obtained in return for slaves captured while crossing the steppes.

From the outset, Abbott was normally 'dressed in the Afghan attire consisting of a double set of stiff petticoats'. Throughout his journey he continually changed clothes: whenever he encountered anyone of authority, he changed into his East India Company military uniform and on special occasions – notably when meeting Russians – he donned gold-braided epaulettes which, although only those of a subaltern, approximated in grandeur to those of a Russian colonel and always created a gratifying effect. On one occasion he had to apologize for not having 'a large cocked hat and plume' (which the khan of Khiva had expected of him) because he 'had just come from the wars and lost all my finery'. A smart uniform and a richly engraved, gilt-hilted sabre were always the essential tools of his role as an envoy, but when travelling or spying, his Afghan attire was more appropriate and attracted less attention.[1]

---

1. Uniform was to remain an important adjunct for travelling in these parts: when the Hon. George (later Lord) Curzon as a young Member of Parliament was travelling in Afghanistan some half-century later, he went so far as to purchase a gaudy uniform and decorations from a theatrical agent in London before setting out.

Once the mountains were behind him, it was necessary to navigate across open steppe. Abbott had a compass and his watch to help him take bearings for the early stages of the journey, but later he was to suffer from the fact that he had to give away his watch, while too much close study of his compass or any instrument aroused suspicions of 'necromancy' which unnerved his companions.

Tamarisk trees provided some night shelter on the steppes, while large fires had to be lit to keep predators at bay. But this was not always adequate: on the first stage of his journey 'he heard a panther prowling round the camp' so close by that it alarmed his followers. Abbott took his rifle and went in search of the animal, but was defeated by the darkness and density of the trees. He recorded that the panther's mewling cry reminded him of a tigress he had encountered in India on a genuine shooting trip. Although he thought his party were not in danger as they slept close to the fires, he feared for the horses and camels tethered further away. However, all survived the night.

As Abbott and his party approached Merv, they found that rumours had preceded them about their being on a mission to free slaves at Khiva. The Turkoman tribal chiefs whose camps they passed chained up their slaves to discourage any ideas of making a dash for freedom. Abbott's Afghan steward – Summud Khaun (who was to stay with him for several years and even accompany him to Russia and England) – recognized one of the slaves as a fellow tribesman, but was unable to do anything to help him. As they went on their way they passed slave caravans also heading for Khiva, and Abbott remarked on the desperate plight of these unfortunates – cramped, cold, inadequately clothed and heading for 'a prison house girded with trackless deserts whose sole inhabitants are the sellers of human flesh'. The male slaves – mostly Afghans from the Herat region – were chained together by the throat at night 'so that rest is scarcely possible, whilst the contact of the frozen iron with their skin must be torturous'. Not surprisingly, Abbott's deeply held Christian beliefs were disturbed by these encounters – although he was writing at a time when slavery was still generally practised in the British West Indies.

Abbott sent messages ahead to advise the governor of Merv of his imminent arrival and, as usual, he was offended that he 'was suffered to approach the castle without any symptom of a greeting'. In a huff, he decided to camp outside the town, but was eventually prevailed upon to accept the governor's hospitality. He managed to contact a Jewish merchant at Merv who was prepared to cash his letters of credit, and who told him of a recent massacre of Jews close by, at Meshed in Persia, following an accusation that they had killed a dog in ridicule of the nephew of the Prophet. A number of the Jews in Merv were refugees from this pogrom.

Abbott's brief stay in Merv provided a foretaste of the problems he was face at Khiva. The Bey – or governor – had a reputation for brutality which was vividly illustrated when the Jewish merchant was struck over the head in Abbott's presence by one of the Bey's officers; when Abbott objected that such behaviour was an insult to him, he was warned that if he persisted in his complaint the offending officer would be promptly decapitated. Even Abbott decided that this was an excessive response to the insult and decided to drop the matter.

Later he was convinced that the Bey was trying to trick him into showing some knowledge of the Russian language, which would reveal him to be a Russian spy. Abbott attributed this suspicion to a message which he thought his discharged escort commander had sent ahead – 'carried by a Turkoman who passed me in the night' – to undermine his position. There was a general reluctance among those whom he met at Merv to believe that two Christian nations – Russia and England – who were not at war with each other could be anything other than collaborators in invading Central Asia.

Ever alert to his brief to spy out the potential of the land, Abbott observed that Merv was a very considerable crossroads for caravans between Bokhara and Persia, Khiva and Afghanistan. He predicted that it had the possibility of 'rising from its dust into wealth and consequence', but nevertheless he was glad to quit 'the much vaunted plain' and enter the desert.

Abbott hired six more camels at Merv as he was warned that the desert crossing to Khiva might involve up to ten days 'when the wells happen to be dry'. As well as purchasing skins for their water, he took on fodder for the horses and extra supplies for the whole party. He even bought a Persian sabre and a Turkish flintlock musket as presents for the Bey, feeling that – however much he disliked and mistrusted him – it was better to leave him conciliated.

The supply of appropriate gifts was a continual problem for Abbott. The budget for his mission allowed for some presents for the khan of Khiva, but both expense and the practicalities of transport kept these to a minimum. The vizier of Khiva was to ask him specifically whether he had any presents for him too, 'such as a brace of pistols, pen-knives that cut steel, telescopes and watches'. Abbott was travelling with all these things (as the vizier well knew) but they were essential parts of his kit, and although he was prepared to part with his trusty telescope and thermometer it was only in extremis that he was later prevailed upon to part with his watch. On a later occasion when he wanted to reward those who had befriended him, he was reduced to giving away his crested silver spoons; and – as we shall see – at one point he was virtually stripped of every-thing he had.[2]

After leaving Merv, Abbott established a demanding daily routine which he described in detail. He and his party would rise at midnight and breakfast over a blazing fire, drinking tea, while the camels were being loaded up. He would then follow the camels on horseback, quickly overtaking them, and then break for another rest over a fire for half an hour – firewood being readily to hand 'and so dry that when the hoar frost or snow is shaken from it, it kindles instantly'. Remounting, the party would continue in single file by a narrow track across the plains, while their breath froze 'upon one's beard and mustachios, rendering the motion of the jaw singularly unpleasant'. When dawn broke, they would halt and light a fire to thaw out. At this point the Muslims would spread out their cloaks, work out the direction of Mecca, and say their prayers. The whole process would be repeated until finally they would pitch camp at around four in the afternoon, when they would retire to sleep until midnight again. The long hours constrained in the saddle and the exces-sive cold paralysed the nerves in their legs so badly that for three weeks after his arrival at Khiva Abbott had 'scarcely the use of my right foot'.

----

2. Exchanges of presents still present thorny diplomatic problems. When the author was at the British embassy in Moscow and Prime Minister Harold Macmillan arrived to visit Nikita Khrushchev, there was prolonged debate about a suitable gift for Khrushchev. Shot-guns and silver were considered. Khrushchev had brought the Queen a bear cub when he visited England three years before, and it was said – possibly apocryphally – that the Queen had suggested 'give the man a lion'. But no suitable lion could be found in London zoo or elsewhere.

As they progressed towards Khiva, the sand dunes increased and the wind effaced the path. At night the best they could hope for as confirmation they were on the right track was stumbling across the bones of a camel. At one midnight start they found the path covered in a foot of freshly fallen snow; they lost their bearings and sent out scouts in the wrong direction to find the camels which had gone on ahead. It was only by use of his compass that Abbott got the party back on course. Losing the camels was particularly disturbing because the guides generally relied on them to find the way: 'the camels never go astray', said Birdler Beeg, the head guide.

At this point a new hazard arose. Birdler Beeg warned Abbott that marauding bands of Tartar horsemen tended to swoop on the wells and rob, kill or enslave any travellers they found there. So water stops had to be kept to a minimum. On one occasion on a night march, they heard voices ahead and 'loosened their sabres'. Birdler Beeg asked Abbott what they should do. Abbott was for advancing and 'cutting down half a dozen . . . the rest will run'; but Birdler Beeg said 'it is much better to run . . . it is the Turkoman custom'. Fortunately, on this occasion the voices turned out to be those of their own camel party, but Abbott concluded that his guide was not to be depended upon in a crisis. He was later to discover how right he was.

When the oasis trees of Khiva came at last into sight, Abbott sent the guide ahead to contact the khan and explain that Abbott was the bearer of a letter to him from the British envoy at Herat. The guide was to add that Abbott had heard that a Persian ambassador had been received by the khan 'with much distinction' and that, as his own government 'was infinitely more powerful than that of Persia', he trusted he would be honoured accordingly.

Birdler Beeg returned the next day having achieved an audience with the khan. Abbott cross-questioned him closely about the meeting as he was nervous that either the vizier from Herat or the Persian ambassador would have already prejudiced the khan against him. However, it appeared this was not the case. Although the khan had already received intelligence of his approach and was suspicious of what the English were up to at Herat, he said he would welcome Abbott and sent an escort of a hundred horsemen to accompany him into the capital.

This was the cue for Abbott to change into his 'only full dress suit – an embroidered surtout with golden epaulettes' and to proceed into the city, with his local escort discharging their firearms and wheeling their horses around at speed. Abbott was shocked by the general lack of discipline in the Khivan escort, but impressed by the appearance of Khiva itself with its 'gardens and dwellings of the gentry', with its lofty walls, spacious gateways and ornamental towers, giving every house the aspect of a castle. He noted that the whole valley was well irrigated with canals flowing from the nearby Oxus river. He was also gratified that the population turned out to stare at this western envoy. He noted that the women showed their faces boldly but that 'their countenances were too round or square for beauty . . . and their eyes ill opened'.

Abbott was conducted to a palace which had been set aside

for him, but found it had 'miserable rooms' with no windows.
It was then that he complained of the need for more spacious
quarters to entertain the local nobility, but it was soon made
clear to him that social intercourse with locals was not to be
encouraged. Indeed, an agent of the vizier was installed in another
part of the house to note and report on his activities. In effect,
he was not so much a house-guest as under house arrest. Abbott
sent a present of cashmere shawls to the vizier, but was convinced
that the latter was helping himself to the house-keeping allowance
which the khan provided for Abbott's party. Meanwhile, he was
told that the khan would probably receive him the following day.

Abbott was clearly excited at having got so far on his mission:
he had at least reached 'Khiva, that capital so famous, yet so
little known, of which half the existing accounts are fabulous
[fabled]'. However, he went to sleep pondering the enormity of
the task confronting him: to gain the confidence of the khan,
when he had no adequate gifts to bring, no firm promises he
could make, no proper command of the language and an unreliable
interpreter, while his position was possibly already undermined
by the vizier of Herat and the recently arrived Persian ambassador. It was against these odds that he received a summons to
his first audience.

Once again the streets were lined with onlookers, curious
to see a foreigner and his retinue in all their finery on their
way to the palace. Abbott was subsequently told that a decree
had been issued that – on pain of death – he was not to be
molested, otherwise he would certainly have been in trouble.
There was no love of foreigners in Khiva. Ever alert for military intelligence, Abbott noted – even as he was riding to his
meeting – that the massed artillery of Khiva was assembled
near the gates of the city and consisted of 22 brass field guns

of 6- to 12-pound calibre, poorly mounted on carriages with wooden axles.

On arrival Abbott shed his shoes and then was embarrassed at mistaking the vizier for the khan, 'however no harm was done'. Eventually, he was admitted to the royal presence where he found the khan seated on a rug propped up by cushions. To his annoyance, he was kept standing. He explained that he had come in response to the khan's own envoy at Herat. The khan, smiling amiably at Abbott's inadequate Persian, listened to his presentation of British interests and his warnings about the Russian incursions.

In his published account, Abbott is somewhat coy about exactly what he said, explaining that even after the event he would not want the Russians to know precisely what he was up to: these were war and peace issues of the greatest magnitude. In reality, he exceeded his instructions and persuaded the khan to agree – at least verbally – to a treaty providing for the establishment of a British agent in Khiva and British mediation between the khan and the Tsar of Russia.

Abbott's assessment of the khan (or 'old King Cob' as he irreverently refers to him) is somewhat patronizing. He judges that there is 'an absence of vigour, for which at the present crisis nothing can atone'; he was always 'ungraceful and unkingly'; his courtiers were of undistinguished appearance; his only vice was smoking his hookah 'for he neither snuffs nor drinks, and has no more than four wives at a time'.

At his second audience, the khan was more specific in complaining about the lack of firm commitments to his defence by the British government. But as the conversation continued, it became clear just how confused and ignorant the khan was about both Britain and Russia, even asking whether it was true that Englishmen could tell 'by looking at a hill, whether or not it contained gold'.

Abbott responded as best he could to the bewildering barrage of questions and the conversation then turned to the vexed matter of Colonel Charles Stoddart. He had been sent as an emissary of the British government (but without the hoped-for signed letter from Queen Victoria) to the emir of Bokhara and had been detained and imprisoned by him. Both the khan of Khiva and Abbott were well aware of this sequence of events and the latter had been nervous from the start that it set a dangerous precedent for his own reception at Khiva. Abbott explained that the prolonged detention of Stoddart would inevitably lead to military action against Bokhara by England, although Britain was extremely reluctant to enter into hostilities with any Muslim state in Central Asia. Surely, he suggested, the khan might use his influence with the emir to obtain Stoddart's release. However, the khan declared he had no influence with the emir, who in any case was mad.

Later the same day, the khan's vizier followed up this part of the conversation by suggesting to Abbott – clearly on behalf of the khan – that a small party of Turkoman horsemen should be sent to Bokhara to rescue Stoddart by force and escort him across the desert back to Khiva. Abbott thought seriously about this daring plan but concluded it would not work: to start with, Stoddart was almost certainly not allowed to ride around Bokhara as the khan imagined; secondly, the horsemen who would be entrusted with this task were 'men of whose sagacity, courage or fidelity' he knew nothing; and lastly, if the emir of Bokhara got any hint of such a scheme, he would in all likelihood either execute or further torment Stoddart. So this exciting but wild idea was rejected.

Meanwhile, Abbott was learning much from the vizier and others about recent skirmishes between the Khivan forces and the Russians. It appeared that the Khivans had been trounced and returned to base having suffered losses both in the fighting and as a result of extreme frostbite that had taken a toll of feet, noses, lips and ears. It also seemed that the Russians had advanced from Orenburg to capture forts near the Aral Sea. Estimates of the strength of the Russian forces varied from 5,000 to 100,000.

Abbott took the opportunity to urge as strongly as possible that the khan should pre-empt any Russian invasion by immediately releasing all Russian subjects enslaved at Khiva. Such an act would not only remove the Russian pretext for invasion, but would make it much easier for Britain to come to Khiva's assistance. The vizier assured Abbott of the khan's intention to meet his request, but the khan later told Abbott that he had unsuccessfully tried to arrange an exchange of prisoners in the past and the Russians were only playing games with him. Abbott failed in this aspect of his mission.

At a subsequent audience with the khan, Abbott presented him with a map of the world and tried to convince him of the relevance of British India to the defence and independence of Khiva and Persia; he also tried to justify British intervention in Afghanistan (the First Afghan War was currently under way) as necessary for the defence of India. He gave the khan a lively account of British fire-power on land and sea, a subject on which – as an artillery officer – he was something of an expert. The khan for his part gave Abbott a detailed account of Khivan skirmishes with the Russians and even showed him one of the latter's cannon balls which had been fired at his men and kept by the khan as a reminder of Russian aggression.

According to Abbott's account, the khan proposed that

Abbott should continue his journey northwards and be more successful than his own ambassadors in dissuading the Tsar from pressing on with his campaign against Khiva. It seems more likely – from other India Office sources – that the idea came from Abbott himself; if so, he was going well ahead of his instructions and indulging in an early form of 'mission creep'. At all events, Abbott readily accepted the task while ruefully reflecting – with some scarcely concealed pride – that he was now not only the envoy of Britain, but also the envoy of 'a khan of Tartary to the court of the Muscovites'. The rest of his stay in Khiva was devoted to trying to leave as soon as possible.

The irony of Abbott's position was that although the khan was requesting him to represent his interests to the Russians, the khan clearly did not really trust him and still harboured suspicions that Abbott was himself a Russian agent. He was watched like a hawk. Even his brief walks in the garden of his palace-prison were viewed with concern: was he measuring out the ground for some sinister purpose? If he was spotted writing, he was assumed to be making intelligence notes. To some extent, of course, the khan was correct in these suspicions: Abbott was indeed noting everything of strategic interest and, when he could not risk being found with notes, he paraphrased them 'in verse, and committed [them] to memory, destroying the paper'. This was no innocent tourist.

The khan continued to set traps for Abbott. A French-language account of travels from Orenburg to Bokhara was handed to Abbott by the khan with a request that he should translate aloud a few sentences into Persian, which he did. It then transpired that the book had been taken from a Russian caravan and the khan probably thought it was in Russian – a language of which Abbott had previously (and truthfully) denied any knowledge. The khan also regaled Abbott with tales of other recent travellers who had claimed to be English but, under cross-examination, appeared to be Russian spies; the khan had them executed. Abbott was to be haunted by such tales as he felt, even after he had left Khiva, that the khan might suddenly decide that he was a Russian spy after all and have him murdered in the desert.

Meanwhile, preparations for Abbott's departure from Khiva were now under way. He asked the khan for three or four Russian slaves to be attached to his party as a sign 'of the khan's intention to free the remainder'. Discussion then followed about what route Abbott should take to make contact with the nearest Russian outpost. Abbott favoured going west across the steppe for some 450 miles to a Caspian port at which Russian ships regularly called, and getting a passage onwards on one of these. An alternative would be to go north across the Kirghiz Steppe to Orenburg, a distance of some 900 miles. The khan said the Caspian would still be frozen and, although the track might be under five feet of snow, he appeared to favour the Orenburg route. Abbott still preferred the shorter Caspian route.

The khan wanted a Khivan envoy to accompany Abbott so that he would have his own observer present when Abbott encountered the Russians and could determine whether he was a Russian spy. Abbott himself was anxious to have a guide who could accompany him all the way; he did not want to be 'bandied from guide to guide and from tribe to tribe'. In the end, after much debate, Abbott's chosen route was agreed, and it was further decided that if he did not encounter Russian shipping at the Caspian port, he would press on to Nuovo Alexandrofski – a larger port. Right up to the moment of departure there were uncertainties, not least about how Abbott was going to pay his way. Local merchants refused to cash his letters of credit (was this a sinister sign?) and the khan declined to finance him. He eventually had to accept that once he reached the Caspian he would starve for lack of funds unless he could sell his horses, tents and equipment and throw himself on Russian hospitality. So at last he set out on the second major leg of his journey – from Khiva to the Caspian – with his original retinue of seven servants and various Khivan armed guards, none of whom he trusted.

The first days were spent travelling northwards along the wooded and cultivated valley of the Oxus, before turning west and into the bleaker desert. He was soon falling out with his senior Khivan guide – Hussun Mhatoor – who was 'insolent' in not being ready for a 2 a.m. start one morning. Abbott left him behind to catch up, but as a consequence managed to get lost. Further friction was caused by Hussun Mhatoor halting the expedition for three days when he passed through his own home village. Abbott's threats were useless and his capacity to bribe non-existent. Money was becoming a real problem and he became increasingly frustrated. Abbott's servants offered to chip in with their savings to help finance the trip, but he declined the offer ('the cause on which I was embarked was my own and not theirs'). Instead, he hoped to meet with some Afghan or Jewish merchant to cash his credit notes, otherwise he 'would most probably perish in the wilderness'.

More worrying still was the fact that he was told by local inhabitants that, since he had left Khiva, he had been denounced to the khan as a Russian spy and that the khan had therefore sent instructions for Abbott to be 'murdered in the wilderness'. Also, he was worried at the obvious procrastination of his guide, who seemed to be hovering within reach of fresh instructions from Khiva. It was at this point, too, that he was told of two supposed Englishmen who had been previously tortured and executed in Khiva as Russian spies: 'your case is exactly like theirs', he was told ominously. Abbott consoled himself with the thought that they were probably not Englishmen after all.

Each day some modest progress towards the Caspian was made and, although the stretch of water which Abbott imagined to be the Aral Sea turned out only to be a lake, before long he reached Kazakh country – the dangers of which were all too soon to become apparent. At least there were some diversions here: a herd of wild asses and flocks of antelope provided the focus for hunting excursions, which was probably as near as Abbott got to any real 'shooting leave'. The terrain became marshy; the camels 'sank at every step'; melted snow accumulated in the ravines; and wolf-fur stockings (worn 'hair inwards') had to be donned as a protection against the excessive cold.

From the start, Abbott took against the Kazakhs: their manners were horrible; the men were ugly; the women 'at a short distance resemble peonies, their faces are furiously red, their features extremely coarse, they have the figures of bears and the dress of toad-stools'. An Afghan boy, who belonged to one of the Turkoman slaves travelling with Abbott, was exchanged for some sheep with some local Kazakhs. This added to his prejudice against them, but he was soon to have even greater reason to hate them.

When Abbott heard stories designed to cheer up the party, they usually had the opposite effect as they relayed gruesome evidence of local cruelties. One such tale, recounted by his faithful steward Summud Khaun, enumerated the grisly details of how the vizier of Herat had been trapped, blinded, and then had his ears and nose cut off; apparently (and this was the point of the story) the vizier only broke down when he suffered the final indignity of having his beard cut off. Such tales were not good for the morale of an officer who had good reason to think he might fall into the hands of similar persecutors.

Abbott began to be seriously suspicious that he was being set up for an ambush. He observed his mistrusted guide Hussun Mhatoor examining all the fastenings of his tent and recalled the practice of 'cutting down the tent over the person whom it is desirable to murder, the tent serving as a net to prevent resistance'. Abbott made a rule of never retiring to bed without having his pistols and sabre immediately to hand; he knew he could not save himself if attacked, but comforted himself with the prospect of taking a number of his assailants with him.

It was in this frame of mind that he got his initial glimpse of the Caspian. This was the first time most of his party had ever seen any sea and they tended to mistake waves for sails. However, it was a disappointing moment: not a ship in sight. This was where he had been assured he would find an 'abundance of vessels and no difficulty whatever in embarking' for Russia. Instead, Hussun Mhatoor suggested that he should sell all his horses and purchase a boat 'and two Russian slaves to man it' to take him to an island some five hours' sail away where his slippery guide promised him, with no great conviction, 'there were always vessels'. Abbott realized this would be a fatal plan: he would have shot his bolt completely and still might not get a passage to Astrakhan, in the Volta Delta, or elsewhere. He decided to wait one day — setting up a flagpole and lighting a bonfire on a promontory to attract attention — to see if a ship turned up, and if not to move on to Nuovo Alexandrofski, where there was known to be a Russian presence. This was thought to be some five days' camel march away.

Not altogether surprisingly, Hussun Mhatoor – who had hoped to profit from the selling of Abbott's horses and tents – refused to accompany him any further, so Abbott replaced him with a Kazakh guide. He had barely set out when a totally unconvincing messenger overtook him and said that some Russian ships had arrived at the point he had just left and that he should turn back. Abbott was sure this was a false report to lure him back and place him at the mercy of Hussun Mhatoor while his supplies ran out. He pressed on, convinced that some of those who remained with him were conspiring against him and sending back messages to reveal his exact location: 'more than once my hand was upon my pistol with intent to shoot [his treacherous guides] and prudence alone prevented the act'. Parties of armed Turkomans loomed up on the horizons and appeared to be shadowing them; he was convinced they were also agents of Hussun Mhatoor.

To add to the tension, his party was obliged to camp in the open where it was vulnerable to attack. Abbott was acutely conscious that his few servants, including Summud Khaun, 'had never seen the gleam of more deadly steel than the metal of a carving knife'. He was depressed too by their fatalism: 'whatever is to be, will be'. Abbott found that while his loyal servants were 'heavy and determined sleepers', the treacherous guides spent the nights conspiring together and continually glancing at Abbott to see if he were sleeping or off-guard. 'My wakefulness saved my throat,' he concluded. And so, tired and apprehensive, Abbott and his party pressed on across the stony, barren landscape to another glimpse of the northeastern corner of the Caspian Sea. Some camel drivers wanted to defect, others to turn back. The camels themselves were failing and the horses nearly exhausted: it was a vulnerable little group of men and animals.

It was at this juncture that Abbott spotted one of his more suspect guides taking off his coat and waving it conspicuously. Although he claimed he was signalling to other members of Abbott's party, it was clear that he was in fact sending covert signals to the circling Kazakh horsemen who were shadowing their progress: 'I felt there was no safety in company of this villain'. In order to move faster towards Nuovo Alexandrofski, Abbott shed all but their essential equipment; but unfortunately a redistribution of his remaining silver coins only served to arouse the cupidity of the guides. There was more covert signalling by them – under pretence of saying their prayers – to lurking figures in the surrounding rocks. Abbott was so sure that an attack was imminent that he 'laid his ear along the earth, the better to catch the sound of hoofs'.

His fears were not groundless. After their camp fires had been put out on the night of 22 April 1840, the Kazakh bandits struck. Abbott had heard a commotion and, thinking the horses were being stolen, went towards the scene of the action. It was too dark to risk shooting in case he hit one of his own men, and then 'suddenly I was struck from the rear by three clubs falling together'. Though stunned, Abbott struggled on against four Kazakhs, who knocked his pistol out of his hand and grabbed at his sabre; he raised his arm to shield his head from a sabre blow and 'the sabre fell upon my hand, severing two fingers'. Although only semi-conscious and 'beaten to a jelly', Abbott prayed fervently 'not for deliverance, but for the constancy and strength to encounter the worst, without faltering or disgracing my country or my name'. This was the Addiscombe cadet's finest hour and he was determined that the

Bengal Artillery should have reason to be proud of him.

Meanwhile, in the general scuffle, passing Kazakhs struck at him with sabres, hatchets or clubs. He very nearly lost his other hand, when a sabre stroke was only diverted by glancing off a ring on his finger; the ring had been a present from his sister and 'her gift saved him from being utterly crippled'. As he looked around as best he could, he recognized that the attackers were 40- or 50-strong. No resistance – apart from his own – had been put up, but he was convinced that his assailants were bandits rather than agents of the khan of Khiva.

He had resigned himself to death when a remarkable thing happened. A passing Kazakh, on finding him still alive, took it on himself to ward off other blows. Abbott pretended to be dead, and the chivalrous Kazakh – one Cherkush Bae – conspired with him in this deception until the assault had eased off. The bandits then realized there was no point in unnecessary killing, as their victims could more profitably be sold as slaves. Some of Abbott's servants had already been badly wounded and beaten up. Abbott himself, with the help of Cherkush Bae, produced his credentials from the khan of Khiva and managed to sow some doubts in the minds of his assailants as to whether it was prudent to kill someone with apparently powerful connections.

There followed a period of several days which were alarming, painful and bizarre. Cherkush Bae used a blunt dagger to amputate Abbott's forefinger ('which hung only by a sinew') and managed to conceal the ring on the other hand 'which – as it was impossible to draw it off otherwise – might if seen have cost me another finger'. Meanwhile, another young Kazakh was cavorting around decked out in Abbott's ceremonial uniform. He could see and hear discussions going on about what to do

with him; one Kazakh glanced at him meaningfully and 'drew his finger significantly across his throat'. At times it seemed likely they would stage another attack by 'unknown' assailants to avoid responsibility for killing Abbott themselves. One of the thoughts that haunted him was that, if he were to die or be killed, his servants would inevitably be sold into slavery 'under the severest taskmasters in the world'; this thought strengthened his resolution to 'cherish my hold on life'. All the while, Abbott and his servants were being systematically stripped of everything of value, including the clothes they needed to keep them from freezing at night.

The days of captivity dragged on. One poignant incident particularly affected Abbott. One of the young camel calves had died and the Kazakhs stuffed its skin with straw and showed it to its mother when they wished her to produce milk. The mother camel howled with distress each time on finding the calf was only a stuffed skin, and Abbott had visions of his own mother lamenting his loss similarly. Sometimes there were incidents which had an element of humour, such as when some of Abbott's servants decided to swallow his few remaining gold coins to hide them from plunder and all sorts of internal complications followed. During this period, Abbott also managed to discover the reason for Cherkush Bae's unexpected kindness to him: the Kazakh had a son who was a prisoner of the Russians and he thought Abbott might intervene on his behalf. There was vague talk of going on to Nuovo Alexandrofski or of going back to Khiva. But always the threat of murder hung in the air and every day seemed likely to be Abbott's last.

Then, literally out of the blue, rescue arrived. A handsome young Afghan on a grey horse with a silver bridle appeared on the horizon. He was Saleh Muhummud whom Abbott had befriended at Merv. He bore supportive letters from the khan of Khiva and gave instructions to his abductors to release him. 'Lift up you head, Sir. Your sufferings are at an end!' he declared to Abbott.

It seemed that the khan had indeed undergone a further spell of doubts about Abbott's status – a British envoy or a Russian spy? He had purloined a packet of Abbott's letters which, when translated to him, persuaded the khan that Abbott was what he said he was after all. Hence the khan's decision to send Saleh and a Turkoman escort after him, along with letters and gold coins. Saleh had heard news of Abbott's plight while he was on his way to overtake him but had bravely pressed on regardless and arrived just in time.

It was, however, only with the greatest difficulty that Abbott persuaded Saleh to accompany him on to Nuovo Alexandrofski rather than return to Khiva. Abbott felt he had to press on or else render pointless all the risks and sufferings he had undergone. Little by little most of Abbott's sequestered horses and equipment were returned to him and a start was made towards the Russian port. For company, Abbott now had Saleh, a small but unreliable escort consisting of some dozen Turkomans and half a dozen Kazakhs, and some of his own original servants. The terrain was high steppe, covered with wormwood.

When they came within sight of a Russian fort at the approaches to the port, the Turkoman and Kazakh escorts refused to go further for fear of being held prisoner by the Russians. Only Saleh offered to stay with Abbott, but the latter dissuaded him as it was too dangerous. It was therefore a very depleted and vulnerable little party that eventually – after all their tribulations – came within sight of the Russian lookout posts at Nuovo Alexandrofski.

Not surprisingly, the Russians sent out a few Cossack scouts to find out who they were and what they were up to. Abbott and his party were ordered to halt while more senior officers came forward to interrogate them. 'I addressed them alternately in French, English, Latin, Persian and Hindustani, but they shook their heads in reply,' Abbott recorded.

After this initially wary reception (they had feared Abbott might be the forerunner of an army of 10,000 Turkomans) the Russian garrison at Nuovo Alexandrofski turned out to be hospitable. One of the first things they did was to find a doctor to tidy up Abbott's lacerated hand: this involved amputating another finger, but this time under far more reassuringly clinical conditions.

Abbott now concentrated on three matters. Firstly, to arrange an onward passage for himself across the north of the Caspian Sea and on to the Russian garrison town of Orenburg. Secondly, to try to secure the release of the son of Cherkush Bae: Abbott offered to buy the boy's freedom for 200 sheep and eventually succeeded in getting this. Thirdly, he was up to his usual practices of spying out military details which might be of interest to Britain in the event of a confrontation: he recorded the size of the garrison, the limitations of the port, the nature of the fort ('square, with bastions, flanks and curtains; but with neither ditch, outwork or glacis'), the morale of the Cossacks and so on. He dismissed Russian boasts that the fort was 'unassailable' by commenting that they would be astonished to know what feats the British had achieved against Indian fortifications. The artillery officer in Abbott was never far below the surface.

He was put out by the Russian insistence that they should report his arrival only by his first names and patronymic – 'James Henry Alexiowitz' – and not by his rank, full name and regiment: 'I imagined there might be something of a slight in this . . . and was disposed to resent it'. All his adventures had not made Abbott any less prickly about social status.

While en route to Orenburg, Abbott heard for the first time about the abortive Russian attempt to invade the territory of the khan of Khiva. Owing to the severity of the weather and the heavy toll in horses and men, the Russians had abandoned their attempts to reach Khiva itself in February 1840. Later, when he reached Orenburg, he became convinced – rightly as it turned out – that there would be further Russian attempts to take Khiva.

Abbott was greatly impressed with what he saw of Russia. The senior officers were gentlemen with whom he felt a natural rapport. And, although he went on spying on every aspect of their military preparations, he scrupulously kept his promise to the governor not to 'hold intercourse with Tartars' during his stay.[3]

From Orenburg, Abbott was allowed to travel further into Russia – first to Moscow and finally to St Petersburg. He was courteously received, but nothing that he could say or do was going to deter the regime from their firm intent of absorbing Central Asia, and in particular Khiva, into the Tsar's empire. The advance towards British India was an objective that no warnings or pleadings by a junior British officer – however remarkable and courageous his story – was going to deflect. Nor was it Abbott who succeeded in freeing the Russian slaves and thus removing a major pretext for the invasion: that achievement and its attendant honours were left to Lieutenant Richmond Shakespear only a few months later. After hearing of the knighthood and honours afforded to Shakespear in London and St Petersburg, Abbott was to record wistfully, 'all the sufferings fell to my lot, all the laurels to his'.

Abbott was forgiven his tendency to overreach his instructions and was welcomed home to London in 1841 as an officer who had gallantly survived a remarkable mission. He was promoted to captain, personally thanked by Lord Palmerston, the Foreign Secretary, and awarded a pension of the lordly sum of 50 pounds a year for the loss of his fingers. He was finally awarded his own knighthood, just two years before he died in 1896.

Reflecting on his experiences he commented remarkably wisely that 'the strength of Russia is in the boundless extent of

---

3. Like their Soviet successors during the author's own early visits to Central Asia in the late 1950s, the tsarist Russian authorities were more alarmed at the prospect of western envoys stirring up sedition among the indigenous population of these regions than they were at the likelihood of them discovering specific military secrets.

her dominions . . . the thickness, so to speak, of her shell . . . she is a tortoise who can be molested only when of her own accord she protrudes some vital part'. He went on to become a general, but his Khivan mission was – as was the case with the early adventures of so many young officers – his finest hour. Not for nothing did Sir Henry Lawrence (later to be the hero of the siege of Lucknow) describe him as being made 'of the stuff of the true knight errant'.

# Chapter 4

## John Wood: The Reluctant Spy

'And the river jumps over the mountain'
– W. H. Auden (1907–73), in
'As I Walked Out One Evening'

Unlike most of the young men who set out to explore the passes of the Pamirs, Lieutenant John Wood was not a smart cavalry officer or an officer in the East India Company's army; in fact, he was not a soldier at all but an officer in the Company's navy. He was unusual in other respects, too. Although a passionate hydrographer and surveyor, he was less interested than his military counterparts – such as Henry Pottinger – in strategic intelligence and espionage. Unlike Abbott, he did not see himself as having any political agenda. For him, the pursuit of knowledge for its own sake was in marked contrast to the objectives of his mentors and sponsors. This dichotomy was eventually to lead to his resignation, but all that lay some years ahead when he set off up the Indus and then the Oxus rivers in 1836.

The background to his trip was one of intrigue and political ambition. As mentioned, Sir Alexander 'Bokhara' Burnes, then a young and unknown subaltern, had first surveyed the Indus in 1830 under cover of the excuse of needing to deliver a gift of a coach and five enormous horses to Ranjit Singh, the ruler of the Punjab. The real objective was to survey the Indus river as a possible line of advance for the British to take over Sindh, Lahore and the Punjab.

That successful voyage had been the launching pad for Burnes's accelerated promotion and early fame. However, six years later more intelligence was required and when Burnes led a second expedition up the Indus in 1836 he gave some of the responsibility to Lieutenant Wood. He drafted careful instructions for Wood, as they were to be separate most of the time. The lieutenant was to ascend the Indus as far as Attock in Afghanistan to gain a more perfect knowledge of the river 'for the purposes of commerce as of war'. He was also to keep a careful note of latitudes and longitudes throughout (for this Wood was to have the help of an engineer officer) and 'the facility which the neighbourhood of the river affords for the supply of coal' as the Royal Navy was always on the lookout for local refuelling facilities. If coal were not available, then he was to try to assess the prospects for wooden fuel for steamers. He was to send his notes regularly back to the superintendent of the Indian navy, in case he lost them or – since his task was 'not altogether free from risks' – he himself perished before getting back. Finally, he was to look out for anything else of interest in a country which was so unexplored. It was an ambitious programme.

As was customary on such military-sponsored expeditions of exploration and reconnaissance, there was to be a large element of shooting leave built in to the programme. Early on their voyage up the Indus they were involved in a jackal hunt, organized by the local emir, and Burnes distinguished himself by shooting 'a grizzly looking patriarch' of a wild boar. Later, the sport turned to hawking and archery.

Wood detached himself from the rest of the party for most of the time. His comments on the navigability of the Indus are a useful corrective to earlier estimates: 'there is no known river in either hemisphere, discharging even half the quality of water the Indus does, which is not superior for navigable purposes to this far-famed stream'. So much for loose talk by others (including, incidentally, Henry Pottinger) of the river being accessible 'to a line-of-battle ship'.

When he reached Kabul and accompanied Burnes to an audience with the Emir Dost Mohammed – the ruler of Afghanistan – he was greatly impressed with the latter's dignity: 'there was that in his manner and tone of voice which enforced attention'. Wood compared this favourably with the 'vapourings' of the rulers of Baluchistan. Burnes had earlier established good working relations with Dost Mohammed on his visit to Kabul (en route for Bokhara) in 1832.

There was not much more to detain Wood in Kabul. Burnes decided to send him north to Kunduz province on a new mission to undertake a survey of the Oxus, the last major river between India and Russia. It had always been reckoned that a Russian army could be transported up the Oxus from the Aral Sea as far as Kunduz, but from that point up to its source in the high Pamirs the route of the Oxus was uncharted. This provided a challenge that appealed to Wood enormously.

There were, however, two snags to pursuing the proposal. The first was that Kunduz was the other side of the Hindu Kush range of mountains and winter was closing in. The second was that British relations with the brutal but effective ruler of Kunduz – Murad Beg – were strained to say the least. The answer to the first problem was to set off as soon as possible. The answer to the second problem was more complex. Murad

Beg had a brother – Mohammed Beg – who was elderly and going blind. Their close relationship was unusual in a part of Central Asia where brothers were more often inclined to rivalry and fratricide than mutual support. Murad Beg wanted a European doctor to attend his brother. Dr Lord, who had been another member of Burnes's expedition up the Indus, was the obvious choice. He was invited to Kunduz with a safe-conduct order and Wood – whose survey of the Oxus was the main British objective – was able to go along with him. They set off on 5 November 1837.

Crossing the Hindu Kush, even in November, was not easy. The first attempt – although they followed the least difficult route, through Bamian – failed. However, they finally got to Kunduz on 4 December. Mohammed Beg's eye condition was indeed serious and Dr Lord proposed a long course of treatment which would need to be carried out under his supervision throughout the coming winter. It was suggested to Murad Beg that Wood might occupy himself by satisfying his urge to trace the famous Oxus to its source – as a harmless act of curious exploration rather than military reconnaissance.

He set off hurriedly on 11 December, before the ruler had time to change his mind. Wood recorded, 'we adopted the costume of the country, as a measure calculated to smooth our intercourse with a strange people [not as a disguise], and we had little baggage to excite cupidity or suspicion'. The most valuable articles he took were his chronometers and other surveying instruments. His supporting staff were also fairly minimal considering the magnitude of the task and the nature of the terrain he had to cross: he took one Munshi, who was a cook and personal servant, a bodyguard supplied by Murad Beg who had belligerent tendencies, two or three porters for the heavy instruments and three Afghan grooms to look after the horses.

They had only been going for a few days before they reached the home village of the bodyguard, who had a disturbing experience. He found a stranger on horseback riding off with a beautiful female slave behind him on the saddle. He explained his grievance to Wood: 'Alas, alas, my Lord! When I left my house the very last order I gave was, that she whom you have just seen should not be sold . . . my other slaves were all for sale: this one! This favourite one! I had thought of taking to wife!' Wood commiserated with him, but found that after prolonged remonstrations and threats of revenge, his bodyguard was quickly consoled on hearing that the sale price had been 'twenty-two gold tillas (about £17 sterling)'.

Soon they were climbing to serious heights. At Kila the Afghan governor greeted them around a great bonfire outside his castle. When they were invited inside later on, Wood became worried about the safety of one of his men who had fallen behind the rest of the party. The governor was afraid he might have fallen victim to the packs of wolves that ranged around and he told Wood that he himself had recently been confronted on the track by a pack. The wolves had a distinctive local trick: they would go ahead of the horses and 'by scratching with their hind feet, threw up snow so as to frighten the animal and bewilder its rider'. The governor reckoned that had some local villagers not arrived three minutes later, the wolves 'would have eaten both horse and rider'. In these circumstances, Wood sent out a search party for the missing man, but they had not returned by midnight, and Wood went to sleep deeply concerned. But all was well: the following day it transpired that the missing man had lost the track and sensibly sought shelter in a nearby village.

As they pressed on over ever higher passes towards Fyzabad, they were struck by the extreme desolation and emptiness of the mountainous terrain in winter: for 80 miles they saw no signs of life except occasional partridges and the flattened snow which provided evidence that herds of wild boar had passed that way. All this contrasted with the legends of a once prosperous region where, Wood relates, a nervous ruler once formed a human chain of servants to pass his food from the scorpion-infested valley to his mountain retreat – only to be stung to death by a scorpion concealed in a bunch of grapes that had been passed up the line.

When he reached the fort of Jerm, he made a diversion – with the encouragement of the governor – to visit a lapis lazuli mine. However, the guide who had been provided turned out to be crazy: 'to every question he replied by a quotation from Hafiz' about blighted love. When Wood sent the man back with an escort, he was accused of having 'conjured the spirit of a poetical guide into a jackass ... for it was known in the bazaar that you left this place with only four donkeys and have brought back five'. These were superstitious and unstable people among whom he was travelling and he found them less than cordial.

A further instance of the strange beliefs of the villagers around Jerm was provided by the curious case of a pilgrim who had fallen sick there and unwisely promised the local chief that, if he could cure his ulcers, he would impart the secret of making gold. When the cure was completed and the pilgrim failed to deliver on his promise, the chief clapped his guest in chains and branded him daily with red-hot irons to make him divulge his secret. Wood rescued the pilgrim and sent him back downriver for medical attention.

They soon found themselves 'approaching the haunts of the Kaffirs, a nation of unbelievers occupying the most inaccessible portion of the Hindu Kush', who regularly massacred not only foreign intruders but neighbouring Muslims. Consequently, Wood's Muslim guides afforded no protection; rather the reverse because, since it was Ramadan, they were disinclined to eat and became enfeebled, although one of the party eventually succumbed to an enormous daytime meal and declared that he would expiate the offence by freeing a slave on his return.

The intrepid Wood got somewhat depressed by the gloom and hostility: on 23 December, the shortest day of the year, he recorded that 'as we listened to the warring elements without, my thought reverted to Scotland and the social gaieties of her winter'. The nearest they got to such social gaiety was a partridge shoot. Wood found that although the cold was intense, when well wrapped up 'a brisk canter through heavy snow on such a day gives a new impulse to the spirits, a new value to existence'. A combination of horsemen, beaters on foot and dogs flushed out a remarkable number of birds and 'we bagged nearly five hundred'. Despite not being an army officer, Wood enjoyed his shooting as much as any of them.

Wood was an enthusiastic explorer but embarrassed by the requirement to look out for strategic information and military intelligence that later might be used against his hosts. When he dined with a prosperous merchant near Jerm, he was delighted to glean information about the upper course of the Oxus which he was exploring; he also noted down the fact that coal was being used for fuel in the Chinese city of Ecla beyond the Karakorams. On the whole, though, he preferred to keep military and economic intelligence out of his published account of the trip. Instead, he expatiated on anthropological matters: the ritual attending Afghan brides and the provenance of cooking pots get more space in his narrative than fortifications and the defensive significance of natural phenomena. It makes for a very different read from Abbott or Pottinger.

Wood's curiosity about local practices often focused on the macabre. When crossing a bridge near the Kokcha river he records that local criminals were thrown to their death from the centre of the bridge – a recent case being an unfortunate man who had been rash enough to criticize Murad Beg. A few villages further on, one of their fellow travelling acquaintances was found dead – apparently poisoned by a local chief. Life was not held dear in these parts.

Natural hazards were also increasing with the altitude. On a diversion to look at some ruby mines, they crossed the Oxus 'upon the ice, or rather on bridges of frozen snow' where it was some 35 yards wide and soon gave warning of its instability. Landslides and avalanches had destroyed both men and animals in this region only a few days earlier. When they reached the ruby mines they found them unworked because a local chief had been so disappointed in their low production that he had decided it would be more profitable to sell off the miners and their families in the slave market at Kunduz.

Wood was now entering what is known as the Wakhan Corridor – a narrow tongue of land in Afghanistan which runs between what are now Tajikistan and Pakistan. Along with the Oxus, it was to form a buffer between the Russian expansion from the north and the encroaching advance of the British Raj from the south. However, political frontiers interested him less than natural ones and his main preoccupation and puzzle was to sort out which was the main stream of the Oxus where it divided at Qala Panja. He took the task very seriously and clambered around with his instruments at the confluence, taking measurements of volume of water, speed of current, temperature and anything else that seemed relevant to the decision. There could be no categorical certainty, but in the end he came down on the side of the northern stream which was known to originate in the lake of Sirikol.

Unlike Abbott, Wood also took much trouble to remain on good terms with his retainers. However, being a man of high principles himself, he found it hard to countenance the corruption of his steward, who extracted bribes and payments in goods from all the villages they passed through on the grounds that it was a tribute due to the emir – his native master. When Wood protested that this got the whole expedition a bad name, the steward pointed out that what he was doing was no more than accepted practice, and in any case Wood was entirely dependent on him for the supply of food, guides and all local contacts. Wood diplomatically patched up their relationship and found that as they moved out of the territory of Murad Beg he stopped his bullying tactics anyway.

Wood was entranced by his first encounter with yaks. He found that – like an elephant – the yak had an instinctive judgement of what ice, snow or other ground-cover would bear its weight: 'he avoids the hidden depths and chasms with admirable sagacity'. A score of yaks driven through a pass would create 'a king's highway'. Wood was fascinated by the way they would roll down a snowy slope to scatter the snow and expose the edible grass below. He even managed to ride one and get some riding trousers made out of yak hair.

He was equally intrigued by the Kirghiz nomads and their yurts (round felt tents), which no one had described so evocatively to English readers before. He collected some good stories about the Muslim Kirghiz and their disdain for the Christian Kazakhs. One Kirghiz bearing a grudge gave a covered jar containing a swarm of bees to his slightly dim-witted Kazakh chief with instructions not to open it until all the headmen of the Kazakh horde were assembled in a sealed yurt. He was to wait until they were all undressed and then place the jar upon a fire and remove the lid. The chief, predictably, was 'literally stung to madness'. Wood was obviously the sort of traveller to whom people enjoyed telling tales.

He was now reaching a point so far upstream that the authority of Murad Beg, the ruler of Kunduz, could no longer be relied upon for his security: the local chiefs had stopped paying taxes and communicating with Murad Beg and the despot construed this as 'looking like rebellion'. Wood was also reaching a point where the extreme cold, particularly at night, was taking a toll, and where they were glad to be able to follow the tracks of earlier travellers through the snow. He had difficulty getting his horses over the chasms and reported that caravans from Yarkand (on the Chinese side of the Pamirs) frequently had to transfer their merchandise from camels to yaks at this altitude. Firewood – essential for getting through the night – was also running out and they had to load the 'already jaded' horses with branches dug out from under the snow. At one point the Kirghiz guides insisted on leaving the Oxus riverbed to camp 'in a cold, ugly-looking spot' because they knew there were reserves of burnable camel dung under the snow there. 'We had great reason to thank our escort for bringing us to such a favoured spot,' Wood reflected as he stoked up a fire through the night at an altitude of some 16,000 feet. Nor were the passes without human hazards. On more than one occasion when they spotted groups of tribesmen watching them, they 'dismounted and prepared our firearms'.

When they reached a halt some 20 miles from the estimated source of the Oxus, most of the escort went on strike and refused to go further, despite Wood 'working myself into a towering passion' and accusing them of cowardice. He decided to go on regardless, with a much reduced party. Had the river not been frozen, Wood reckoned he could not have gone further. They took turns to lead and when the leader's horse collapsed with exhaustion in the snow, the next man took over. The ice was not always thick and one mule went through. It was rescued by a Kirghiz 'who wrapped him in felts, took off his own warm posteen, and wound it round the shivering brute'.

Finally, on 19 February 1838, they reached 'the roof of the world . . . a noble but frozen sheet of water, from whose western end issued the infant river of Oxus'. Wood rapidly worked out the precise coordinates. He knew that Marco Polo had reached this lake in 1271 and had found the wild sheep here which were to be named after him as Ovis Polo, or Marco Polo sheep, and which were to become one of the most prized trophies of those on shooting leave. However, he realized he was probably the first European since then to reach this source of the famous river and he contemplated renaming Lake Sirikol: 'as shortly before setting out on my journey, we had received the news of her gracious Majesty's ascension to the throne, I was much tempted to apply the name of Victoria to this . . . newly rediscovered lake'.

Wood then walked out some 600 yards on to the surface of the lake and started making a hole in it with a pick axe. The ice was two and a half feet thick and when pierced sent up a jet of freezing water. All this diligent activity resulted in acute mountain sickness. This, together with a feeling that his mission had been accomplished, encouraged Wood to set off on his return without delay. By 11 March he had reached Kunduz again and was reunited with Dr Lord, the expedition's medical officer; they sat up talking all night, recounting their experiences.

The next morning he set off with Dr Lord to attend another of Murad Beg's relatives who needed medical care. He took the

occasion to thank the ruler for the degree of effective protection he had afforded them in his domain. However, Wood had few illusions about the character of his protector: when he reached his court he discovered Murad Beg had just murdered a local chief who had arrived without delivering a proper tribute and with an inadequate gift. The unfortunate man had been clubbed to death in Murad Beg's presence, but this was not allowed to interfere with a shooting party at which Wood admired the locals' dogs – 'a breed which, for strength and symmetry, vie with our own greyhound and in beauty surpass it'. When he moved to Said on the frontier of Murad Beg's dominions, the sport was even better. In addition to pheasants, there were plenty of deer which were hunted by the somewhat brutal method of setting fire to the forest and scrub-land, and 'when an animal breaks cover he is speared by a horseman or pulled down by dogs'.

This far downstream, the Oxus was muddy and was no longer the clear stream which had been 'my old friend in the mountains'. Wood meticulously noted the places where it could be forded by troops and recorded points on the river where guns had been conveyed across. He related that Murad Beg's 'mounted banditti' had swum their horses across in summer in the course of one of their celebrated raids.

Wood decided they had better move on before they risked 'being kept prisoner here longer than was convenient'. Even as it was, they were considerably delayed by the fact that the passes of the Hindu Kush were still blocked with snow in March. It was only in mid-April, after attending a durbar given by the ruler, that they finally quit 'that metropolis of thieves'. The elderly chamberlain who saw them off was himself murdered shortly afterwards. Wood (for once allowing himself a political comment) remarks that every Tajik in the region would welcome an escape from the tyranny of Murad Beg and a return to the more benev-olent rule of Kabul. However, for the present the protection of Kabul was less effective in securing a safe crossing of the Hindu Kush than a 'holy man of great influence' whom Dr Lord got to escort them through the pass and down the Panjshir valley. Despite the beneficial influence of the holy man, Wood had a bad fall when his pony missed its footing and, together with Wood, went head-over-heels down a hillside.

When they finally reached Kabul to report back to Captain Burnes, they found that he had already left – disillusioned by the reception given to a Russian emissary there. Again, Wood ventured into the murky world of Afghan politics and found that the mass of the population – both Afghan and Tajik – were disconcerted with their sovereign Dost Mohammed's flirtation with the Russians; but Wood did not share Burnes's ready incli-nation to abandon all support for Dost Mohammed in favour of the exiled Shah Shujah. However, it was Burnes's view that prevailed with the hierarchy of the Raj and resulted in his returning three years later with the British Army of the Indus to instal Shah Shujah as their puppet, with all the subsequent disasters – including the murder of Burnes by a disaffected mob in Kabul – of the First Afghan War. But all that lay in the future.

For the present, Wood was preoccupied with getting home. He embarked for Jalalabad 'on a raft of inflated skins, and dropped down stream to Peshawar', where he rejoined Captain Burnes. His mission had been – to outward appearances – a total success: he had traced the Oxus to its source (and it was to be another 56 years before Lord Curzon disputed his findings). However, he was unhappy about the British abandonment of Dost Mohammed and somewhat embarrassed by the degree to which his exploration and scientific discoveries had been sponsored and overshadowed by military and strategic considerations. Despite the acclaim that greeted his return, he decided to resign his commission in the Company's navy and to give up the prospect of further intelligence reconnaissance missions. He was not forgiven and never offered another post. He returned to the highlands of Scotland where no doubt he enjoyed that winter gaiety which he had missed so much while plodding over the frozen Oxus towards its source in the Pamirs. The Royal Geographical Society awarded him its gold medal, but he was too shy or embarrassed to attend any ceremony to receive it.

Such a retiring figure is not one which invites immediate comparison with such an extrovert figure as Lawrence of Arabia, but he had one thing in common with the First World War hero: he felt that the relationships which he had established – whether with rulers or simple people who had helped him – and the information he had so painstakingly gathered had been used to the advantage of his masters in a way which constituted a betrayal of his good faith. This had been the result of a change of British policy in which he had had no hand. He did not want to be part of that betrayal, so he left the public service. This might be the world of Henry Pottinger and Charles Masson, of James Abbott and Alexander Burnes, but it was not the world of naval Lieutenant John Wood of Argyllshire.

# Chapter 5

## Charles Masson: Absent Without Leave

'Gentlemen-rankers out on a spree,
Damned from here to Eternity'
– Rudyard Kipling, in 'Gentlemen-Rankers'

Most young officers who took 'shooting leave' did so with the encouragement and blessing of their own governments. This was not the case with Charles Masson. The missions of discovery he undertook were as hazardous and the contribution he made as substantive as anybody else's, but they were frequently achieved in defiance of authority. This was because Masson had not only broken the rules, but he had broken the most basic code of conduct for a gentleman: he had deserted from the army and acquired a new name, nationality and occupation.

He had been born as an Englishman called James Lewis, the son of an oil merchant in London. He had enlisted in the ranks of the East India Company's infantry in 1821, later transferring to the Bengal European Artillery (where pay was good and a number of educated men enlisted in the ranks in the hope of promotion). He had been present at the siege of Bharatpur in 1826, but had become increasingly disaffected and critical of British policies and finally decided the army was not for him. He deserted in 1827 and to cover his tracks – the penalty for desertion could be death – he assumed the name of Charles Masson and claimed to be an American citizen from Kentucky. His adoption of a new persona was made easier by the fact that rumours were circulating that he had committed suicide. But it was made more difficult by the fact that everywhere he went – particularly in Persia or Afghanistan – he was mingling with East India Company officials and he had to conceal any knowledge of British India or the British army, as well as avoiding any reference to his own upbringing in England. He must have been an accomplished deceiver and a high degree of duplicity and secretiveness became part of his personality. However, at least one person – a certain Dr Harlan with whom he had briefly travelled – did know who he really was.

Masson – in his new identity – made himself a considerable authority on the antiquities, languages and customs of Central Asia and became a collector and dealer, amassing some 80,000 ancient coins and many other artefacts. As a scholar and local expert, he became a useful source of information on out-of-the-way places to the authorities and began sending confidential reports to agents of the British Raj. When he settled in Kabul his reports on all aspects of life there – particularly the political aspects – became of special value in the years leading up to the First Afghan War. The officer to whom he was reporting was Captain Claude Wade who became sufficiently intrigued to indulge in some research into Masson's background: in January 1834 Wade was in Lahore and encountered Dr Harlan and it seems from then on he knew the truth about Masson.

Wade now realized that he had an interesting asset with whom any official contact would have been highly irregular. He was unwilling to forgo the relationship, so in April 1834 he wrote to

Sir William Macnaghten (then in charge of the secret and political departments of the British government in India) about his suspicions and argued for permission to continue to correspond with Masson: 'Desertion is a crime which is viewed I believe by our government with a degree of rigour that scarcely ever admits of pardon but . . . I hope that I shall be excused for the correspondence I have opened with Mr Masson . . . he has enjoyed opportunities of making his observations which no other European travellers have hitherto possessed.'

Macnaghten agreed that Masson was too valuable to be arrested and brought to justice. Quite exceptionally, with the King of England's approval a process was put in place to pardon Masson in return for his becoming a 'newswriter' and continuing to send in reports.

It was in this capacity, as well as being a scholar and collector, that he found himself in Kabul alongside Alexander 'Bokhara' Burnes in 1835. His advice was usually well-informed and intelligent, but frequently ignored. Part of the reason for this was that because of his record many officers distrusted and disliked him, or were suspicious of his motives. He was an opponent of the policies that were to lead to the First Afghan War in 1839 and eventually decided – once again – to detach himself from his official associations and leave Kabul.

So it was that in 1840 he found himself in Karachi, having dispatched to Britain a wad of erudite manuscripts for publication, and feeling (as he put it in his subsequent journal) 'as I supposed free to move where I pleased . . . to continue my antiquarian researches – with the due prosecution of which government employment had interfered'. This was the somewhat vague and unconvincing explanation he gave for setting off to Kalat on the Afghan border of Baluchistan. He later wrote that this trip was to prove 'more pregnant with singular incidents than any other I had made throughout my career'.

Since Henry Pottinger had been at Kalat in 1810 much had changed: there had been an armed struggle for the mastery of the town with a lot of local casualties, and there was now a British agent installed there – in the form of an officer called Lieutenant Loveday – to keep an eye on a supposedly compliant khan. But the British control of the region was still tenuous and Masson must have known that he was heading into a troubled border area without any official backing or obvious credentials.

Masson set out from Karachi on 30 April 1840, attended by an old Kashmiri servant and two local guides; a chance companion in the form of a pilgrim – a 'Hadji' – also attached himself to the party for company and safety. Masson himself rode 'an excellent Kabul horse' and had five camels to carry the luggage while his companions went on foot. He had a quick eye for any archaeological remains or collectors' pieces, such as old coins, and there was no doubt about his genuine interest in these artefacts. He wore Afghan costume but never intended to conceal for a moment that he was an Englishman.

From his description of his journey to Kalat, it is clear that Masson was busily engaged in talking politics with the local chiefs of all the small places through which he travelled; at the same time, he was actively recording the features of the landscape from a military viewpoint. For instance, as he approached Kalat he entered 'a defile which . . . although in its actual state might be barely practicable to artillery, a good road could easily be made through it'. He regularly makes the point that, while the terrain through Sindh and Baluchistan towards the Afghan frontier presented relatively few problems to a caravan of camels such as his own, it would cause difficulties 'where armies with their encumbrances [would] perish'. His horses and camels were permanently hungry, and a larger caravan which was following on behind his lost two-thirds of its animals through hunger and thirst. He also concluded that although 'serious opposition need not be apprehended' from the tribes, any army passing through could expect to be the subject of harassment and the stealing of their horses and equipment.

In some of the villages, Masson heard the inhabitants debating 'whether or not it was lawful to kill me, in retaliation for the blood of those slain a few years earlier at Kalat; but it was generally conceded to be unlawful, as I was not present at the slaughter, and because I had appeared unarmed amongst them'. At one moment, he was actually accommodated in the house of 'a chief who had fallen at the hands of my countrymen'. At another moment he identified a local chief who he was advised would always be a source of trouble unless he was lured to Karachi or Quetta and detained there. The countryside was clearly still very anti-British and, although the traumatic shock of the Indian Mutiny was still 16 years ahead, Masson sensed that there was nervousness in the air of many parts of British India and its neighbouring territories.

From the moment of his arrival at Kalat, Masson fell out with Lieutenant Loveday, the British representative. He failed to pay a courtesy call on his first evening and Masson quickly heard that this had given offence to Loveday who had remarked that 'I must be a low fellow, for, if I had been a gentleman, I should have come to him.' The mistrust was mutual, as Masson had heard on his journey many ill reports of Loveday's conduct and had concluded 'that it was difficult to avoid the suspicion that he must be a strange person'. Things did not get better when the two men met the following day. Masson was offended by

Loveday's heavy-handed approach to local problems: the latter 'took much credit for the opening of the Mulloh Pass, by blowing from a gun the petty chief who infested it', and said he wished he could get hold of other local chiefs to treat them in the same manner.

Loveday's position was anomalous: he was committed to the support of the local ruler, Shah Nawaz Khan, who had been put in place by the British, and he had some 60 native troops as a personal guard (of which 25 had been sent to Quetta). But, for reasons which Masson explained at inordinate length in his book, there was widespread unrest and resistance to the Shah. In these circumstances Loveday would have done well to avoid giving any unnecessary provocation, but he did just the opposite: he made a practice of setting his dogs on any native who offended him, and not only did this sometimes cause fatalities, but it gave huge insult on account of the 'uncleanness' of the act.

Very soon after Masson's arrival at Kalat there were reports of an uprising at nearby Mastung. The son of a deposed former khan was said to be marching on Kalat. Lieutenant Loveday was advised to stay within the walls and fortify his house; Masson was told by his friends to leave quickly and, although he declined to flee, he did move into secure accommodation after hearing that two of the late khan's servants had 'buckled on their arms, intending to have assassinated me that evening'. Everyone was in a state of alert.

In the event, the insurgent tribes first made an unsuccessful assault on Quetta. Only thereafter did they turn their attention to Kalat, where the khan and Lieutenant Loveday were busy collecting 'a supply of water in the citadel, in expectation of a siege'. The greatest problem was that neither the khan nor

Loveday could rely on the support of the local garrison: many people wanted Loveday removed before, as they speculated, 'he would be dragging them all about by their beards', and there were accusations that the khan was acting as a puppet of the British.

At this juncture, Loveday – who had earlier been so patronizing – invited Masson to join him at his residence and clearly sought his advice and support. Despite his dislike of the man, Masson agreed to throw in his lot with Loveday during the expected siege, although all his local friends warned him he would be more at risk in Loveday's company than he would be on his own. 'I thought I might be useful; and I by no means considered the defence of the place as hopeless,' he wrote.

Masson now turned his long-neglected military experience to assessing the means of defending Kalat against a rebel assault. He urged the khan to patch up the walls and start urgently manufacturing bullets from the 'many pigs of lead' in his store. He even persuaded Loveday to leave his fortified residence long enough to inspect some of the work himself. Masson tried to get the khan to level the walls around an orchard on the edge of the town as he feared that this might provide a venue for 'a parley between the besiegers and the besieged, which it was part of our plan to prevent if possible'. Mistrust of their own garrison remained at the front of everyone's mind.

Loveday for his part was actively trying to restore his relationship with Masson, now that the latter was a useful and necessary go-between with the khan and the garrison. Masson recorded that 'when I briefly related to him my reason for resigning the service of government [an explanation of his leaving Kabul in 1839 rather than a euphemism for his earlier desertion, one suspects] he told me he admired my feeling of independence'.

At this point, the scouts from the insurgents appeared on the horizon and a brief skirmish took place. Masson was relieved by the fact that casualties were inflicted – 'two or three men were slain on either side' – as he thought this would make it less likely that the garrison would do a deal with their attackers. He estimated that the attackers numbered some 1,200, about twice the number of the garrison, but that the latter had more firearms: 'Certainly we could have overpowered them on the plain, had it been prudent to trust our men so far; unhappily, we could not.' Meanwhile, Masson toured the ramparts telling the garrison that the East India Company would not forget to reward their efforts. It soon became clear that the rebels intended to storm the walls with specially constructed ladders, ironically sourced from the site of a summer house which Lieutenant Loveday had been building just outside the town.

The assault took place on the fourth night of the siege and the fears of the khan, Loveday and Masson that they could not count on their supporters proved to be well-founded. The intruders were 'assisted over the walls by those stationed to defend them'. Indeed, some of the supposed defenders transpired to have been passing ammunition to the enemy while they themselves fired blanks. Even the artillery guns on the ramparts were found to be loaded with blank cartridges by disaffected defenders. Although the night attack was repulsed – largely by the personal efforts of the khan – Masson recorded that, 'we were not long allowed to rejoice at the events of the past night, for the symptoms of a general panic were too clear to be mistaken'.

Things went from bad to worse in the following days. Lieutenant Loveday was advised that 'it was dangerous to continue the defence, and it was necessary to negotiate', while the khan appeared downcast and dejected. Much to Masson's dismay, envoys from the rebels were received by the khan and Lieutenant Loveday, and they in turn sent envoys back to the rebel camp outside Kalat. This predictably resulted in a patched-up agreement by which the khan gave up his sovereignty of Kalat in return for other territory, and Lieutenant Loveday was to be escorted with his bodyguards and belongings back to Quetta. Despite Masson's urgings that such an agreement would not be approved by the British nor adhered to by the rebels, 'Lieutenant Loveday expressed his satisfaction'. With all the increased traffic between the rebel camp and the town, it became even more apparent just how weak, poorly armed and unsupported the rebels were. Consequently, the khan tried to retract his agreement and joined Masson in urging Loveday to continue the defence of Kalat. But to no avail. Loveday was busy sending ever more frequent messages to the rebels, while at the same time professing friendship to the khan. Masson witnessed all this 'with shame, I was going to write horror'.

At this stage the rebels were offering Loveday a choice between safe-conduct to Quetta or, if he stayed in Kalat, a splendid residence would be built for him. Loveday hovered in indecision and eventually declined to leave, even when the rebel forces occupied Kalat. Masson attributed this decision to an exaggerated 'desire to preserve his property' and concluded that 'from the commencement of the revolt [Loveday] had been overpowered by a languor which incapacitated him from any effort of mind or body'.

It was not long after the rebel takeover that Loveday and Masson were summoned by the rebel leader and promptly incarcerated in a room which was known as the Chamber of Blood, as state offenders had been executed there in the past. Loveday underwent the agony of seeing his house and possessions – to whose preservation he had attached such exaggerated importance – plundered by rebels. Unsurprisingly, his nefarious bulldogs, which he had used so offensively, were cut to pieces. Both Englishmen were heavily guarded, but not protected from 'the taunts, menaces and ribaldry with which we were assailed'. They had to sleep on the floor on a coarse carpet, but were fed and watered. Meanwhile, one of Loveday's former servants was tortured by the rebels in an attempt to find out if the English officer had a store of hidden jewels (always a supposed possibility after the British had captured Kalat and its princely inhabitants).

The rebels must have been puzzled by Masson's role. Loveday had told some of his native confidants that Masson was a spy – hardly a helpful remark, but one which probably reflected Loveday's own suspicions about the motivation of his cell-mate. When later Masson got a chance to read some letters sent to Loveday by Captain Bean at Quetta, he found they included the sentence: 'The mystery of Mr Masson's appearance at Kalat at the period of the present outbreak, combined with his clandestine residence at that place, has given rise to suspicions in my mind of that individual, which I have not failed to communicate to government.' These doubts about Masson were to have worrying repercussions.

It was decided by the rebels, for no very clear reason, that Loveday and Masson were to be taken away from Kalat to their headquarters at the nearby settlement of Mastung. Their progress through the streets, bazaars and gates of Kalat provided an opportunity for the population to revile them with 'yells and hootings . . . the very women spitting on us'. When encamped on the way to Mastung, Loveday had his legs put in fetters and he was chained to the tent pole. The following day they were denied

stirrups for the ride, presumably to lessen the chances of their escape, and were later lodged in a bug-infested room. If they attempted to leave the room, they were pelted with stones and clods of earth: the manner of their detention was becoming more unpleasant all the time. As Masson remarked, 'In this, the third stage of our confinement, our situation had become desperate indeed.'

Eventually, after a very confused correspondence between Captain Bean and Lieutenant Loveday, in which most of the letters were intercepted and either mistranslated or suppressed, the rebel leaders agreed to release Masson to go to Quetta and try to reach a peaceful accommodation with the British authorities. Masson assured Loveday that he would come back and not desert him for good. After crossing a bleak plain between Mastung and Quetta, Masson duly arrived and was received by Captain Bean, who clearly did not like the content of the letter from Loveday which Masson handed over.

The next morning, Masson had a long talk over breakfast with Captain Bean. He instantly took against him, as he had initially taken against Loveday; he decided he was 'a weak man, puffed up with absurd conceptions of his official importance'. Bean was unresponsive to ideas which Masson put to him about how to help Loveday in his predicament, and he even declined to allow Masson to return to Mastung in the supposed belief that no harm would come to Lieutenant Loveday.

No sooner was their breakfast talk over than Bean placed an armed guard on the house where Masson was staying. Masson reflected wryly at 'the oddness of a man inviting me to breakfast, and then sending me into confinement'. He also reflected that it was a strange reward for all the efforts, risks and hardships he had undergone at Kalat in his attempts to be useful to the British government.

Further meetings and the exchange of frigid formal letters resulted in Masson learning that there had been reports of a Russian agent operating in the region, with the implication that Masson might be that agent. Masson's presence at Kalat at the moment of the insurrection was apparently viewed as being no coincidence. His track record as a deserter was catching up with him and he suspected resentment in high places of the fact that he was travelling independently and not under the protection of the Raj. He identified as his particular enemy Sir William Macnaghten, the British envoy and minister at Kabul (who was to be murdered there the following year).

Masson sent off a raft of letters to the governor-general's private secretary and others in authority, but while he awaited some response Captain Bean was treating him with more cruelty than the rebels in Kalat had done: 'I passed two entire days and three nights without food,' he recorded. Sustenance eventually arrived in the form of 'three farthings' worth of sheep's entrails from the bazaar'.

On 10 October 1840, Macnaghten wrote to Masson saying: 'I did authorize Captain Bean to detain you at Quetta, until the pleasure of the Governor-General in Council should be ascertained as to your being permitted to prosecute your travels in countries subject to the crown of Cabool [Kabul], since, so far as I know, you are without permission to do so, either from the British Government, or from His Majesty Shah Shooja Ool Moolk.'

Meanwhile, a British force under the command of Major-General William Nott had marched on Kalat. Alas, it was too late to save Lieutenant Loveday from being slaughtered by the rebels. As Masson wistfully wrote in his volume of travels: 'the malice of my enemies had unwittingly saved me from a similar end, – my certain portion had I been with him [Loveday] in the camp'.

The malice of Captain Bean persisted even after all the evidence from Kalat exonerated Masson of having had a sinister part in the uprising; the most he would concede was that 'nothing further had transpired by which the disloyalty of Mr Masson as a British subject could be established'. But as more and more evidence emerged from the recaptured Kalat of Masson's role in its defence and of his attempts to support and rescue Lieutenant

Loveday, the government eventually wrote to him, regretting his detention, and copied the whole correspondence to the governor-general in Calcutta. Masson was cleared and freed. It was even recommended he should receive compensation. The whole matter was referred to a 'secret committee' in Britain who 'suggested the hush system, commending the acquittal and release, but disrelishing the point of compensation'. When his book was published in 1843, Masson was still pursuing the question of his vindication and compensation. His memoir is understandably bitter about those in high office in India who felt that 'their pleasure stood in place of law'.

It is interesting that one of those who tried to dissuade him from pursuing old vendettas in his book was none other than the same Henry Pottinger whose adventures are the subject of an earlier chapter. Pottinger, who was much more of an establishment figure than Masson, had written to him two years earlier, saying: 'No-one of the respectable Booksellers in England will publish any work (at their own risk) animadverting on [criticizing] public men or measures. They justly say, that that is the duty of the daily Press and that such criticisms are quite out of place in Books of Travel.' Masson may have modified his vitriolic remarks slightly, but what was 'out of place' in polite society had never unduly worried him.

Indeed, Masson was the odd man out in any account of British officers or political agents travelling purposefully through the wilder parts of Central Asia. He had his own agenda and did not fit the pattern prescribed for agents of the Raj. This was despite the fact that he did many commendable things on this, his greatest adventure: he had used his scholarly knowledge and experience to collect useful information about tribal unrest and made it available to the authorities; he had surveyed with a military eye the little-known territories over which he travelled; and he had attempted to come to the aid of a British officer who had proved to be unsuitable for his task as a resident political agent and inadequate to face the crisis which confronted him.

However, Masson did all these things without orders, authority or support from on high, and so he ran up against resentment and suspicion. Freelance adventures were to be encouraged if – like those of Pottinger, Abbott, Burnes or Wood – they fell within the broad purview of the Raj. But if they did not, if they were unknown to the governor-general in council or to the British-sponsored local rulers, then they would bring down the wrath of the powers that be, in however remote a corner of the fringes of the Raj such adventures might occur: the tentacles of power stretched far. Like Rome before it, Queen Victoria's empire could be unforgiving to those who got out of step. Masson was a man with a past that could be officially pardoned but which could not be altogether forgiven. His trip looked less like 'shooting leave' than like going 'Absent Without Leave'.

# Chapter 6

## Stormy Interlude: All Leave Suspended

'War is nothing but a continuation of politics with the admixture of other means.'

— Carl von Clausewitz (1780–1831), in *On War*

During the first half of the nineteenth century, the Great Game was warming up. Although the threat of Napoleon joining the Russians in an assault on India soon evaporated, the Russian threat itself not only continued but increased. So did the number and quality of the young British officers sent out to gather information and intelligence, map the passes, penetrate the deserts and stiffen the resistance of the khans and emirs of Central Asia to the Russian incursions.

However, in the mid-1850s, the focus of Russian–British confrontation changed: Russian aspirations now appeared to have shifted to Constantinople and the Ottoman empire – the vulnerable 'sick man of Europe' who held the key to access to the Mediterranean for the Tsar's fleet. The Crimean War which ensued in 1854–6 absorbed all Tsar Nicholas I's attention and resources. One person who tried to take advantage of the Tsar's preoccupation was the Muslim rebel leader Imam Shamyl of the Caucasus, who wrote to Queen Victoria, 'England must know of our ceaseless struggle against Russia . . . we urge you, we beseech you, O Queen, to bring us help.' But Britain was also fully extended in the Crimea and Shamyl's appeal fell on deaf ears. Meanwhile, faced with British and French armies in front of Sebastopol and a series of bloody battles, the Russians eventually found the war unwinnable, the Tsar died and the Russians signed a peace treaty which – while excluding them from naval power in the Black Sea – enabled them to concentrate on retrenching and consolidating. They had realized how vulnerable they were to 'the enemy within' in the Caucasus and, as soon as the Crimean War was over, it was there – rather than in Central Asia – that the new Tsar Alexander II concentrated his military efforts. He sent his friend Prince Alexander Bariatinsky as viceroy and commander-in-chief to the Caucasus in 1856 to confront and overcome Imam Shamyl.

From the British point of view it was providential that this was still the position in 1856–7 when the Indian Mutiny (alternatively known as the First Independence War) broke out. Had the Russians been in a position to take advantage of the chaos and confusion in northern India during the Mutiny – and they did consider it – they might have intervened, claiming to support a native revolt against imperial rule and to offer a more benign protection from the north. As it was, Britain was able to suppress the Mutiny in its own time without outside interference.

However, the Mutiny had administered a severe shock: never again would the British army allow itself to be quite so heavily outnumbered by native troops – the sepoys; never again would sepoys be entrusted with artillery; never again would there be such a relaxed relationship – including mixed marriages and casual intercourse – between the British rulers and their Indian subjects. The East India Company, with its separate army and distinct lines of command, was replaced by direct British governmental rule.

The governor-general was designated 'viceroy' and given greater prestige and power. The British retreated into their compounds and clubs and, as John Masters puts it in his book *Bugles and a Tiger*, 'some chased polo balls and some chased partridges, some buried themselves in their work, and all became unmitigated nuisances through the narrowness of their conversation'.

However, once the Russians had got over the setback of the Crimea, and once the British had recovered from the shock of the Mutiny, the Great Game was to resume with added vigour. Although little or no 'shooting leave' was permitted while these events were unfolding in the late 1850s and the early 1860s, by the end of that decade young officers were once more volunteering for political services beyond the frontiers of the Raj. The period of most intense activity was about to begin: these were the years when, one after another, the Central Asian khanates and emirates fell under Russian occupation or at least under Russian sway. The horizon was also extending eastwards as the Chinese province of Sinkiang (better known at the time as Kashgaria) was fast becoming an arena of rivalry and confrontation between Russia and British India, just as Afghanistan and the formerly independent territories of Central Asia had already become.

During the first half of the nineteenth century, the court of the Tsars in St Petersburg had watched – with varying degrees of concern, anger and amusement – the activities of allegedly independent young British officers circulating around the periphery of their domains. Now they were to begin sending out their own young – and sometimes not so young – officers on similar quests for knowledge and influence. The courtesies were usually observed, but the rivalry was intensifying as the physical boundaries dividing the empires narrowed.

The character of the officers on both sides was also changing. Whereas the Russians had previously been based at garrison towns such as Orenburg or involved in full-scale military campaigns such as those against Khiva, now they were beginning to branch out into more individual exploits, just as the British had always done. Some were at heart explorers, some were individual adventurers, some were surveyors or military engineers intent on extending lines of communication across the steppes and – as they saw it – bringing the civilizing influence of European Russia into the heart of Asia. Like the British, almost all of them were keen sportsmen.

The British were changing in some respects too, although much remained the same when the East India Company's officers were transmuted into servants of the Crown. It was still the case that most of them were modelled on Squire Brown's expectations for his son in Thomas Hughes's *Tom Brown's Schooldays* (published, incidentally, in 1857 – the year in which the Mutiny was put down): 'If he'll only turn out to be a brave, helpful truth-telling Englishman and a gentleman and a Christian, that's all I want.'

There was still some interchangeability between military and civilian officers. The civilian administrators – or district officers – developed a high degree of self-reliance and self-confidence (not always associated with civil servants): in an emergency they would turn their hand to taking command of a company of Indian infantry, preaching a Sunday sermon in church, administering medicine and first-aid, or building bridges and roads. An officer in the political service – often attached to semi-independent Maharajas – increasingly had (in Philip Mason's words in his book *The Men Who Ruled India*) to 'keep his head among the splendours and barbarities of an oriental court . . . to judge when he must, and how far he might, interfere'.

Meanwhile those in the army increasingly grew bored with the routine of barrack life on the sweltering plains, however much this might be punctuated with pig-sticking and polo, by tea dances in the clubs and by amateur performances of Gilbert and Sullivan operettas.

It was the brightest and best from these different branches of public service that volunteered or were selected for 'shooting leave', and they were supplemented by officers of private means from smart regiments of the British army at home.

Both British and Russian officers were increasingly well supported at the highest level by their royal patrons, as interest in India and Central Asia grew in London and St Petersburg. With Queen Victoria's assumption of the title of Empress of India in 1876, she increased her affection for the people of India (she even had an Indian personal servant in the form of the Munshi). And with the encouragement of his father, the new (and last) Tsar to ascend the Russian throne – Nicholas II – had an early and persistent curiosity about his Central Asian territories (the explorer and Great Game player Nikolai Przhevalsky was to tutor him about the subject at an impressionable age). In the high era of Victorian supremacy and self-confidence – the age of Tennyson and Disraeli – the British lion felt more than a match for the Russian bear: the end of neither empire was in sight and there was all to play for.

# Chapter 7

## Valentine Baker: The Doomed Sportsman

'We found them to be very badde and brutish people, for they
ceased not dayly to molest us, either by fighting, stealing or begging:
and they forced us to buy the water that we did drinke.'
— Anthony Jenkinson (1529–c.1610) on the Turkomans, in
*The Voyage of Master Anthony Jenkinson from Moscow to Bokhara*

Valentine Baker was a soldier of some reputation before he
embarked in 1873 on his private exploration of the country
between the Caspian Sea and the very eastern corner of Persia
where it touched Afghanistan: the no-man's-land of Turkmenistan.

Establishing his military career in the 12th Lancers (not for
him some native infantry regiment where officers were expected
to live on their pay) he had quickly risen to command the dashing
10th Hussars, by a mixture of ability – particularly distinguishing
himself in the Crimean War – and judicious use of his considerable wealth to purchase promotions. In the process he had
become a good friend and shooting companion of the Prince
of Wales (later to be King Edward VII). Although he did not
know it at the time, when he handed over command of his regiment to undertake his adventure, it was to be the last substan-
tial job he ever had in the British army, as his career and reputation
were to founder more dramatically than he or anyone else could

possibly have imagined. The fashionable cavalry commander was to be dubbed a common criminal and sentenced to prison. But all that lay two years ahead.

Baker was drawn to the venture by a variety of factors. Although a number of intrepid officers had traversed the flanks of this region during the pioneering epoch of the 1830s, they had almost all travelled north–south or south–north: the idea of a lateral survey of this Russian-Turkoman-Persian border region was a new one. It was a natural frontier formed by the highlands of Khorassan, and one which was much in the minds of the British high command as General Konstantin Kaufman and the Russians moved towards Khiva.

Baker also wanted a break from regimental soldiering. In fact, he wanted shooting leave in the most literal sense – a chance to hunt wolves and wild boar (and possibly even tigers) in the Caucasus; to pot at pelican over the Caspian Sea; to shoot partridges, bustards and woodcock in Persia; to go deer-stalking in the hills of Khorassan; to bag ibex and mouflon in the mountains of Central Asia; to gallop after wild asses with the Turkoman on the steppes. To him, field sports were just as important as strategic reconnaissance.

It was with these twin motives that Baker enlisted two like-minded officers to accompany him: Captain Clayton of the 9th Lancers (who was later to be killed during a polo match in Delhi) and Lieutenant Gill of the Royal Engineers (who was later to be murdered by the Bedouin). Baker had been very keen to have an engineer with him who 'could make all observations and surveys of additional value', while he hoped Captain Clayton's 'genial energy' would be demonstrated in the hunting parties.

The main problem the party expected to face in crossing the wild and uncharted region was explained to them by a leading

Persian authority on Central Asia who said: 'The Turkomans will take you for Russians, while you can expect no sympathy or support from the Russians themselves.' However, Baker had an answer to this. He enlisted the support of his old friend the Prince of Wales and obtained a letter to the Grand Duke Michael, the Russian viceroy of the Caucasus, which proved invaluable: he was to receive support from the Russians to a remarkable degree.

Leaving London on 20 April 1873, the three officers went by train to Vienna where they boarded a river boat down the Danube to the Black Sea and along the coast to Constantinople. Baker was not one to travel light or uncomfortably if he could help it. He had to be 'equally ready for the needs of sport or the observations of science . . . breech-loaders entailed an immense supply of cartridges, and surveying instruments filled a large and ponderous box'. The porters at Charing Cross 'stood aghast as they had to register considerably more than a ton of luggage for only three passengers'.

The immediate objective was Tiflis (Tblisi), the capital of Georgia in the Caucasus, where the Grand Duke Michael had his headquarters. So Baker and his party spent only minimum time en route, pressing along the Black Sea coast to Trebizond at the eastern end of Turkey. Here, Baker allowed himself a short pause as there were high hopes of some good sport: bears and red deer were reported to be found in large numbers. After one of his carriage wheels came off during the expedition, he had to be content with some quail shooting and was 'rather disgusted to meet a native sportsman with a bigger bag than our own'.

He cheered up a little, however, on the Russian ship taking them from Trebizond to the Caucasus when he found the caviar superior to any he had ever tasted – except that provided 'by Messrs Fortnum and Mason in their glass barrels'. Such frivolous thoughts were set aside when he reached Batumi on the Caucasian Black Sea coast. The strategist in him took over: 'The fortifications are miserable . . . both [redoubts] are completely commanded from the high ground in the rear . . . a Turk never thinks of this . . . Russia could walk into Batoum whenever she chooses.'

From Batumi they progressed as best they could by river boat and train through the heart of Georgia. Baker noted that everyone was armed with cartridge belts, 'large Damascene knives and any number of other arms'. The train was superseded by carriages until eventually they reached their destination of Tiflis, which Baker found disappointing apart from the fact that a salmon river flowed through the town. This was the starting point for the serious part of the expedition, but they had to pause for several days as the Grand Duke Michael was away in St Petersburg.

Baker did not waste his time. He dined with Prince Mirsky and found the region alarmingly close to being on a war footing. Mirsky explained the thinking behind the Russian advance on Khiva and 'pointed out how difficult it would be for Russia to stay her advances until she had some well-defined frontier'. This sounded like an excuse for continual advance towards India. Mirsky also admitted to considering plans to use the old bed of the Oxus river, which it seems had once flowed into the Caspian, as a canal or railway line to open Central Asia to Russian trade and military supplies. At Prince Mirsky's suggestion they also made various excursions out of Tiflis by the new Georgian military highway and Baker had a chance to see the Russian forts and blockhouses which had been constructed during their campaign to subjugate the Caucasus and defeat the Imam Shamyl some 15 years before. He was initiated into the culture of the

Cossacks and when visiting their villages found that most of the men of military service age were away on the Khivan campaign. Thanks largely to the Prince of Wales's introduction, Baker was seeing the tsarist military machine from an extraordinarily privileged viewpoint.

Finally, the Grand Duke returned to Tiflis and Baker was received in audience. Baker was interested in what he was told of the agricultural and mineral potential of the Caucasus, but he was clearly even more fascinated by what one of the Grand Duke's staff – General Shehavskoy – showed him of the 'spoils of the chase' and told him of his adventures on shooting trips in the region. The general even invited him to return in the autumn when he promised some excellent sport. Baker noted the bush country round Tiflis was full of wild boar: 'there never was such country for boar-spearing'.

Having secured all the required official documentation, Baker and his party set off by carriage – with an order for escorts wherever necessary – towards Baku. 'As darkness came on the first day, we were told we were in a dangerous neighbourhood,' he recorded, but he declined the suggested 12-man escort because he thought that three Englishmen armed with revolvers and rifles could hold their own against any attacks they were likely to encounter.

From Baku they sailed southwards down the Caspian coast towards Persia, sharing the ship with the wives of the Shah of Persia who had been sent home from Moscow while the Shah proceeded on a state visit to Europe.[1] Baker was more interested in their attendant courtiers who were keen sportsmen and, when

---

1. It was on this occasion that the Shah visited Queen Victoria, but he did not greatly endear himself to her: he was reported to have blown his nose on the curtains at Windsor Castle, to have attempted to buy Lord Salisbury's wife, and to have advised the Prince of Wales to cut off the Duke of Sutherland's head before the latter became too powerful.

an immense flock of pelicans flew over the vessel, they opened fire with their guns which – he noted – included 'a very nice old two-groove rifle by Purdey'.

The coastal voyage was punctuated with short overland trips, including to Astrabad, where the Persian governor wanted to deflect Baker from making an incursion to an area that was out of bounds to foreigners. Instead, he suggested a hawking expedition to the banks of a nearby river where they 'found some young pheasants that could not fly far; and the hawks behaved admirably, striking their birds beautifully'. Baker was much gratified, particularly when he was shown some large hawks 'like small eagles, for hawking antelopes', and he decided not to press the point about the forbidden visit.

Despite these diversions, Baker did find time to study the troubled area of the Persian-Turkoman frontier between the Caspian and Afghanistan, along which he was about to travel. He found that the Turkoman tribes from the north – who formed a buffer between Russia and Persia – regularly mounted raids on the Persian villages and carried off men, women and children 'to sell them, or hold them until a ransom can be extracted'. But the Persians were just as aggressive, since they too made regular raids 'killing and destroying, or capturing and holding Turkomans of note'. He concluded that the whole frontier was both undefined and in a state of continual warfare. This was his chosen field of exploration.

A journey by carriage and horseback over the Elburz (Alborz) mountain range, through steep defiles and across fast-flowing rivers and arid plains eventually brought Baker and his party to the Persian capital city of Tehran, where they were welcomed and accommodated by the minister and his staff at the British legation. The route onwards was – as so often with Baker –

largely decided by sporting considerations: 'Hearing that there was very fair shooting and excellent trout-fishing to be had in the mountains, I determined to make our way slowly towards the East at a high elevation.' There was the prospect of mouflon and ibex in the mountains, red deer and tiger in the jungle, wild asses and partridges on the plains around Meshed, and in the winter 'enormous quantities of swans, geese, ducks and all kinds of wild fowl'.

Baker halted in Tehran to equip himself and his party for the opportunities ahead. All three of them bought horses, took on extra servants and, 'what with tents, guns, ammunition and supplies, we reckoned our party would require nineteen mules'. He enumerates in his book the enormous armoury of sporting weapons loaded on to the mules, including 'my old shoulder single-barrelled duck gun No 4, which carried a ball beautifully up to eighty yards, and with 8 drachms of powder would be a formidable weapon for tigers'. Other provisions included Worcester sauce, Liebeg's extract of meat, chests of tools, boxes of surveying instruments and salmon rods. The dual purpose of the expedition – sport and surveying – was well reflected in the inventory.

Baker was also taking his personal security very seriously. He wore his revolver at all times, commenting that the fact that everyone knew he was never to be found unarmed 'produces a very salutary effect'. This might be attractive hunting terrain, but it was also dangerous for reasons unrelated to sport.

The chapter in Baker's book describing the first stage of his more rigorous journey on from Tehran, again across the Elburz mountains, reads like a passage from John Buchan's novel *John Macnab* about deer-stalking in the Scottish highlands. He tells us of the frustration of not being able to move across the mountain side without the loose shale setting off 'a musical tinkling sound'; of the thrill of stalking a stag and killing it with a long shot at 200 yards; and of the problems of getting the dead buck down the rock slopes. He was also embarrassed at wounding a stag and the difficulty of following it on foot over the precipitous ground, while in another incident two mules with their loads fell into the river below.[2] They had left Tehran on 13 July and hunted for 11 days: for Baker, this was a trip with a proper sense of priorities.

When Baker and his party moved on from their sporting delights in the Elburz, things quickly took a more serious turn. The first sign of trouble was when one of his tent-pitchers went into the local village and was set upon by a group of Persians, severely beaten and cut. The next bad omen was when one of the guides was disinclined to continue travelling with them; he clearly thought there was trouble ahead. Meanwhile, Captain Clayton had turned back to Tehran, as his health had collapsed and he was unable to continue.

They had nearly finished their breakfast halt the following day when one of Baker's horsekeepers came galloping into the camp to report that while he had been with some of the baggage party 'a large band of robbers, upwards of a hundred, had suddenly stopped and surrounded them . . . they were beating the muleteers to death and pillaging the baggage'. Baker and Lieutenant Gill immediately jumped on their horses and rode back to the scene of the incident. They found their baggage party 'had formed a sort of breast-work of the baggage . . . firing whenever the attacking party attempted to advance'. The

2. The author lost no mules when crossing the Elburz, but did lose two in the same circumstances when crossing the Andes in a party of similar size to Baker's: they are less sure-footed than reputed.

approach of the heavily armed English officers had the effect of chasing them off, leaving two of Baker's men 'lying groaning and apparently in extremis'. Some 20 of the robbers attempted to block the path while the others remained close, waiting to join in any affray. Baker and Gill charged the road-blocking party at full tilt and they 'broke in all directions, running for their lives'; the others took up positions behind a swamp, but Baker – ever the cavalry officer with an eye to the lie of the land – outflanked them and scattered them too.

Baker was determined to take some prisoners so that the robber band could be identified to the Persian authorities. He pursued one of the fleeing robbers and, when threatening to shoot failed to stop the man in his tracks, he passed his weapon to Gill and wrestled him to the ground, securing his hands with his own handkerchief. Thus tied up, the unfortunate prisoner was dragged off, together with one or two others.

It transpired the attack had been carefully planned as the visitors had been spotted and were considered to be rich plunder. However, no great harm had been done: the injured men recovered and the firearms and money bags had not been taken. Baker and Gill had proved themselves more than a match in courage and nerve for their assailants. To their chagrin, though, the prisoners escaped the first night because Baker had considerately slackened the cords binding them and the Persian sentries had fallen asleep ('how is it that no men of Eastern race ever make efficient sentries?'). There was one bonus from the incident: Baker's Persian support staff had been greatly impressed by his resolute handling of the events which had 'evidently given them great confidence in us, and everyone was on his best behaviour'.

Both Baker and Gill had trouble with their horses at this stage. Not surprisingly they had gone lame and were suffering from saddle sores, so it was necessary to hire ponies at the villages they passed through. This proved difficult because the villagers feared that they would not hand the ponies over at the next village: 'this was often done by their Persian masters; and, never having seen any European before, they could not believe that they were likely to prove more just and honest'. So great was this fear that it led to a nasty incident only a few days after the earlier attack.

A dozen men, some armed with guns and some with spears and sticks, were standing round a great old oak tree on their route through Mazenderan. Baker fondly imagined in his innocence that they had been shooting game. However, this was no sporting party but an ambush, intended to force Baker to give back the hired ponies. In vain he and Gill protested that they had paid in advance and were not stealing the horses. While the altercation went on the rest of the party caught up and a general skirmish followed in which the leaders of the ambush had their weapons wrested from them. While this was going on, it became apparent that there were others involved – gunmen aiming at the travellers from the safety of nearby rocks and banks, but unable to fire because the scrimmage was so close and confused that they might have shot their own people. Baker and his supporters 'got possession of the great oak which gave partial cover from any fire'.

Very calmly and sensibly, Baker gave orders that his side was not to fire first, as he was 'most anxious the English name should not be associated with violence and bloodshed'. At the same time, he was determined that they should not appear to give way: 'Never halt or retreat in the face of an Eastern enemy: it is always fatal,' he remarked. He worked out a plan of attack, creeping round to a point from which he could completely outflank the bank and ridge. Before he had to put this tactic into action, he managed to involve his opponents in a parley which was just about to reach an impasse when by chance two servants of the local governor appeared on the scene, and good sense prevailed. But it had been a close call, and Baker was convinced it had only worked out well because his own staff had rallied to him after seeing his performance at the earlier attack.

Even when this incident was behind them, the prospect of fighting their way through the mountains, lumbered with a long trail of mules and facing hostile, armed mountaineers, was not an attractive one. At the next village, they observed that all the women were leaving for the mountains, indicating the possibility of an attack. They heard that a messenger who had been travelling with a small escort had been murdered by Turkomans the previous day on the same road to Meshed as they were themselves taking; when they came to the spot 'the clothes of the murdered man were still lying there covered with blood'. Nearby, they also found a 12-year-old Georgian boy who had been kidnapped by the Turkomans and carried off for 150 miles through the mountains, until his family paid the ransom. This, they were told, was a frequent occurrence in these parts.

It was hardly surprising in these circumstances that Baker and his party welcomed the chance to join up with a larger pilgrim convoy. They also accepted with alacrity when a local governor offered them an escort of around 60 irregular cavalry. It was therefore at the head of a sizeable column that Baker set off for Meshed. He was soon to find out the frustrations of travelling in such a large group: no one was ready on time; the bugler sounded off at the wrong hour in the middle of the night; the pilgrims either straggled behind or pushed themselves forward inappropriately; the caravanserais were so filthy that they preferred 'the risk of the Turkomans to the dirt within'; some of the escort offered to defect and join Baker permanently if he would pay them European rates; and the whole caravan moved within a dense cloud of dust. This was not how the 10th Hussars had conducted themselves under his command.

His path now lay through the plains of Nishapur, which he decided 'would form an admirable place for the concentration of an army . . . a hundred thousand men could be assembled here and watered'. As he approached closer to Meshed, the British agent there (an Afghan known as a 'news-letter writer' because he kept the legation in Tehran informed of local happenings) came out to meet him and brought him some disappointing news: the Persian governor of Meshed was on bad terms with the Turkomans of Merv and it was consequently impossible to pass from one place to the other. So the agent suggested that as Baker could not go on through Sarakhs towards Merv, he should divert southwards and go on to Herat in Afghanistan. The only snag was that Baker had no authority from the British government to enter Afghanistan.

Baker was furious: he had applied for papers for Afghanistan but had been refused by the Liberal government of William Gladstone on the grounds that if he met a violent death there, the government might feel obliged to do something about it. And the last thing that Mr Gladstone wanted, with his policy of masterly inactivity, was another Afghan war. Baker felt that Benjamin Disraeli's Conservative administration (which had now taken over) might have been more robust and he had already written to Lord Northbrook, the governor-general of India, appealing against the earlier ban on Afghanistan. His letter failed to get through in time. Baker poured out his anger in his book:

'After crossing all this distance, at a considerable risk and expense, to find oneself thwarted, not by difficulties proper to the occasion, but by want of support from one's own government, seemed hard. And the position was embittered by the fact that we had no private object in view – no thought of anything but getting useful information for our country.' (Baker seemed to have temporarily forgotten his sporting agenda.)

He decided to press on to Herat anyway and hope that a positive message would by then have come through from Lord Northbrook, but his health was rapidly collapsing. He suffered from fever, sleeplessness and a conviction that he was 'dying by inches'. He was tempted to turn back to the Caspian while he still had the strength, and reminded himself: 'You are not on duty. You are merely trying to carry out a useful work for your country. Will your country ever thank you for it?' He was even too weak for thoughts of sport. Soon afterwards, Lieutenant Gill managed to shoot himself in the leg while out hunting, but fortunately not puncturing a vein or an artery. They decided reluctantly to return to the environs of Meshed, where a mixture of local medicines and rest restored both officers sufficiently for them to be able to move forward again.

However, a message from the ruler of Herat made it clear that no word had been received from Lord Northbrook and so Baker could not be received there. Consequently, they made a circuit northwards to the fortress of Kelat (not to be confused with the Kalat in Baluchistan which featured in the travels of Pottinger and Masson) and even managed to climb a mountain peak from the summit of which not only Sarakhs but – they fancied – also Merv was visible. Baker promptly speculated, as so many of his contemporaries had done, that Merv was the key to Herat and Herat to India. This was the nearest he would get to either place. His disappointment was mitigated by managing to buy a remarkable thoroughbred Turkoman horse which he rode and eventually took home to Britain. Indeed, he was so impressed with the quality and stamina of Turkoman horses that he made enquiries as to whether they could be bought in large quantities for the Indian army, and was told of a place that could provide 15,000 given three months' notice. This too was useful military information.

When it became clear he would not reach Merv or Herat, Baker devoted himself to long conversations with his hosts about the Russian threat and to even longer hunting trips. He moved on to Mohammadabad, another walled and fortified town on the edge of the Turkoman country, where the governor took him out on partridge and pheasant shoots. However, when he came across the fresh tracks of a tiger and wanted to follow them, he was discouraged by his hosts and 'it struck me forcibly that there was no desire on their part to meet with so dangerous a beast'. But Baker did manage to bag some exceptionally large and fierce wild boar – at times shooting these from the saddle.

His favourite guns were the object of many covetous glances and pointed remarks by his hosts. Baker found this embarrassing and remarked:

> The giving of presents was a great tax. All other English travellers in this part of the world had been sent on special government service, and the presents were given by government; but Gill and I had either to pay the penalty ourselves, or else discredit the English name for liberality . . . valuable rifles and Purdey guns had therefore to be parted with, which made the pursuit of geographical information rather an expensive process.

Before the end of the trip he was reduced to buying the guns of his local retainers to pass them on as presents to his hosts.

During this interlude in his travels, Baker became acutely aware of the friction between Kurds and Persians in this part of the country; his sympathies tended to be with the Kurds as he admired their bold and positive character, while he found the Persians all too often timid and evasive. Indeed, he showed some percipience in his forecast of the future troubles between the Kurds and their neighbours at a time when informed British opinion was almost unaware of them.

A vivid example of this occurred when one of the Kurds they encountered suggested that it would be stimulating for Baker to witness a raid on a Turkoman village. Sixty of the best mounted Kurds and Persians were to swoop down, kill all the village men and capture all the women and children and flocks. To his credit, Baker firmly vetoed this display of aggression: 'we as English officers had no quarrel with the Turkomans . . . I could not permit such an act'. Reluctantly the Kurds and Persians allowed the innocent villagers to continue tending their flocks and weaving their carpets.

Now Baker was heading homewards. He decided to cut his losses: if he could not reach Merv, he could at least survey the river Atrak from its source to the Caspian and explore the northern slopes of the mountain range (now known as the Kopet Dag) which ran along the ill-defined Persian-Turkoman frontier. He consoled himself with the thought that, 'Merv has been visited by several Englishmen, whereas these northern slopes were absolutely unknown, as no Englishman had ever yet set foot on them'. Lieutenant Gill of the Royal Engineers (his leg now fully recovered from the gunshot wounds) came into his own, 'recording every angle in the road for mile after mile'.

In this way they continued through a succession of villages, where they were made welcome and supplied with escorts. One of the Tekke Turkoman chiefs went so far as to tell Baker that his people would like to be under the protection of the British, rather than being under Russia or Persia. Despite the general goodwill, there were always incidents and complications. At one village the locals had just mounted a raid on their neighbours, so no escort could be spared. At another the chief generously sent hampers of food to the visitors but Baker discovered that his cook had been selling the contents in the market and pocketing the proceeds. When he was sacked, the cook stirred up feelings against the infidel visitors, 'which is always dangerous in a Mahomedan country'.

At this point the journey home took on a faster pace. They encountered a messenger from the newswriter in Meshed who (although he had been robbed and stripped of his clothes en route) had letters from Captain Clayton, who had safely arrived in St Petersburg on his way home following his sickness. He warned Baker that the last Russian steamer to cross the Caspian before the ice made it unnavigable was due to set off (it was already November). As they did not fancy spending a whole winter in Persia, or taking the much longer southern route home, they gave up some promising shooting invitations and pressed on, pushing their horses and themselves to the limit. Unfortunately, Baker's fever returned at this point and sometimes this usually excessively energetic officer had to be lifted off his horse and carried into the post-house at the end of the day. They reached Tehran after 26 hours in the saddle, managed to bribe their way in although the city gates had already closed, located the British legation and finally found themselves 'in clean sheets in a comfortable bed'.

The rest of the return journey was not without its excitements. It was a real struggle for Baker, with his health rapidly deteriorating, to get to Enzelli on the Persian coast of the Caspian before the last steamer sailed for Baku on the east coast of the Russian Caucasus. But he just made it. From there, they decided to make the exciting 800-mile dash across the frozen steppes by tarantass ('a little phaeton with a hood but with no seats') to Rostov-on-Don, and thence by train to Moscow and St Petersburg, even though they were warned that they might be caught in violent snowstorms. Hardship had not destroyed their sense of adventure. They decided to travel night and day and calculated that it would take some eight days, during which they largely existed on 'figs, biscuits and some Crimean wine . . . upon which diet we got on famously'.

Just before they were due to set off a snowstorm started and they were told that those in carriages could be 'completely snowed up, frozen to death, and not discovered for weeks'. But they set off anyway, trusting to keep to the road by following what could be seen of telegraph posts. They wrapped their heads completely in thick rugs, but the following day it was snowing so hard that it was impossible to see 20 yards, and finally the tarantass got stuck in a snowdrift: 'all seemed hopeless, for in an hour's time we should be completely buried and frozen to death'. Miraculously, their driver plunged through the snow on foot and came across a building which turned out to be the outskirts of the next post-station. Despite their rashness they had survived. They exchanged the tarantass for two sledges and hired an elderly Cossack to guide them over the snowy terrain.

Even when they reached Rostov, their perils were not quite over. They had to cross the river Don by sledge and 'as we progressed the ice cracked ominously'. Looking back they saw the sledge behind had crashed through the ice and the horses were struggling in the water. After this, the train journeys on from Rostov to Moscow and St Petersburg were a positive rest. In St Petersburg Baker was debriefed at the British embassy and then completed his odyssey by train via the Ostend ferry to Charing Cross station in London.

The fact that his journey had entirely been paid for by himself and undertaken with no governmental support did not inhibit Baker from giving cogent advice to the British government. The final section of his book, *Clouds in the East: Travels and Adventures on the Perso-Turkoman Frontier* (1876), is in the form of a 'political and strategic report on central Asia'. In this he enumerates nine points for action; they all revolve round the perceived necessity of keeping a buffer region between the tsarist Russian empire and the British Raj in India. He argued that Britain should seek to dominate but not occupy Afghanistan and view this cordon sanitaire as being as vital for the defence of India as the English Channel is for the defence of Britain.

The irony of Baker's trip is that the whole enterprise was devoted to trying to alert opinion in Britain to the danger represented by Russia. Yet he had been treated generously and courteously by his Russian hosts and had developed a respect and even affection for them.

Baker returned to an enthusiastic welcome in London; although his book – when it came out two years later – was not to receive as wide a readership as that of his friend Captain Fred Burnaby's *A Ride to Khiva*, published the same year, his tales of his adventures were listened to by the Prince of Wales and London society. His military career looked set to prosper.

Then, on 17 June 1875, everything came unstuck quite

suddenly, unpredictably and dramatically. He had been invited to dine in London with the Duke of Cambridge (commander-in-chief of the army and a cousin of Queen Victoria) and boarded a first-class compartment on a train at Aldershot. He shared the compartment with a Miss Dickinson, the sister of an officer in the Royal Engineers. When the train arrived in London, Miss Dickinson accused him of having raped her. Two gentlemen travelling in the neighbouring compartment gave evidence which appeared to corroborate the charge. Baker was arrested and brought to trial at Croydon Assizes in July. Crowds gathered outside the court room protesting in favour of a lady who appeared to be the victim of a shocking abuse by an upper-class toff. Baker declined to give evidence in his own defence, possibly – his friends thought – because he was too much of a gentleman to claim that the lady had invited his advances. Although the rape charge did not stick, he was convicted of indecent assault. In sentencing him to a year's imprisonment and a fine of £500, Mr Justice Brett referred to Baker's 'sudden outbreak of wickedness'.

Everyone who knew Baker – his wife, family and friends, including the Prince of Wales – thought that the event was completely out of character; most believed him innocent. But this did not alter the fact that he was cashiered from the army. Indeed, the Queen was said to have been unsympathetic to him throughout as apparently she viewed his brother, the famous Nile explorer Sir Samuel Baker, as 'unprincipled'. She was disinclined to give Valentine Baker the benefit of any doubt.

Although within three years of the sentence the Prince of Wales had managed to arrange for Baker to be re-elected to the exclusive Marlborough Club, there could be no question of his regaining his commission in the Queen's army. Instead, he offered his services first to the Sultan of Turkey and later to the Khedive of Egypt; in both services he reached high rank and great distinction. However, for the former commanding officer of the exclusive and aristocratic 10th Hussars, this was not the future he had hoped for.

Valentine Baker was the quintessential amateur gentleman. He did a great reconnaissance with courage and military skill, but he did it in his own way at his own pace, never allowing his self-imposed intelligence task to interfere unduly with his sporting activities. For him, 'shooting leave' was exactly what it said it was.

# Chapter 8

## Nikolai Przhevalsky: The Bully of the Steppes

'Here you can penetrate anywhere, only not with the Gospels under your arm, but with money in your pocket, a carbine in one hand and a whip in the other.'

— Nikolai Przhevalsky (1839–88),
in a private letter to General Tikhmenov

Many of the young British and Russian officers who applied for shooting leave had complicated and unconventional backgrounds, but none more so than Nikolai Przhevalsky. His family origins were in part Cossack and in part from the Polish nobility (indeed the family name had recently been changed from Przewalski to its more Russian form). Nikolai was born in 1839 and brought up on a run-down rural estate in the forests near Smolensk. From his earliest days Przhevalsky was no stranger to bears and wolves, and at the age of 12 he was given a sawn-off shot gun and started hunting.

From an equally tender age Przhevalsky showed signs of developing into the bully he was later to become. When his little brother refused to climb down a well, Przhevalsky flung him down the shaft and walked away, leaving him to be providentially rescued by a passing peasant. While at school he led a revolt against his teachers – throwing the school register book into a river – and was flogged so severely that he was sent home on a stretcher. He needed disciplining and the army seemed the obvious career for him. He was anxious to take part in the Crimean War, but arrived at the front just as hostilities were ending.

Too poor to go to the cadet school, he started as a lance-corporal and later studied for the Academy of the General Staff, giving up duck-shooting to spend 16 hours a day at his books. When he succeeded in getting a place, he took time off to write *Memoirs of a Sportsman* about his early hunting experiences. He was allowed to graduate early if he volunteered to go on active service in Poland where the landowners had revolted against Russian rule. Despite any conflict of loyalties stemming from his ancestry, he volunteered without hesitation, but once again he only arrived after virtually all the action was over. Now, frustrated by soldiering, his mind turned to exploration.

Przhevalsky had long been intrigued by the fringes of the tsarist empire in Asia. He was later to venture into the traditional Great Game territory of the Tien Shan mountains and Kashgaria, but his first project, in 1867, was much further east. Although the Cossacks had opened up Siberia some three centuries earlier, there was still very little detailed information available to St Petersburg about the Amur river and the Ussuri region bordering the Chinese frontier. The Russian government and the Imperial Geographical Society created a joint brief for Przhevalsky's mission: he was to report on the state of the Russian troops garrisoning the border with Manchuria and Korea; he was to study the native population, which included a Cossack element; he was to amend the available maps and make new ones where there was none; and he was to reconnoitre land and water routes from the rivers to the borders. As Przhevalsky himself put it later: 'Scientific research will camouflage the political goals of the expedition and should discourage any interference by our adversaries.' He also had his own more personal agenda: he was to hunt and shoot everything that moved on the steppes and to bring back trophies of the chase.

Przhevalsky was allowed to gather his own team and among them he recruited a 16-year-old boy called Yagunov who was training to be a topographer. On all his subsequent expeditions Przhevalsky co-opted similarly youthful and good-looking young men as his companions and subordinates. He never married, and was thought by most of his later biographers to have been at least latently homosexual – although one of the wilder theories about him (based on his remarkable facial resemblance to Stalin and the fact that he was in the Caucasus at the time when the Soviet leader was conceived) is that he was Stalin's natural father. There could be no denying that there were common characteristics in their courage and ruthlessness. Be that as it may, it was certainly the case that as soon as one of his 'favourites' needed replacing (Yagunov was drowned) another one or two young replacements would be found. He appears to have bullied his protégés mercilessly, writing to one of two lads he was recruiting: 'I know you will be good friends, but then you will be thrashed together. Of course that won't happen often, but all the same it will occur.'

On his first expedition, Przhevalsky was accompanied by a pointer dog (later to be replaced by a setter called Faust which died of thirst on a desert crossing) to function as an active gundog. He rode for eight days from Lake Baykal to a tributary of the Amur river. The Cossack outposts on which he had been asked to report were all linked by rivers – a route for troikas or sledges in winter and for small boats or barges in summer. It was a desolate land, peopled by escaped convicts desperately searching for gold in the rivers and animal furs in the forests. Even the Cossack garrisons were starving: too weary to fish or trap game, too depressed to sing or dance, they fell back on the comforts of the vodka bottle. When Przhevalsky included details of the failed provisioning of these stations in his report, he incurred the displeasure of his military superiors.

Przhevalsky exceeded his instructions by venturing into Korea and parleying with the local commandant, while seated on a Siberian tiger skin. (He saw his first wild tiger shortly thereafter and also stumbled on a dacha whose owner had just been eaten by a tiger.) It was not a happy meeting: the commandant tried to insist that all Koreans who had fled to Russia should be sent back for beheading. Przhevalsky asserted his independence and strength by setting up a target a hundred paces away and riddling it with carbine fire: the message was clear – he was not to be trifled with.

Back in Russia, Przhevalsky was bent on further adventures. One such plan was to explore the rivers along the Manchurian border and to disguise himself as a trader to avoid arousing local suspicions. Before he could do so, he received orders to go back to the Ussuri region where Chinese bandits were attacking Cossack posts and to take command of the situation. So successfully did he destroy the poorly armed Chinese that he retrieved his reputation with the army high command in St Petersburg.

Stuck in Nikolayevsky on the Amur river for the winter, Przhevalsky found himself short of funds. His answer to this was to spend the evenings playing cards with the residents of the town which he described as 'one slop-pit where everything low and disgusting is found from off the whole of Russia'. However much he might despise them, he would resort to restoring his finances at their gaming tables when he was strapped for cash. One suspects he was a daunting competitor at poker as he abstained from vodka while encouraging his opponents to indulge.

Back at last in St Petersburg in 1870, he was soon commissioned to make the first of his further four memorable expeditions. This time he went through the region where the Yangtze river rises and in China, between Mongolia and Tibet. The scientific results of the trip were considerable and resulted in many new specimens reaching the Academy of Sciences in St Petersburg, with Przhevalsky receiving the Imperial Geographical Society's medal. The political results were even more significant, since he was able to report on the emergence of a new force in western China – the Muslim leader Yakub Beg at Kashgar – and for this he received the Order of St Vladimir from the Tsar.

What the expedition did not result in was the growth of Przhevalsky's respect for the inhabitants of these regions. His arrogant disdain found expression in his letters home: 'the Chinaman here is a Jew plus a Muscovite pickpocket, both squared'. Unlike so many of the young English officers engaged on shooting leave in Central Asia, he had not mastered any of the local languages nor attempted to study the religions and customs of the area; he was an essential outsider. For him, the answer to any problem or crisis was 'the spell-binding effect [of rifle fire] on the half-savage natives', even if he 'was sorry to waste cartridges'. On a later expedition, when he was again to insist on demonstrating his marksmanship, he remarked, 'You can't walk here if you don't carry a Nagayka whip . . . this Russian weapon is the only way of putting sense into the exceedingly persistent impudent fellows.'

Przhevalsky's next major expedition was indisputably political in character. Having reported on the emergence of Yakub Beg, he was now dispatched to Kashgar to establish relations and to negotiate with him. The emergent Muslim leader had already spread his breakaway domain as far as Urumchi and, fearing a Chinese counter-attack, was seeking support wherever he could find it – in St Petersburg, London or Calcutta. He desperately needed money and arms to maintain his precarious independence from China. He had in consequence dispatched an envoy – his own nephew, no less – to St Petersburg, but the Tsar had thought it more prudent not to receive him, lest doing so should upset the Chinese. The British – unknown to the Russians – had already been instrumental in sending a number of emissaries to Yakub Beg: Robert Shaw, an independent tea merchant, had gone to try to open up a tea trade of caravans between India and Kashgar; George Hayward, an explorer backed by the Royal Geographical Society in London, had been hard on the heels of Shaw; and Mirza Shuja, one of the celebrated 'pundits' who acted as surveyors and spies for the Raj, had reached Kashgar where he had been temporarily imprisoned by Yakub Beg.

When Przhevalsky set out in 1876 to visit Yakub Beg he had an impressive entourage with him. His nine companions included two new 'favourites' and were accompanied by a number of servants, 24 camels and tons of luggage, including gifts. It was an arduous journey over the Tien Shan range, during which Przhevalsky fell out with and sacked most of his servants. When he arrived, he was duly received by the Muslim leader and did everything he could to impress him. However, Yakub Beg for his part totally failed to impress Przhevalsky, who later wrote home to say that the then-unknown leader was 'a political impostor . . . the same shit as all feckless Asiatics'. With his arrogant manner, his total ignorance of his host's language and practices, and his disdain of everything and everyone he encountered, one feels it was hardly surprising that Przhevalsky was less successful in making friends and influencing people than were some of his British rivals – such as 'Bokhara' Burnes or Fred Burnaby. Nevertheless, Przhevalsky concluded that Yakub Beg's subjects were anxious to come under Russian protection. However, no attempt was made by St Petersburg to follow up Przhevalsky's blustering remarks; in the event it was the Chinese and not the Russians who sent an army. By the following year, Kashgar was occupied again by the Chinese and Yakub Beg was dead.

Most of the rest of Przhevalsky's Asian travels were devoted to trying to reach Lhasa in Tibet: he set out with that intention in 1877, in 1879 and again in 1883. There could be no denying the resilience he showed in the face of extreme hardship and danger. Food was usually short – on one occasion his camels became so hungry they tore up their saddles to eat the straw inside them. Water was also frequently in short supply. Once, having slaked his thirst at a remote desert well, Przhevalsky looked down the shaft to find a decomposing human body at the bottom.

He had to hide out of sight of the inhabitants to take his compass bearings or barometer readings, as technology was viewed with the gravest suspicion: 23 Europeans were slaughtered in one incident in 1870 when they were suspected of stealing local children to extract fluid from their eyeballs to make their cameras work. It was an unfriendly world, but not improved by Przhevalsky's high-handed methods: confronted with some reluctant Mongol guides on one occasion, he wrote: 'We gently invited them to come with us to our camp . . . the Mongols refused . . . then I announced that I was taking them by force . . . in case of flight I warned them I would shoot.'

Although he failed in his main objective of reaching Lhasa,

as the Tibetans not surprisingly decided he was an unwelcome intruder, he nonetheless added greatly to western knowledge of the eastern quarters of Central Asia. In fact, the Royal Geographical Society in London said no one had contributed so much since Marco Polo. And there were some worthwhile by-products of the expedition, including the first identification of the wild horse which was to be known as Equus Przewalski, which – incidentally – only survived to be discovered because it was out of rifle range when first sighted.

Two features characterized all Przhevalsky's trips. The first was a barrage of fire, aimed at the dual purposes of slaughtering the maximum amount of wildlife and intimidating the locals. In the foothills of the Tien Shan range he would hunt wild mountain sheep, which he found so unafraid of men that even after he had fired the survivors would not flee, but stare curiously in his direction awaiting a further volley. He would crawl on all-fours, holding the tripod of his gun above his head, to deceive the short-sighted yaks into thinking he was one of their number.

Then, at short range, he would empty his carbine into them – often only to find the yaks wounded but still alive afterwards. In two months he accounted for over 30 yaks, most of which – some 14 tons of meat – were left on the hillside to feed the wolves. The wolves themselves were frequently his prey, particularly after he found one wolf had carried off and eaten a box of his cartridges. Bears fared even worse than yaks and wolves: on one series of hunts he killed over 60 of them and carried away 35 bearskins to trade later.

On the lake Lob Nor he shot so many duck (743 from one hide) that he ran out of cartridges and had to save his fire for larger birds such as eagles. (On one expedition he had taken 7,200 rounds of ammunition, and on another 9,000 plus four hundredweight of lead shot.) Once he shot eight blue goats and only stopped when his rifle became too hot to hold; in panic the rest jumped over a crag to their death. New Year's Day 1885 was celebrated by shooting 23 Orongo antelope. When shooting wild boar he developed a scheme for making his carbine more

lethal: he drilled the bullets out and filled the hole with a cock-tail of chemicals so that he was firing an explosive dum-dum; it was not a very gentlemanly device or one of which Valentine Baker would have approved.

Added to this somewhat obsessive approach to the concept of shooting leave was the fact that he was collecting specimens and evidence for the Academy of Sciences and it was easier to shoot things than to photograph them. All in all, it was hardly surprising that expectant vultures followed his progress across the steppes as a matter of course.

It was unfortunate that this indiscriminate slaughter of wildlife was occasionally accompanied by a trigger-happy attitude towards the natives – somewhat reminiscent of his almost exact contem-porary Henry Stanley on the Congo river in Africa. On the shores of the Oring-Nor near the Tibetan frontier he provoked an attack by Ngolok tribesmen, which was repelled by his Cossack escort who killed more than 30 of them. He was to describe firearms drill as 'the best of all Chinese passports'.

The second feature which characterized Przhevalsky's trips was his attempt to undermine British influence wherever he could. In his diary for 1879 (quoted by Meyer and Brysac) he explains that 'to incite the Tibetans . . . against the English' he revealed to them maps and surveys of Tibet which had been compiled by the Indian 'pundits' and later published by the Royal Geographical Society in London. He knew that the Tibetans were extremely sensitive about all information regarding their own country, which they viewed as an intensely private fiefdom, and that by reciting to them details of place names and distances, and attributing all this material to 'English spies', he would harden their resolve not to allow any English visitors. It was also later to be rumoured that Przhevalsky had recruited a Russian-born tutor for the Dalai Lama – a certain Dorjiyev – who was alleged to have exerted an anti-British influence on his pupil. None of this resulted in the Tibetan authorities allowing Przhevalsky to approach their capital of Lhasa, but their determination to rebut British approaches precipitated the British invasion of their country in 1904. Przhevalsky had done neither himself nor the Tibetans any service by stirring up their suspicions of foreigners, but he saw it as part of his brief as a player in the Great Game.

The corollary of this anti-British activity was a very militant attitude towards Russian expansion. Although Przhevalsky's experience of commanding troops was virtually non-existent, his military-sponsored journeys led to his regular promotion in the Tsar's army. By 1885 he had reached the rank of major-general and his views on strategic matters carried some weight in St Petersburg. And very aggressive views they were. He urged in a classified memorandum (and later in a published book) that Russia should deploy its Cossack units to annex large tracts of western China, Mongolia and Tibet. This was going far beyond the largely accomplished Russian ambitions towards the khanates and emirates which had formed a buffer between the Tsar's domains and those of the British Raj. It was also flouting every aspect of legitimacy and the sanctity of existing frontiers, but Przhevalsky brushed that aside with the bald assertion that 'international law does not apply to savages'.

It was perhaps surprising that, when he died (predictably on an expedition to the Tien Shan mountains) in 1888, such an insensitive character should have been the subject of an adulatory obituary by that most sensitive of Russian writers Anton Chekhov, who saw in him the personification of a 'higher moral force'. His own view of his legacy was more prosaic: 'My brass cartridge cases, scattered in plenty over the mountains and valleys, will remind the natives for many years that Europeans have travelled and hunted here.' They would indeed.

# Chapter 9

## Charles MacGregor:
## The Disgruntled Staff Officer

'But is there for the night a resting-place?
A roof for when the slow, dark hours begin.'
– Christina Rossetti (1830–94), in 'Uphill'

Charles MacGregor of the Bengal Staff Corps set out at the age of 34 on a prolonged period of 'shooting leave' while travelling home overland from India in 1875. His travels took him through Khorassan in Persia and along the northwest frontier of Afghanistan, over territory seldom – and in some cases never – penetrated by earlier Englishmen. It was a bold and adventurous trip, but one which he undertook with remarkably little enthusiasm. There were two reasons for this.

First, he was in mourning – indeed in shock – from the death of his wife (who was a daughter of the Sir Henry Durand who had so courageously blown up the gate at Ghazni in the First Afghan War) who had died the year before on her way home to England on leave. His two-volume book about this journey is dedicated 'to the memory of her whose loss prompted these wanderings'. Although he had a daughter at home in England, whom he was longing to see, he could not quite face going back home without the prospect of spending his furlough with his wife amid 'the whirl and gaiety of a returned exile's life in England' for which he had yearned for so long. So he decided to put off the moment of return by protracted travels.

The second reason was that he viewed his intended exploration of unknown parts of Persia more as a duty than a pleasure. MacGregor was convinced (and was to become increasingly and ever more publicly certain) of the likelihood of a Russian invasion of India via Persia, Herat and Afghanistan. He speculated that such a campaign might well coincide with other campaigns by other routes. He thought the government of India was asleep at the helm and that it was his duty to provide information which would wake them up to the dangers of their situation. He had 'a feeling that unless some private individual gets information for them, our government will never obtain it for themselves . . . it is the English feeling that if the government won't do it I will, that brings me here'. He was a staff officer whose career (as we shall see) was to lie increasingly in the field of intelligence-gathering work: he wanted to try his hand at it and thought that his services 'might one day be appreciated'. However, this did not mean he relished the task. Quite the opposite. He was inclined to dismiss Persia as 'an uninteresting country'. He was annoyed at what he saw as the Persians' arrogance and feebleness, and he was appalled by their cruelty – 'it makes one quite sick'. He also deeply mistrusted the Afghans as 'quick with a knife, and having none of the chivalrous feeling that would stay his hand if attacking a defenceless foe'. Furthermore, he 'did not like the life [on the journey] in the least, with all its dirt and discomfort'.

These two motives – postponement of his return to Britain and a desire to find intelligence that would shake the Raj out of its lethargy – left little place for some of the altruistic inspiration of other Great Game travellers such as James Abbott. Not for him was the desire to see slaves freed, women emancipated or the Christian faith promulgated. He referred disdainfully to compatriots whose 'hobby' was the abolition of the slave trade. For an educated Englishman (he had already attended three leading public schools – Glenalmond, Marlborough and Haileybury – by the time he was 15) in the age of William Gladstone and Thomas Macaulay, his views were extraordinarily regressive. He referred to Africans as 'the nearest approach to an animal I know of any human race' and argued that they were better off in slavery since a slave 'comes to a country where houses are to him palaces, he is sumptuously fed and has more clothes than the kings of his own country'.

Equally he believed that the women of Central Asia 'see in the huge cloaks in which they shroud themselves far greater freedom than they could ever hope to attain by the adoption of western customs'. He was also given to bouts of facetiousness about veiled women: 'The women of Ghaeen are not so closely veiled as their sisters more to the west, and from this circumstance I am enabled to inform my readers that in this place, at least, the women have noses, a matter regarding which I was before in doubt.' MacGregor is certainly a bigoted traveller who starts out with a curious set of attitudes and grievances.

However, this did not stop him from being both highly observant of the strategic features of the country through which he was passing and extraordinarily brave in facing dangers along the way. His route took him from Shiraz in southern Persia, northeastwards to Yazd, through Birjand and on towards Herat in Afghanistan, and then back to Meshed and Sarakhs in Persia, before eventually heading home via Tehran and overland through Russia, Poland and Austria. It was an eight-month expedition.

Much of the way in Persia was across bleak deserts or through severe passes and, as he got closer to Afghanistan and into Turkoman-infested country, the risk of raiding parties who carried off travellers for ransom or slavery became acute.

Every mountain pass he traversed was assessed as a conduit for an invading force. A typical description reads: 'This pass [the Kotul-y-Koomary] could not be forced in the face of opposition; but I ascertain that, like most mountain passes, it admits of being turned by light infantry. I hardly think guns could be got up . . . elephants could get up but care would have to be taken to prevent any animal coming down while others were going up.'

Equally, every fort which he passes is assessed for its defensive potential. For instance, at Sowgund he noted that the fort 'has high walls that would be sufficient protection against Baloche robbers, but is in too dilapidated a state to offer any resistance to a regular attack'. At Furk, the fort 'is clumsily and unskilfully built and a few rounds of shot would probably bring down an entire side of the structure . . . it is commanded [overlooked] from so many directions as to be quite untenable . . . from one hill to the north you might literally stone the garrison out'. At Ghorian, the parapet of the fort 'could be enfiladed . . . I should expect to be inside in an hour'. At Meshed, the walls had 'very few places that are not practicable for infantry, even without ladders'. At Kulat, although the fort appeared impregnable, there were serious flaws. And so on, and so on. It was quite clear that the Persians, even if they had the will, did not have the capacity to withstand or seriously delay a Russian advance through their land towards India.

As well as passes and forts, MacGregor noted oases and fertile plains where an invading army could rest and recoup.

Writing of Ghaeen (on the way to Herat), he recounted that, 'it would be able to furnish supplies for a small force, and it could draw in more from [neighbouring] fertile districts', whereas Birjand 'could not of itself furnish any supplies for an army'. He pointed out that it was perfectly easy and safe to survey these militarily significant matters in Persia without risk of being considered any more than a mad Englishman. He concludes, 'nothing can justify us in not long ago having had a reliable map of the country, nothing but apathy should prevent us from making one now'. This was the intelligence-staff-officer on his hobby horse.

However much it might be the case that the actual process of surveying was without the sort of risks that some other Great Game players had encountered, it remained the fact that reaching the places was in itself a highly risky business.

Between Shiraz and Yazd he passed through a region known to be prone to Bakhtiari tribal raiders. MacGregor stumbled on a group of Bakhtiari robbers hiding in the hills and told his 'matchtlockmen' (bodyguards) to fire at them – an act of pre-emptive aggression. He was somewhat relieved that none of the Bakhtiari was hit, 'although the skedaddle that ensued was something to behold', because they would very likely have come back to seek revenge.

More serious danger occurred when they entered the Turkoman country along the Afghan-Persian border. His servants 'were in a great funk' and at least one of them deserted rather than venture into territory renounced for the frequency of Turkoman raids. MacGregor was very careful never to disclose in advance details of the route he intended to take, lest word should be passed forward and ambushes laid. At times, he even gave his own people deliberately false information, in the confidence that this would leak and mislead possible assailants. He was also careful never to march on the exact road, but a little off it, so as not to fall into any trap.

One of his narrowest squeaks was between Kohsun and Meshed. They were crossing a typical stretch of country – 'every road in Persia seems to me exactly alike . . . a waste, with barren rugged hills in the distance' – when he spied about three miles away a posse of some 20 Turkoman raiders in dark clothes and black hats, some armed with rifles, others with lances and swords. The raiders were galloping towards them. The only hope of defending themselves seemed to be to reach higher ground – one of the 'rugged hills in the distance'. Some of MacGregor's party instantly fled on foot in that direction, 'quite green with fright', but soon found themselves 'dead beat with their unwonted hurry and ready to drop'. MacGregor, who was also heading for the higher ground on his horse, found that 'despite their unfaithfulness, I could not quite bring myself to abandon them and leave them to shift for themselves'. So – very gallantly – he got off his horse and told them to mount in his place.

MacGregor himself scrambled up the hillside on foot and took up a firing position, waiting for the Turkomans to come within range. As soon as they did, MacGregor fired off a number of rounds from his Snider rifle, 'taking care not to hit anyone' as he wanted to repel them without drawing blood and giving a motive for a retaliatory attack. His firing did the trick; the

Turkomans withdrew into a ravine, shooting a few desultory rounds as they did so. At this juncture, rescue came in the form of a body of some 40 armed nomads who had been alerted by one of MacGregor's fleeing escort. While the nomads' own women and children had fled their encampment for whatever safety they could find, the nomadic men had set off to confront the Turkomans and rescue the travellers. MacGregor for once acted graciously, thanking the headman, presenting him with a pistol and joining him for a dish of curds.

MacGregor was fortunate that the attackers had not been a larger group, as was often the case. In fact, MacGregor had earlier reflected wistfully: 'The worst of these devils is that they sometimes come in such large bodies (200 to 300) that it would be useless to fight; if only they behaved like gentlemen, and came in decent odds, say five or six to one, one would not mind, but enjoy a brush with them rather.' He had not, in fact, greatly enjoyed his brush with them between Kohsun and Meshed, but that was perhaps because his Persian servants and escorts had proved so cowardly that he had had to put himself excessively at risk to compensate. He considered these risks were worth taking because only by crossing the Turkoman-infested country could he 'pick up accurate information as to the real frontier of Persia in this direction, a matter on which the Indian government had no information, though knowledge of the subject may one day be of great use to us'.

He was continually frustrated by the lack of professionalism in the Persian military. On some occasions he could not resist showing them how things should be done. When approaching some bandit-infested hills between Meshed and Sarakhs in the company of some Persian troops, he approached their commander and said: 'You are surely not going to advance with your command jumbled up in this fashion . . . don't you see a couple of hundred Turkomans could put the whole of such a helpless mob to flight?' As usual, his military skills outstripped his tact.

In reality, the risk to MacGregor was exacerbated by the unfortunate fact that he made a practice of making enemies along the way. For someone who set out with such disdainful feelings towards the inhabitants of the lands he was traversing, it only required the smallest frustration of his plans or the smallest degree of incivility by the locals to provoke a diatribe of wrath and insult from MacGregor in return. If the accommodation he was expecting for the night seemed slow in materializing, or if it fell below the standards of comfort or cleanliness he expected, then he would refuse to enter the village or fortress in question. If local chiefs did not send out someone appropriate to meet an English officer, or if they did not receive him in the manner which he felt was his due, he would adopt a haughty and threatening manner. One escorting officer who was 'consistently insolent' was told not to ride alongside him as 'I never care to ride with people I dislike'. When he was – understandably – disappointed at not being welcomed at Herat, he wrote a letter of enormous length and pomposity to the Moostoufee (the local governor) protesting at his treatment. He was surprised, having explained to the governor's agent that he was complaining to the governor about his 'sending a low-bred man like yourself to me', that the agent refused either to transcribe or deliver the letter. MacGregor viewed the governor of Meshed as 'a mild old imbecile . . . a nerveless old mummy', and took little care to disguise his feelings.

In another incident, when the form – a type of bench – on which he was sitting during an audience with the prime minister in Tehran collapsed, and the prime minister laughed, MacGregor responded by saying, 'It is of no consequence, Your Excellency, the form is typical of Iran.' He was gratified to see that this insult to the nation made his escorting officer 'turn green' with horror. Then, at the very moment of leaving Persia, he picked a quarrel with a ferryman and 'jumped off [my horse] knocking him down flat, jumped on my horse, left him howling, and went to ferry and crossed'. All the hostility which such behaviour generated along the route meant that if anything went seriously wrong he had few friends to help him sort it out. An embarrassment was inclined quickly to become a crisis.

One such incident occurred at Tabas in the heart of the Khorassan desert region, when MacGregor was – as usual – short of cash and decided to write an 'order on Tehran for £20 asking [a local officer] to send him the equivalent here'. For this he needed a trustworthy messenger and the man he selected collected the letter and disappeared into the night. An hour later his body was found below an open window in MacGregor's house. His head was smashed in, but the rest of his body was not in the least injured 'nor even his clothes disarranged'. MacGregor realized immediately he might be in trouble, as 'two fugitives' whom he had earlier antagonized were on the loose in Tabas and he 'felt sure they would be on the lookout to make the most of anything they could distort to my detriment . . . here was a story ready . . . a man had last been seen in my company and an hour later was found dead . . . how easy it would be to concoct a story which would be believed by the ignorant scum of this place'. MacGregor feared that his enemies might persuade the dead man's relatives to take revenge on him for the death. He therefore posted a sentry over the body and tried to persuade the 'principal authority in the place' to come and take charge of the inquiry. However, the official in question said it was too late at night to go out on such business. MacGregor was left to make written statements, inform the next of kin, take measurements of the site and draw sketches, and even pay for the burial and some compensation to the widow. Having done everything he could and concluded 'so far so good', he sat down and wrote a long and detailed account of the whole incident to the British minister in Tehran, so that it would be on record if subsequent charges were made against him. The affair would not have been threatening if he had not felt that he was among people he had already antagonized. He was paying a price for his impatience and arrogance.

His behaviour in this respect was in marked contrast to that of Valentine Baker who generally left behind him a legacy of respect for his good manners as well as for his courage and sporting prowess. MacGregor was continually meeting people who remembered Baker's similar – but far from identical – travels of a few months earlier. People 'recounted to me numerous stories of the hills the colonel [Baker] had climbed, and the game he had shot . . . I heard nothing but good of him and everywhere learnt that his conduct had greatly raised the English name in these wild countries'. It was almost at the end of his journey that MacGregor heard reports of Baker's 'affair' – his trial for rape and assault. MacGregor found the reports 'a blow to my national amour propre'.

Having failed to enter Afghanistan at Herat at the first attempt, MacGregor worked out a more circuitous route which would avoid the prospect of a second rebuff from the same quarter. However, to follow up this plan he needed the consent of the British government in India. He consequently wrote a carefully worded letter to the Foreign Secretary in Simla, pointing out what valuable information he had already acquired in Khorassan and going on to say, 'I consider it of vital importance that an English officer should visit this tract [Herat and northern Afghanistan] at once . . . the danger is not worth weighing.' He reported the repeated indications he had received that the locals wanted some protection from the Turkomans and, if Britain did not intervene, then they would welcome the Russians.

It therefore came as a shock as well as a disappointment when he received a 'frigid rejection' of his proposal stating bleakly that the Foreign Secretary 'had the honour, by direction of His Excellency the Viceroy of India, to inform you that you are prohibited from travelling in Afghanistan or Turkestan, or going beyond the borders of Persia'. MacGregor particularly resented this ban as he was not asking for public finance or government protection – in this he was like Valentine Baker. He also suspected that those who had inspired the rejection were 'seized by the curse of jealousy'; he was not going to be allowed to outshine his contemporaries as 'Bokhara' Burnes had done. The rest of his trip was to be something of an anti-climax.

This bleak rejection was to stimulate MacGregor on his return to India (after the much-postponed furlough in England) to make it his mission to arouse concern – if not alarm – in British government circles about the Russian threat. Although the authorities in Simla had reservations about his trip to Persia and efforts to enter Afghanistan, he rose steadily in the military hierarchy. By 1883 he was Quartermaster General of the army in India, with the rank of major-general. In this capacity he was in charge of intelligence gathering and collating, and was in a good position both to assess the threat from Russia and to warn his political masters about this.

He started writing to all his friends and contacts in the military establishment to try to get them to provide material for a major thesis on the subject. Sir Frederick ('Bobs') Roberts VC, the commander-in-chief at Madras, was one recipient of his very pressing letters; General Sir Donald Stewart, the commander-in-chief in India, was another. How soon could the British reinforce Herat? How long would it take the Russians to get there? Should we not be building railways up to the frontier area in the way the Russians were doing? Having thoroughly stirred up the whole question (largely on the basis of his own shooting leave in the region some eight years earlier) he put together a definitive report of some 100,000 words. He concluded this report by asserting his conviction that there could be no real settlement of the Russian threat until they were 'driven out of the Caucasus and Turkestan'. Although the report was classified as secret, he ensured that copies reached influential figures outside government, including opposition politicians and newspaper editors. The report – it amounted to a book entitled *The Defence of India* – and its circulation infuriated Mr Gladstone's government, with its preferred policy of inactivity. MacGregor was duly reprimanded. A couple of years later, like his wife, he died on a voyage back to Britain, at the age of 46.

MacGregor had been frustrated at every turn. Despite his credentials as an outstandingly brave officer – he had distinguished himself in the Mutiny, in the campaign against the emperor of Ethiopia and in the Second Afghan War – he had not been trusted to fulfil his ambition for his shooting leave. He had allowed himself to be infuriated to an exaggerated degree by the lack of respect shown to him by the locals on the travels – even more than James Abbott had been – and he had been frustrated by the suppression of his history of the Second Afghan War on the grounds that 'it contained a critique of Indian defence policy beyond its terms of reference'. The reprimand he received for his work on the defence of India further rankled with him. If he had been a less prickly traveller, he might have enjoyed his expedition more (as Charles Stewart was to do) and influenced the local population more (as Valentine Baker did); and if he had been a less grumpy staff officer he might have been more widely listened to (as was Alexander Burnes) and more widely read (as was Fred Burnaby). As it turned out, his was an example of a protracted spell of shooting leave that left a sour taste for both him and his masters.

# Chapter 10

## Fred Burnaby: The Gentle Giant

'That island of England breeds very valiant creatures; their mastiffs are of unmatchable courage.'

– William Shakespeare (1564–1616), in *Henry V*

Captain Fred Burnaby of the Royal Horse Guards was the popular prototype of a Great Game player. He was rich, paying for his extended travels in Central Asia and elsewhere with no help from the government (though the Russians would never believe this), and he was handsome – James Tissot had memorably painted him lounging on a chaise-longue in his blue and scarlet regimentals. He was also immensely strong – his party trick was to hold out at arm's length two billiard cues by the pointed ends between his fingers without wobbling (the nineteenth-century equivalent of tearing up a London telephone directory). Furthermore, he was daring and dashing, predictably meeting a gallant end when speared to death on a mission to Khartoum.

However, he was not quite such an uncomplicated character as all this might imply. Before he set off on his celebrated ride to Khiva in 1875, he had already given much thought to the whole relationship between Russia and Britain in Central Asia. He rejected the Russian contention that it would be 'a great advantage for England to have a civilized neighbour like Russia on her Indian frontier'; in fact, he viewed 'Russian civilization as something diametrically opposite to what is attributed to it by those [Russians] whom [Englishmen] meet abroad'. He tended – like so many of the subjects of this book – to like individual Russians but deeply to mistrust the state and its policies. His adventures tended to confirm both feelings in a traveller who was certainly no simple soldier.

Burnaby also suffered from some of the prejudices that went with the supreme self-confidence of Victorian Britain. He despised Orthodox Christianity and wrote that 'the Greek faith as practised by the lower orders in Russia is pure paganism in comparison with the Protestant religion'. And recurring throughout his account of his travels is a latent anti-Semitism, or at least a distaste for all things Jewish. He refers to 'a man whose peculiarly-shaped nose showed a distinct relationship to the tribe of Israel'. There are other references to 'the nasal ejaculation of the Hebrews' and to 'a waiter of the Jewish type . . . begrimed with dirt'. One feels that such sentiments were probably all too common in nineteenth-century officers' messes both in British and Russian cavalry regiments.

He also had other, less offensive, Victorian mannerisms. He liked to use what Peter Fleming described as 'the full panoply of nineteenth-century explorers' purple prose'. He does not fall asleep, but rather is 'plunged into the arms of Morpheus'; the sun does not set, but 'the golden orb descends in the far-off west'; and the moon is 'that queen of light, a globe of metallic silver'.

A more positive aspect of Victorian self-confidence was demonstrated in his feeling that – to a British officer like him – all things were possible. His ambition to ride to Khiva clearly had the odds heavily loaded against him from the start. He was

advised by many that the Russian government would never countenance such a trip; the widespread feeling – both among his
British and Russian acquaintances – was that the authorities were
nervous about any word getting out regarding the conduct of
General Konstantin Kaufman's troops on the borders of the
Tsar's empire. The fact that Burnaby was a Russian speaker (he
also spoke Arabic) made it all the more likely he would be in a
position to report Russian misbehaviour, or even stir up trouble
among the newly subjugated citizens of Khiva. (Although the
khan of Khiva's capital was not occupied by Russian troops, he
was obliged to pay a heavy levy to Russia and he effectively
presided over a vassal state.) To get there in these circumstances
seemed a very long shot.

Undeterred, Burnaby set off to St Petersburg to obtain the
necessary permission. He called uninvited on General Dmitry
Milutin, the Russian minister of war, but he nevertheless received
a prompt reply: 'to the effect that the commandants of Russian
Asia had received orders to aid me in my journey through the
territory under their command, but the Imperial Government
could not give its acquiescence to the extension of my journey
beyond Russian territory, as the authorities could not answer for
the security of the lives of travellers beyond the extent of the
Emperor's dominions'.

Clearly, while Milutin did not mind Burnaby travelling through
Russian-controlled territory, he was not happy with his going to
the semi-independent capital of Khiva. Burnaby wistfully speculated in his book whether Milutin was being over-protective
about his security, and whether the general himself – when a
young officer – would have been deterred by such warnings. He
concluded that the answer to both parts of the question was
negative. It followed that Milutin had his own reasons for not

wanting Burnaby to go to Khiva. As he had not explicitly forbidden him to do so, Burnaby decided he would get as deeply into Russian Central Asia as he could and then see what possibilities were open to him.

Burnaby set about equipping himself for the long, cold overland trek. One essential was a heavy waist-belt containing enough gold sovereigns to pay his way, 'and which was a most uncomfortable bedfellow'. Otherwise, he decided to travel as light as possible, but certain requirements could not be overlooked: 'it was as well to have some sort of gun in the event of falling in with wild fowl', so he packed a 12-bore shot gun and made sure that some of the cartridges were loaded with ball rather than light pellets, 'in case I should encounter any bears and wolves'. His box of 400 cartridges ended up being so heavy that it attracted the attention of the railway authorities on the first leg of his journey to Orenburg. He was not making a special point of specifically being on shooting leave (as Valentine Baker had done two years before) but his book describes various shooting

162

and hunting expeditions : wolves, chamois, antelope, foxes, hares and pheasants being among the prey; with horses, hounds, grey-hounds and hawks being among the instruments of the chase. A revolver was also packed in case of the need to repel Turkoman robbers.

Sixty hours of rail travel took Burnaby to Syzran on the Volga (near Kuybyshev) where he transferred to sleighs for the remainder of the road to Orenburg. Now the snowbound steppe was a real challenge. He had not gone far with his horse-drawn sleigh and driver before they were 'so buried in the snow that the horses could not stir it'. He decided that the only hope was to get out and help the driver lift the vehicle back on to the path. This they succeeded in doing, but the driver was astonished, not so much at Burnaby's strength – which was prodigious – as by his being prepared to stir himself into action at all: 'a Russian gentleman as a rule would almost prefer to be frozen to death than do any manual labour', whereas Burnaby had been brought up in a tradition where officers were expected in an emergency

to set their hand to anything they might ask their men to do.

When eventually they got back on the road, they had an unexpected encounter with the governor of the Orenburg district, who was on his way back to St Petersburg. The governor was clearly already aware of Burnaby's impending arrival at Orenburg and of his knowledge of the Russian language. The governor lost no time in telling Burnaby that he 'should on no account go to India or Persia' but must return the way he came. Sensitivity about the regions beyond the borders amounted to paranoia.

On arrival at Orenburg, one of Burnaby's first tasks was to recruit a servant to go with him for the rest of the journey. The first Tartar he hired asked for wages in advance to support an aged mother during his absence, and then absconded with the money. Eventually, he discovered a replacement – a diminutive Tartar called Nazar who spoke Russian and Kirghiz. Packing a sleigh with all the necessary provisions for the next stage of the journey to Kasala (known as 'Number One Fort') proved a tricky task: Burnaby's legs were just too long to fit in. Consequently, Nazar was made to balance on top of the gun-case and saddle-bags, and the harnessed horses galloped away.

They followed the line of a frozen river but the driver lost his way and they became stuck. He informed them that they would have to sleep out and that 'in all probability we should be frozen'. There was no wood to make a fire, no shovel to make a shelter and no remaining food. Fortunately, Burnaby had kitted himself out with massive furs which he generously distributed to the driver and Nazar. The big problem was to keep awake through the night, and whenever Burnaby lost consciousness he was violently shaken by Nazar who declared: 'Do not close your eyes, Sir, or you will never open them again.' Somehow, they all survived the night and in the dawn the driver rode off in search of help. By midday a local farmer appeared on the scene and together with some peasants dug out their sleigh and set it on the road again.

When they reached the next staging post, there were other benighted travellers – including an official courier – who told them that the storm conditions were too severe to allow them to go on. The next day, Burnaby joined forces with the courier as he was aware that he had a good supply of shovels and would get priority access to good horses – which Burnaby hoped he might share if he distributed 'tea-money' generously to hostel keepers and drivers. In the event, considerably more money had to be shelled out than he had expected, while the number of people lying around drunk in the snow did nothing to speed up either negotiations or progress.[1]

The winter of 1875–6 was acknowledged to be the worst on record and Burnaby was soon to have his most traumatic experience of the trip. Between Orenburg and Kasala he fell asleep on the sleigh with his bare hands folded into the sleeves of his fur-trimmed coat. As he slept, his hands slipped from the warm covering in which they had been inserted, 'resting themselves on the side of the sleigh, unprotected by any thick gloves, and exposed to the full power of the biting east wind'. He awoke after a few minutes in intense pain: his fingernails and the backs of his hands were blue, and his wrists and arms 'of a waxen hue'. This was frostbite of a serious order. Nazar rubbed his hands and arms with snow – a traditional cure for

---

1. Russian rural habits changed little in eight decades. When the author would drive back to Moscow in winter from hunting or skiing in the forests, every aul or hamlet would have at least one drunken 'comrade' wandering dangerously on the road or collapsed in the snow. It was an additional hazard to add to many others.

mild frostbite – to no avail. So they drove on with all haste to the nearest staging post seven miles away. By the time they arrived Burnaby – for all his strength – was in a very bad way: he thought he would rather be dead as the pain wracked through his forearms and he poured with sweat.

Fortunately for him, when they reached the staging post he fell into the hands of a band of Cossacks who knew the best first aid: they plunged his arms into a tub of ice, but still feared that it was too late: 'brother, you will lose your hands, they will drop off'. One of the Cossacks asked if they had any spirits and Nazar produced some naphtha (intended for cooking) with which they rubbed his arms until the skin peeled. They then plunged his arms into the ice again and sensation – extremely painful sensation – returned. The Cossacks told him it had been a close-run thing as to whether he lost his hands and arms. When Burnaby pressed on them some remuneration, they remonstrated that they were sure he would have done the same for them if they had been in a similar predicament. Although his relationship with the Cossacks was to be strained on various future occasions, Burnaby never forgot their kindness to him in his hour of extreme need. He also had a high regard for their military skills: they were now highly trained troops and he warned that 'in the next war . . . the Cossacks will be found a very different foe from those undisciplined and badly armed horsemen whom we encountered in the Crimea'. Captain Burnaby might have been on extended leave, but the cavalry officer was ever alert to professional considerations.

Although it was some weeks before Burnaby was fully recovered from this experience, the party pressed on regardless. He noted the potential of the various forts they passed. On one occasion he got out his gun and thought he would get a shot at a wolf, but the wary animal 'slunk away . . . at a good jog-trot'.[2] At least he felt it had been worth bringing the heavier cartridges with him all this way.

The rough going – rocky terrain covered in snow of unequal depth – was taking its toll on the sledge so Burnaby decided to abandon it in favour of a more robust vehicle, but not without 'feelings of regret . . . for it had carried myself and fortunes for more than a thousand miles'. The new sledge was even more cramped than the last, and he had no possibility of stretching his long legs between halts.

He reached Kasala – 'Number One Fort' – just after the Russian Christmas. This was a junction for camel caravans from Khiva, Bokhara and Tashkent, and was also a garrison town with 350 infantry and 400 cavalry stationed there, as well as an equal number of sailors from the Russian fleet of the Aral Sea. Every detail of the defences was assiduously noted down by Burnaby, including the ominous fact that barracks had been built for a very much larger force. He had considerable difficulty finding any accommodation. He records in his somewhat aggressively Gentile mode that he even tried in vain to find quarters 'among the tribes of Israel . . . Abraham, Isaac and Jacob'. Luckily for him, the Russian commandant eventually offered him an apartment in his own house.

Burnaby took advantage of the access which his lodging gave him to Russian military gossip. He soon learnt that a steamer had been designed with a specially shallow draft to ascend the

---

2. Shooting wolves from sleighs was still practised when the author travelled in these parts in the 1950s. The somewhat brutal practice was to drag a piglet in a bag behind the sleigh, and when its squeals tempted the wolves out of the forest, the hunter would wait until they were silhouetted against the snow and then shoot them with a rifle from the moving sleigh.

Oxus to a far greater distance than previously possible, while a commercial fishing fleet on the Aral Sea could also be used as troop-carrying barges up the river into the heart of Afghanistan and near to the Indian frontier. His Russian hostess, who quietly poured out these military indiscretions over tea, shocked Burnaby's Victorian etiquette by lighting up a cigarette as she did so: 'fortunately the girls have not yet taken to the habit', he comments.

When he called on the governor, he was ordered to move out of the commandant's house and into the governor's own residence. Here he attended a Christmas assembly where he met 'all the beauty and fashion of Kasala'. The talk, though less strategically informative than that of the garrulous commandant's wife, was blatantly jingoistic and assumed that a Russo-British confrontation was all too imminent: 'when we fight you fellows in India then we shall have some promotion . . . if we do fight we will shoot at each other in the morning, and liquor up together when there is a truce'. Burnaby did not take these outbursts too seriously as he noted that 'few of the party could speak French' which showed that they were not a very upper-class bunch of officers, and so unlikely to be influential in policy matters. Those who were from the upper echelons of society were usually only in Kasala because of some fall from grace.

The day after the party, Burnaby broached the delicate question of his onward journey with the governor. He was offered an escort of Cossacks. Burnaby immediately sensed that these would be not so much bodyguards as minders, who might well prevent him reaching his target of Khiva. When he declined and inquired what would happen if he went there on his own, the governor did his best to scare him off any such idea: 'Why, the khan would very likely order his executioner to gouge out your eyes, or would keep you in a hole in the ground for five or six days before he admitted you to an audience. The Khivans are very dangerous people.'

Burnaby and the governor now compromised. He could have a guide rather than an escort, but he must go via Petro-Alexandrovsk, the Russian fort just inside Russian territory and across the Oxus from Khiva. The governor was also helpful with suggestions about provisions: he recommended 'cabbage soup with meat cut up in it . . . frozen and easily carried in iron stable-buckets'. There was no need to bother with water: he could collect snow off the ground, and if the snow thinned out anywhere he could 'put some in sacks and carry it on camels'.

Before leaving Kasala, Burnaby got Nazar to take him on a tour of the markets. As a bachelor, Burnaby always had an eye for the girls but was seldom attracted by what he saw, 'although on horseback they appear to perfection'. However, on a later occasion he did encounter a good-looking and prepossessing Kirghiz girl and made an attempt to express his admiration via an interpreter. He was somewhat disconcerted when he realized that his compliments were being translated as 'thou art lovelier than a sheep with a fat tail . . . thy face is the roundest in the flock . . . thy breath is sweeter than many pieces of mutton roasted over bright embers'.

A more urgent occupation was to equip himself for the next and final stage of the journey. He bought the ingredients of the governor's soup and then set about the harder task of finding horses and guides. He had to pay over the odds for the former and accept 'a cunning and avaricious' character as a guide; but the guide's avarice was to be turned to good advantage by Burnaby.

He decided to take the most direct route south across the frozen steppe, relying on snow for water as there were no wells; this route had not been travelled by any Englishman before.

Because he had to take everything he needed with him, he, Nazar and the guide required three camels and two horses between them. This small party set out, ostensibly for Petro-Alexandrovsk, with the blessing of the governor, the commandant and the garrison of Kasala.

Burnaby had not the slightest intention of going to Petro-Alexandrovsk if it could be avoided. He felt sure the Russian commandant there would stop him crossing the Oxus to Khiva, interpreting General Milutin's qualified permission to travel within Russia as a ban from going beyond the frontiers. The problem was going to be to persuade the guide to bypass Petro-Alexandrovsk. On departure the guide did not endear himself to his cavalry-officer employer by eyeing his horse up and down and speculating on its potential as good eating material: 'We will all have such a feast!'

The first obstacle was the Syr Darya river (the Jaxartes of ancient history) but as this was frozen solid it presented no difficulty. The steamers of the Russian Aral Sea fleet could be seen embedded in the ice and reminded Burnaby of the possible role of these ships against India.[3] His powers of observation were restricted by the fact that he had to pull his fur hat down over his eyes and peer out through the fringe of it, as wearing dark glasses (which he had prudently brought) was impossible as the steel rims froze to his face 'as if [they] had been seared with a red-hot poker'. More seriously, his moustache 'was frozen into a solid block of ice'. The horses were even worse off; their

---

3. The author's own first sight of the Aral Sea was when alighting for a break on a five-day train journey from Moscow to Tashkent at Aralsk. The custom was then for the passengers to change into pyjamas on the first day and stay in them for the duration of the train journey, so one was easily identified – even under a fur coat – as a passenger, and Russians would approach one in the market near the station and warn one when the train was about to depart.

nostrils became entirely stuffed up with icicles.

It was several days' further march before Burnaby hit on the idea that was to enable him to bypass Petro-Alexandrovsk and go directly to Khiva. The conversation, as so frequently, had turned to horses, and the guide said that he had a brother-in-law who could supply 'beautiful animals, round and fat'. These were available – at a price – at Kalenderhana, a village off the road to Petro-Alexandrovsk but directly on the route to Khiva. Burnaby records: 'A thought suddenly occurred to me. Why not try to persuade the fellow to take me to Kalenderhana under pretext of buying horses from his brother-in-law?' So Burnaby set about suggesting that if he went to Petro-Alexandrovsk he would take the opportunity to buy new horses. This produced the expected reaction from the avaricious guide (who would clearly get a slice of the profit he brought to his brother-in-law). First, he suggested that he sent for the family horses and, when Burnaby declined this, proposed on his own initiative that they bypassed Petro-Alexandrovsk in favour of going straight to Kalenderhana and on to Khiva. It was not only the prospect of profit but also the sheer love of all Kirghiz for horse-dealing that spurred him on. To make sure he got the support of Nazar in this plot, Burnaby offered him some financial inducements, too.

For part of the way, Burnaby's party joined forces with a Khivan caravan, but both the guide and Nazar were nervous about being in the company of armed men who were more numerous than themselves. Although this part of the country was normally free from Turkoman raiders, since now the Oxus was frozen over no one could be quite sure that some robber bands had not crossed the ice. This added to the tension. What security the Russians had managed to impose on the region,

Burnaby concluded, was 'based on the sword and the gibbet rather than on Christianity and the Bible'.

More alarming than any appearance of Turkomans was a confrontation between the Kirghiz guide and some Khivans they encountered. The latter recognized the guide as the one who had also guided General Kaufman's Russian occupation force on its way to Khiva nearly three years earlier. They called him 'a dog of an unbeliever' and a fracas ensued which was only ended by Burnaby drawing his revolver and calling them to order.

When they reached Kalenderhana the guide's brother-in-law was not slow in presenting the merits of his horses. Much bargaining ensued, but finally it was agreed that Burnaby would buy horses and the guide would take them straight on to Khiva, avoiding Petro-Alexandrovsk altogether. The deal was celebrated in a manner least likely to appeal to Burnaby: they slaughtered and ate a horse which had been ill.

On the following day the guide explained that they would have to send a messenger ahead to seek the khan of Khiva's consent to their arrival. A mullah was produced who knew the correct and subservient language in which such a missive should be couched. He inquired Burnaby's rank and insisted that he described himself as a colonel rather than (more truthfully) as a captain: rank implied status and status was essential.

As they approached Khiva, they encountered various caravans of Khivans and Burnaby warmed to them greatly. He admired their red dressing-gowns, made partly of silk and thickly quilted, which reached down to their heels. Even more, he admired their tall black lambskin hats – 'taller even than a footguard's bearskin'. He liked the confident way they crossed frozen streams, although some of these were so solid they 'would have safely borne a battery of eighteen-pounders'. The visitors were offered hospitality and given the place of honour, seated on sumptuous carpets. The Khivans saluted them politely, and Burnaby was enchanted and hugely looking forward to entering their capital.

Before they finally entered the city of Khiva, Burnaby decided he should seek out a barber at Urgench and be shaved so that he would look smart and not 'with a beard of thirteen days' growth' when he met the khan. Only with the greatest difficulty did he persuade the barber that it was his chin, and not the top of his head, that he wanted shaved; and he had some anxious moments (remembering the governor of Kasala's warnings) as to whether the barber might not think that slitting the throat of an infidel would have been 'a good deed in the eyes of Allah'. The important thing was that his smart military moustache remained intact.

For the first time, Burnaby was hearing directly of the barbarity of the Russian invasion of two years before. Colonels and even generals had proved corrupt; women and children had been killed. This was just the sort of damaging information that the Russian authorities had wanted to prevent him hearing, and why they had not wanted him to stray beyond their currently occupied domains.

However, the conversation was not restricted to horror stories of the Russian invasion. Burnaby spent the next night with a sportsman who regaled him with tales of hawking and hunting. Burnaby in turn tried to explain English fox-hunting to his Khivan host, which evoked the question: 'Which do you like best, your horse or your wife?' There was no doubt that there was no surer way of building bridges than talking about field sports; those who forgot that they were – at least ostensibly – on shooting leave, put themselves at a disadvantage.

The next day started well: the messenger whom they had

sent ahead to the khan met them, accompanied by two Khivan nobles sent to accompany Burnaby into the capital. Richly painted minarets and domes of coloured tiles appeared above the trees; orchards and avenues of mulberry trees opened up; tall gallows warned of the dangers of misbehaviour; walls were studded with cannons, but appeared to be more decorative than defensive: this was a destination worth the journey. To make sure that Burnaby was suitably impressed with the size of the capital, the accompanying nobles took him on a circuitous route around it, beating off inquisitive locals with their whips. They delivered him to an elegant but not particularly comfortable apartment, which was a government guest house.

Partly because he felt he needed a bath after his travels, and partly because it was a sociable thing to do, Burnaby immediately visited the local Turkish baths. Here, he encountered a mullah who remembered Captain Abbott's visit 40 years before: 'such a nice gentleman', was the mullah's verdict on Abbott.

His next call was on the khan's treasurer, who was surprised that the Russians had not prevented him reaching Khiva; he said that if Burnaby had gone via Petro-Alexandrovsk he would certainly have been stopped. The talk quickly turned to the likelihood of the Russians invading India, where – the treasurer observed – 'you have not many white men'. Burnaby told him there were more than enough to see the Russians off. The treasurer made an appointment for Burnaby to be received by the khan the following day.

The question of how Burnaby was to be dressed for his audience gave some anxiety: Nazar brushed down his black shooting-jacket and a relatively clean white shirt was found, but he bemoaned Burnaby's lack of decorations: 'if only you had a few crosses to attach to your coat, it would look so well'.

Unadorned he might be, but at six-foot-four Burnaby's unusual height made him stand out as a remarkable figure in Central Asia.

He was royally conveyed to the khan's palace, his escort pointing out a deep hole where criminals had their throats cut from ear to ear. Burnaby, who was well aware of the fate of Stoddart and Conolly in Bokhara just 32 years before, was hardly likely to have relished the sight of such deep holes, particularly when on his way to see a ruler who would be likely – the Russians had told him – 'to gouge out your eyes and keep you in a hole in the ground'. The approaches to the palace were adorned with the predictable mixture of guards in silk robes bearing scimitars and 'good-looking boys of an effeminate appearance . . . dressed a little like the women, lounging about, and seeming to have nothing in particular to do'.

However, the khan's welcome could not have been friendlier and Burnaby took an instant liking to him. The khan was propped up on cushions sitting on a Persian rug and invited Burnaby to sit beside him. (His predecessor had made Abbott stand.) Burnaby suspected he was in his late twenties and had an unexpectedly 'merry twinkle in his eye'. The conversation which ensued was conducted through a variety of interpreters and was not dissimilar from some of the conversations that Abbott had with the earlier khan, including the same complaints that Britain had not responded to Khiva's requirement for protection against Russian ambitions (though now this was part of history as far as Khivan independence was concerned). At least Burnaby was in no danger of being suspected of being a Russian spy, as Abbott had been. Between the two visits, the Crimean War had occurred and, because of English support for the sultan of Turkey, the khan had hoped that the khanates and emirates of Central Asia might have enjoyed the same support, but this had not proved to be the case. Would England do anything to protect Kashgar? Burnaby had to plead that – unlike Abbott – he was not an agent of his government and could not answer for them about these things. But despite this slightly disappointing response on the part of Burnaby, the audience ended on a friendly note with the khan telling Burnaby he should feel free to look at everything he wanted to in Khiva.

Burnaby took advantage of this offer and toured the little walled city extensively. He concluded that the khan and his dominions were comprehensively under Russian domination, but some barbaric practices persisted – so the Russians could not really claim that spreading their civilizing influence was a justification for invasion.

Until now, Burnaby had still hoped to go on from Khiva to Bokhara and Merv, but this was not to be. On returning to his apartment he found two strangers who produced a letter sent to him 'by order of the commandant at Petro-Alexandrovsk'. Clearly, the Russians had tracked him down. So that there could be no excuses that the message was not understood it was written 'in Russian on one side of the paper, and in French on the other'. And the message was clear enough: a telegram for Burnaby had been received and he must go directly to Petro-Alexandrovsk to read it. Not only did the commandant's message not tell him the content of the telegram, it did not even tell him whom it was from.

What, Burnaby wondered, could all this be about? Had General Milutin had second thoughts? It must be something urgent, he reckoned, to justify sending the telegram by special messenger from Tashkent (the end of the telegraph line) to Petro-Alexandrovsk, not to mention the subsequent couriers who had been dispatched to Khiva. Burnaby pleaded that he needed some shopping time before leaving Khiva and set off to the jewellery market. Ominously the couriers shadowed him consistently for the rest of the day, clearly determined that he should not escape Russian surveillance again.

The khan granted him a farewell audience and expressed his sorrow that Burnaby had been called to Petro-Alexandrovsk; as a parting gift he presented him with a long silk robe or dressing-gown which Burnaby (perhaps rather ambitiously) described as being the equivalent of being awarded the Order of the Garter in England. He concluded that the khan 'was the least bigoted of all the Mohammedans' he had met.

On the ride back to Petro-Alexandrovsk, Burnaby encountered some Cossack cavalry units who, despite the winter weather which resulted in the horses 'having coats like bears', had clearly been stationed there to keep an eye on Khiva. When they reached it, Petro-Alexandrovsk turned out to be little more than a fort. He was greeted with the words 'we expected you before this' and given the much-travelled telegram.

It was an important message and a disappointing one. It came from no lesser person than Field Marshal His Royal Highness the Duke of Cambridge, the commander-in-chief of the British army. It was a peremptory command that he should immediately return to European Russia. The adventure was over: Bokhara and Merv were out of bounds. In fact, if he had gone via Petro-Alexandrovsk as originally directed he would never have reached Khiva as the message would have intercepted him. Burnaby reckoned that the Foreign Offices of St Petersburg and London had probably been responsible for prompting the order. It was a bitter disappointment – but at least he had Khiva under his belt and a great deal to tell on his return.

Considering that Burnaby had clearly hoodwinked the Russians and slipped through their net to reach Khiva, the commandant and officers at Petro-Alexandrovsk were remarkably friendly and entertained him as a brother officer. He was invited to a dance with the garrison wives and to a day's coursing with greyhounds and hawks. He described the sporting event at great length and obviously enjoyed being able to hold his own on a wild gallop across the steppes. He was also able to demonstrate, at an officers' mess party, one of his favourite tricks: he invited a fellow officer to tie him up with ropes and then 'the time I took in escaping from my bonds was not half so long as the officer had taken in tying me up'. Burnaby certainly sang for his supper as a mess guest.

Despite all the camaraderie, the commandant was implacable about his having to go back to St Petersburg by the shortest route through Kasala – the way he had come. He was also very frank about Russian ambitions: he said they could take Merv at any time, but that the Turkomans were a lot tougher and more tiresome than the Khivans. He also told Burnaby about a Russian soldier who had been captured by the Turkomans and – because he had falsely claimed to be an officer – had been made the subject of an unreasonably high ransom demand. (A similar story was to be told to Colonel Charles Stewart four years later – possibly referring to the same incident.) It was quite clear that the garrison at Petro-Alexandrovsk not only thought that Russia and Britain were on a collision course for a military confrontation in Central Asia, but that they were positively looking forward to it.

The commandant was taking no chances with Burnaby this time around. He dispatched him to Kasala with an escort of Cossacks. One positive aspect of this, from Burnaby's point of view, was that it gave him a chance to see something of the operational methods, discipline and morale of a Cossack long-distance patrol. It was a fairly brutal regime, with the slightest idleness being rewarded by a lashing with a knout (a Russian whip). However, Burnaby was already well-disposed towards the Cossacks – they had, after all, saved his hands and arms from being lost to frostbite – and he retained his respect for them, which was not surprising when they were averaging 40 miles a day across often snowbound steppe. Burnaby was doing for fun, and at his own expense, what was a testing professional experience for some of the toughest soldiers in the world.

When they reached Kasala, Burnaby caught up with a lot of gossip and intelligence. Some officers had been placed under arrest for duelling; some Cossacks – fed up with being so far from their homelands – had mutinied and their leaders been condemned to be shot by firing-squad; the Aral Sea had been charted and found free from dangerous rocks; 800 Cossacks had left Orenburg for Tashkent and more battalions were to follow; and the Tsarevitch (the heir to the Tsar) was shortly expected in Tashkent to earn his spurs in a campaign against Kashgar. No other British officer, agent or spy had gleaned nearly as much highly classified information so easily. Burnaby obviously inspired a degree of confidence in those who met him, as was dramatically demonstrated by one Russian officer entrusting to his charge (rather than to that of one of his compatriots) a large sum of cash for the purchase of horses. Burnaby was perceived as a gentleman who was to be trusted – even if he did occasionally give them the slip.

The rest of his journey home was relatively uneventful, but his homecoming was not. He was fêted as a great adventurer. Queen Victoria expressed an interest in meeting him, while the

Duke of Cambridge had a long session with him – being at pains to explain that it was not really his fault that Burnaby had been recalled prematurely – and was much impressed by the young officer's courage and judgement. The public lapped up the book he wrote, which had to be reprinted more than ten times within its first year of publication in 1876. The political and military establishment's suspicion of Russian intentions in Central Asia was fuelled by his reports and comments, and other travellers and writers like Valentine Baker found him a hard act with which to compete. The six-foot-four guards officer had shown the world that he was not only capable of wriggling free when bound with ropes while at a mess party, but capable of wriggling across borders when he was bound with regulations.

# Chapter 11

## John Biddulph: The Viceroy's Protégé

'It is the natural right of a Briton to get his throat cut when and where he likes.'

— Lord Salisbury (1830–1903), in a letter from the India Office to the viceroy in 1876

For the first half of the nineteenth century those concerned with the protection of the frontiers of India from Russian expansion had tended to concentrate their efforts on the north-west frontier, on Afghanistan and Persia. Consequently, most of the young officers who had been encouraged to combine their leave with more serious reconnaissance or espionage missions had headed in that direction: in particular Baluchistan and the Karakum Desert had been heavily reconnoitred. However, by the 1870s it was clear that not only did the Tsars have their eyes on Merv, Herat and the Khyber Pass, but also on the more northeastern fringes of India – on Kashmir, Kashgar and Eastern Turkestan. While Nikolai Przhevalsky had been officially commissioned by his Russian masters to explore and make contacts in these regions, British activities had mostly been conducted up to that time by less official travellers such as Robert Shaw (the tea merchant) and George Hayward (the Royal Geographical Society explorer).

All this was to change with appointment of Lord Northbrook as viceroy in 1872. Northbrook was a Liberal politician who had served as an under-secretary in both the India Office and the War Office and was to go on to be First Lord of the Admiralty under William Gladstone. Unusually for a Liberal, he was in favour of generally 'forward' policies in India, but not in favour of further expeditions against Afghanistan; in this he disagreed with Lord Salisbury. Northbrook was more concerned about the Pamirs and the possibility of a Russian invasion of India through passes to the northeast that were unknown to the British authorities in India. When he was looking for a young officer to scout out this region, he looked no further than his own staff.

Captain John Biddulph was on secondment from the Bengal cavalry and was aide-de-camp to the viceroy, who was to become a personal friend with whom he was to continue to correspond long after Northbrook had left India. Biddulph was a spirited officer who was genuinely fond of shooting and had a reputation for hunting wild yak in Tibet and ibex in the Himalayas. Northbrook had other intentions for his protégé: he wanted him to explore the passes of the Hindu Kush from the northern side, from where any Russian intrusion would come. Precedents for exploring the region were not promising: Hayward had been murdered in those parts in 1870 and buried nearby at Gilgit,[1] inspiring Sir Henry Newbolt to write in his popular Victorian poem 'He Fell Among Thieves' that as,

'He drank the breath of the morning cool and sweet;
His murderers round him stood.'

---

1. The author managed to find the grave, with the help of a local cobbler, when visiting Gilgit in 1996; it was overgrown but well-preserved.

Another such murder of a British subject on the fringes of the Indian empire would present problems: imperial dignity would require some retribution.

In these circumstances, the best way of infiltrating Biddulph into the region seemed to be as part of a reconnaissance party for a mission (the second of its sort) by Sir Thomas Forsyth to Kashmir in 1874. While this mission – authorized by Lord Northbrook – had political and commercial objectives, the important feature from Biddulph's point of view was the potential for investigating the unknown mountain passes on India's northern frontier. This was all the more relevant because it was considered in London to be premature to leave a permanent representative in Kashmir, outside the frontiers of the Raj. Lord Salisbury at the India Office had noted that any such envoy 'will probably get his throat cut, and . . . we shall have to go to war across the Himalayas in order to avenge him'.

Biddulph's mission produced some startling intelligence regarding these northern passes. Hitherto, knowledge of the Pamirs had been largely restricted to the findings of Lieutenant John Wood some 40 years earlier. Now Biddulph and the mission's surveyors reported that 'an excellent road' ran south from the Russian base at Osh to Sariqol which – with a little repairing over a 20-mile section – could carry artillery. From here there was perceived to be a gateway to India through Hunza, forming a new angle of threat. The sinister passes were those of Ishkoman and Baroghil and it was to these that Biddulph turned his attention. He concluded that 'there is nothing to prevent the rapid advance of an army fully equipped . . . no road making for the passage of field artillery [was] necessary . . . along the whole distance there is an unlimited quantity of the finest pasture in the world'. And it was not only for a restricted season that these passes were open: he estimated that they were negotiable for ten months of the year.

So great was the anxiety caused by these reports that in 1876 Biddulph was sent back to the region – now rapidly outstripping the northwest frontier as the main source of imperial concern – to examine the southern exits from the passes. Lord Northbrook, who again was responsible for sending him on this mission, realized that he himself would have left India before his protégé could report his findings, but he was confident that they would be taken seriously by his successor as viceroy – Lord Lytton. In this he was correct: Lytton – who was himself a Conservative appointment and therefore more naturally associated with a forward policy for the region – concluded that 'should the Russian power, resting along the northern frontier of Kashmir, overflow the mountain range . . . the moral effect of such a position would be as injurious to the tranquillity of our power as if Russia were at Merv'. (Indeed, in another six years Russia would be at Merv.)

Biddulph did not write the sort of narrative account of his travels which so many of his predecessors and successors penned. His official reports in the India Office archives are equally uninformative about the day-to-day hazards of the journey, and his published work – *The Tribes of the Hindoo Koosh* – is more anthropological and didactic than the works of Abbott, Wood and Burnes, which were designed for the general reader.

Despite this, some flavour of his adventures comes across in his accounts of travelling conditions in the Pamirs. He described leaving the protection of British territory to enter the refuge of 'the Hindustani Mussulman irreconcilables, whose avowed object is unceasing war against the Christian power of the British Empire'. He found them spending all their working hours practising military drill outside their forts, but derived some comfort from the fact that their cannons were made of leather 'which became useless after a few discharges'.

However, it was the physical conditions of the terrain to which he devoted most attention. In the Hindu Kush and the Pamirs he found that the valleys, even though they were up to 30 miles long and supported a population of anything up to 5,000 people, were guarded by 'an embouchure so narrow that it is difficult to find a pathway beside the torrent which issues between overhanging rocks'. The roads were of such a crude kind that the inhabitants become obliged to be 'intrepid cragsmen', and pass over precipitous terrain which would deter experienced mountaineers. As for crossing bridges, this required particular stamina since a bridge would normally be 'formed of nine plaits of twigs' suspended across the river where the stream flowed between precipitous rocks. Three plaits formed the foothold, about five inches wide, while the others created a handrail on either side. Crossing them involved a certain amount of courage: 'The whole bridge sways about with every gust, making it very unpleasant to cross in a high wind; and when the river, as often happens, requires a span of over three hundred feet, the steadiest nerves feel the trial.' He went on to explain that such bridges were often left for two or three years without repair 'and become very dangerous'.

Biddulph found the danger of bridges was nothing compared to that of some hill paths 'where precipitous rocks overhang the boiling torrent' and a rough log would be thrown across a chasm. He added that the sangfroid of the natives was only matched by that of the wild goats.

Biddulph contemplated trying to follow the upper reaches of the Indus river on part of his route back to the passes, but

he found that these stretches were 'subject to the same conditions as the smaller streams', and had the added risk that their
banks were inhabited by fanatical and warlike tribes which barred
the way to travellers. Further north, he found a 'colony of convict
horse-stealers'. Neither man nor nature was accommodating.

As a sportsman, Biddulph noted that in addition to the goats
there were packs of wild dogs, but the local
tribesmen – mostly Dards – were not keen
hunters and did nothing to keep the dogs under
control. Further up the mountains, Biddulph,
who had maintained his enthusiasm for
hunting, found ibex, Marco Polo sheep, red
bears, snow cock and even snow leopards.
As he approached Hunza, he found the
going harder than he had done on any of
his earlier shooting trips, and for half a mile
he followed one stream by 'holding on by
corners of rock, working along rocky shelves
three or four inches wide, and round projecting knobs and
corners where no
four-footed animal
less agile than a wild
goat could find a
path'. At times he
was down on the
riverbed, at other times
several hundred feet above
a gaping chasm.

Hunza itself was not
strictly part of his official

assignment, but when the mir (emir) of Hunza discovered he was nearby and sent an invitation, he could not resist visiting this hidden kingdom. However, he realized he was venturing through territory which had proved fatal for Hayward, and he decided that before he went further it would be prudent to insist that the mir sent his own son to Gilgit where he would effectively be held as a guarantee for the safe return of Biddulph. After much prevarication, the mir consented. Biddulph found Hunza hard to reach – on account of the natural hazards already described – but even harder to leave. The mir tried to get Biddulph to help extend his territorial sway, but Biddulph declined despite ominous references to the fate of Hayward. The mir then resorted to other pressures such as trying to separate him from his porters and putting further obstacles in the way of his departure. This political pressure was every bit as alarming as the physical pressures of the trek into Hunza. But he extricated himself.

Eventually, when Biddulph resumed his designated objective of exploring the passes he found – somewhat to his embarrassment – that his conclusions from the southern side were very different from his original observations from the north. He trekked again up to the Ishkoman, Darkot and Baroghil passes and this time, approaching from a different direction and with more time to form an independent judgement, he found these passages through the mountains less of an open door than he had earlier assessed: the Ishkoman Pass had a much more restricted open season than he had calculated; the Darkot was after all impassable for artillery; the Baroghil was 'closed at the south side by an easily defended gorge'. In fact, this second expedition largely reversed the findings of the earlier report of the Forsyth reconnaissance in which he had played a key role. There was no denying that from the south the passes looked less threatening than they did from the north, and although the conventional military wisdom would remain that passes were better defended at the point of entry than the point of exit, the strategic situation now looked less panic-inspiring than it had done.

One reason why Biddulph did not write up the results of his second expedition was that his earlier – alarmist – conclusions about the passes had been circulated too widely. News of the vulnerability of the Punjab to incursions from the north had even reached the Russians, and there was evidence that they were taking this into account in their forward planning regarding the region. The period between 1874 and 1878 (when the Congress of Berlin was to cause a temporary halt on expansionist plans) was one of intense speculation and nervousness. But even without his writing a popular account of his exploits, news of his second expedition reached the public; a publication called the *Pall Mall Budget* was one of those which revealed details that it would have been more prudent to leave under a pall of secrecy. The India Office in London had been upset by the earlier leaking of Biddulph's gloomy news about the passes in the Pamirs, and they were doubly bothered by the further press coverage. One official minuted that in the currently critical times:

it is necessary that researches in those countries [on the northern borders of India] should be conducted by secret Agents, and secrecy is incompatible with the publication of the adventures of our Agents, whose very names, before long, became by-words in the mouths of persons interested in watching their movements . . . it is scarcely necessary to remark that the premature publication of such information and comments, before we are ready for action, may prove of the utmost political embarrassment to us.

Biddulph might have been tempted in 1880, when he published *The Tribes of the Hindoo Koosh*, to have made it into a more personal and racy narrative like those of Burnes, Baker or Burnaby. His fame and fortune might have been advanced by this, but he would have incurred official censure – as had Charles MacGregor. It was therefore ironic that he should receive no official recognition for his exploratory services. However, he had other ambitions – or rather one particular ambition – in mind.

By now Biddulph's own thinking had moved on. He had become convinced that there ought to be a permanent British presence at Gilgit (on the Indian side of the Pamirs) and that he was the right person to provide that presence. No one at this juncture had more knowledge of the terrain or of the tribes and their chiefs. He also had the right connections in Simla to influence the appointment, but these connections had grown more tenuous since his patron – Lord Northbrook – had been recalled to London in 1876. However, Lord Lytton was open to persuasion that a British agent at Gilgit would be a useful spokesman, reporter and spymaster. Lytton had considerable difficulty in allaying the suspicions of the Maharaja of Kashmir about the appointment, but eventually persuaded him that a resident British agent would not interfere in Kashmiri affairs.

So Biddulph – now in his mid-thirties – was given the job and proceeded to Gilgit in 1877. His official task was to 'furnish reliable intelligence of the progress of events beyond the Kashmir frontier . . . and to cultivate friendly relations with the tribes beyond the border'. He was also to be a doorkeeper for the southern exits from the passes which led towards Hunza, Yasin and Chitral, and to be the one who should sound the alarm if any incursions appeared imminent. In fact, he was to be the guard dog at the gate of empire.

Biddulph had probably underestimated the difficulty and loneliness of the job he had so assiduously sought. Not only was the geography of Gilgit claustrophobic, as it was surrounded by formidable rock-faces, but the lack of any companionship and society was even more so. The few outward routes that existed were subject to landslides on to the paths and landslips off the paths. At one point he wrote to Lord Northbrook saying he had not seen a white face for ten months; this sociable cavalry officer was several weeks' journey from his nearest fellow countryman and even further from the nearest polo field.

To add to his troubles, the Maharaja of Kashmir did nothing to help: Biddulph was made to feel unwelcome and more like a hostage than an envoy. He recorded that 'my baggage was openly plundered by an official' and that 'false reports of an alarming nature were made to me . . . the governor would not be responsible for my safety'. When Biddulph visited Yasin and Chitral in 1878 all sorts of obstacles were put in his path and objections raised. He began to fear that there was a plot afoot to assassinate him and thus terminate his mission. However, none of this prevented him from organizing a network of spies whose tentacles stretched out from Gilgit across the Hindu Kush as far as Osh and even Samarkand in one direction, and down the Indus valley to the Pathan tribal lands in the other.

Meanwhile, officials in Simla and London thought that Biddulph did not do much to help himself: his attempts to 'cultivate the tribes' deteriorated into getting involved in intrigues between them. Just as earlier he had rushed into unsubstantiated reports about the usability of the passes, so now he rushed into judgements about the Maharaja of Kashmir, the governor of Gilgit and the tribal chiefs. At times he let his temper run away with him. This was an officer who – however brave an explorer – lacked the personal skills of Burnes or Abbott. In many respects he was a liability rather than an asset, one who might at any moment have his throat cut and necessitate a retaliatory expedition, in the same way as the murder of another envoy – Sir Louis Cavagnari in Kabul – was to do just one year later. However firm the grip of the Raj within the frontiers of India, there could be no denying that beyond these frontiers support was not readily forthcoming: communications were just too extended and precarious. (Even 15 year later, as G. J. Adler recalls in his *British India's Northern Frontier*, a caravan of 300 mules and muleteers could be wiped out by a storm in a single night.)

Biddulph ended up thoroughly disillusioned. It transpired that the Maharaja was in secret correspondence with the Russians. The surrounding tribes and their chiefs would never be reliable allies who could be counted on to guard the backdoor into India. Occupation and permanent garrisons were the only way to secure the region. But worse than any of this, from Biddulph's point of view, was the fact that Lord Lytton was refocusing his attention away from Gilgit and the Pamirs and towards the old stamping ground of Afghanistan and the Khyber. The Second Afghan War was about to begin and attention in high places had returned to the northwest frontier. Biddulph had proved a gallant if erratic surveyor and an unfortunate envoy.

However, if any doubt remains as to the real fears the open passes through the Hindu Kush and the Pamirs presented to the authorities in Simla and London in the last decades of the nineteenth century, and if any doubt remains as to the vital contribution of daring (even rash) young officers to solving the problem, then one need look no further than *The Half-Hearted*. Written by John Buchan in his last year at Oxford and published in 1900, this is a fictional account of the Russian threat in the Gilgit/Hunza region and of the efforts of one young man to regain his self-esteem by holding a previously unknown pass through the Hindu Kush until he had alerted 'an awakened empire'.

*The Half-Hearted* was written 15 years before Buchan made his name as a thriller writer with *The Thirty-Nine Steps*, and it is seldom read or even remembered now. However, it is not only a gripping yarn in the genre for which he was to become famous, but it tells in graphic detail a story of shooting leave in the remotest corner of the Pamirs, of reconnoitring near-invisible defiles though the mountains, of Russian and tribal intrigues just beyond the fringes of the empire, of courage by the young men on the spot and of disorganization and alarm by the authorities further back from the frontier.

Buchan spells out the dangers as perceived in London; one of his characters remarks, 'I've always been held up to ridicule as an alarmist about the Kashmir frontier . . . the way into the Punjaub [sic] is as clear as daylight for a swift force, and the way to the Punjaub is the way to India'. When asked why no one has explored the passes more thoroughly, he answers that the officers there 'only care about shooting, and there happens to be little [game] in those rocks'. An Islamic tribal leader points out that the English are no longer alert to the danger, and by constructing roads and a rail link towards the frontier have actually increased the risk of a sudden incursion. All that stood in the invader's way were 'isolated garrisons of Goorkhas and Pathans, with a few overworked English officers at their head'. This is a snapshot of how Biddulph's world was seen from an Oxford college or a London gentleman's club at this juncture – the penultimate phase of the imperial history of the Raj.

Another snapshot, this time of how a young Scottish upper-class adventurer views this scene as the natural backdrop for his exploits, is equally vividly brought to life by Buchan. 'Is the north the best shooting quarter? I am just as keen on some geographical work, and if I can join both I shall be glad,' says his hero, Lewis Haystoun. He goes on to add that while he can 'understand the difficulties of the Khyber, the Kashmir road looks promising' for a Russian invasion. And always present is the romance of the whole Central Asian backcloth: 'names rang in his head like tunes – Khiva, Bokhara, Samarcand, the goal of many boyish dreams born of clandestine suppers and the Arabian Nights'. Haystoun realizes too late that he has missed spotting a strategic defile in the mountains: 'the long nullah on which he had looked from the hill-tops had, then, an outlet and did not end, as he had guessed, in a dead wall of rock'. In the end he defends this undiscovered defile single-handed against the invading Cossacks and disaffected tribesmen: 'he brought his rifles forward to the stones . . . they were all dear-loved weapons, used in deer-stalking at home and on many a wilder beat'. Inevitably, he is overwhelmed and killed, but not before he has sounded the alarm and gained precious time for more solid defences to be activated behind him. He had 'walked steadfastly in the direction of his dreams' and had achieved the patriotic aim of his ambition – a noble death defending Queen Victoria's India.

Captain John Biddulph had done much of this in the real world, and had risked the same fate. However, his lengthy, informative book about the Hindu Kush and his carefully drafted reports to the viceroy do not altogether deliver the flavour of his quest. For that, the reader must turn to John Buchan's fictional work of nearly 20 years later.

# Chapter 12

## Nikolai Grodekoff: The Big Bold Russian Bear

'Approach thou like the rugged Russian bear.'
– William Shakespeare, in *Macbeth*

In the months before the Congress of Berlin in 1878, the prospect of a Russian invasion of British India seemed perhaps greater than at almost any earlier stage. Setbacks in the direction of Constantinople and the Ottoman empire had fostered a Russian desire for territorial progress elsewhere. General Mikhail Skobelev had marched to the Bokharan frontier with an army who cherished dreams of watering their horses on the banks of the Indus river. However, the treaty emerging from the Berlin conference called a halt to their march and a suspension of their dreams. The need for reconnaissance, remained, nevertheless, foremost in the minds of many of the Tsar's generals and staff officers.

One such officer was Colonel Nikolai Grodekoff. He already had a great deal of active service under his belt: he had marched to Khiva in 1873; he had been with General Skobelev in Kekand in 1875; he was well known as a courageous commander and an officer who was ambitious for himself and his country in Central Asia.

With an indefinite hold on military campaigning in the region, Grodekoff decided to put aside his already elevated rank of

195

colonel and behave as a younger and more junior officer might have done. He would take leave from the army and not accept any government funding for the journey he had in mind (although he did agree to accept a few handsome silver objects as presents to bestow along the way). He would undertake a one-man recce of the route which he hoped one day to take with a Russian army from Samarkand, through Herat and into India.

By a one-man expedition Grodekoff meant one officer; in fact, he took along with him an interpreter, a native servant and a groom – a very small party for such an enterprise. They had seven horses: the four they rode, two for the kit, and one in reserve. Nor did he take an array of weaponry: one cavalry rifle and one revolver, with a limited supply of ammunition for each, was their entire arsenal. With this modest team, Grodekoff intended to spend his leave crossing some 1,200 miles of wild, largely unknown country which was infested with unpredictable and predatory tribesmen. He set out on 9 October 1878.

Unlike most of the young British officers who had embarked on similar escapades, Grodekoff rejected the idea of disguise: 'I travelled in my uniform, concealing neither my nationality nor my rank,' he wrote. He possibly did not have much alternative to this plan, because – unlike Abbott and Pottinger for instance – he did not have a great knowledge of the local languages and he was not conversant with the finer points of Islamic practices. He was also convinced that the Afghans would welcome a Russian officer as a friendlier and more congenial face of Europe than the more familiar British officers of whom they were more suspicious.

The first stage of the journey was relatively uneventful. He rode from Samarkand to Bokhara (both places by now having been effectively brought within the purview of the Tsar's domains) and on to the Oxus river. It was here he entered Afghanistan, being met on the far bank of the river by a chamberlain of the emir and a cavalry escort. This boded well, but soon things started to go wrong.

When invited to enter a tent by the chamberlain, one of the sentries made a pass with his sword over Grodekoff's head in a distinctly menacing way. It transpired that the tent contained prisoners under arrest and was not one a visitor should have tried to enter. When Grodekoff remonstrated with the chamberlain, the latter reacted by striking the sentry, who had just been doing his job. Grodekoff may have been of slight and short stature himself but he was not used to people threatening him with arms and was unimpressed by the whole affair.

Worse was to follow. The chamberlain wanted him to camp in a swampy marsh rather than go on to the local centre of government at Mazar-i-Sharif. The chamberlain prevaricated: he would not be kept there long, a calf would be slaughtered for his evening meal, messages would be sent to the local governor, and so on. Grodekoff would have none of it: either he was allowed to press on, or he would recross the Oxus and leave Afghanistan – informing the emir of the chamberlain's discourtesy and insulting behaviour. The chamberlain gave in, but the friction was not over. When Grodekoff rode on ahead of the cavalry escort, they shouted at him and then pursued him: 'I replied to them that it was not my place to conform myself to their wishes, but their place to conform themselves to mine. Did they not know who I was? Did they think I meant to run away?'

By adopting this sort of arrogant manner, Grodekoff was pushing his luck. When they halted for the night, two sentries were placed on his lodging and he overheard one of them saying to the other, 'If I had my way, I would cut that infidel to pieces.'

Although the remark was made within hearing of the Afghan officers, neither of them remonstrated. No wonder Grodekoff locked his room, barricaded the door with boxes and kept his pistol to hand. The next morning his interpreter reported that he too had heard threats made on Grodekoff's life. One soldier had repeated the suggestion of murdering him and gone on to say, 'what matters what happens afterwards – you know what awaits us in future life if we kill an infidel' (the prospect of heavenly rewards seemed as vivid then as to a suicide bomber over a century later). Another soldier had cautioned that the Russians would exact vengeance for any such murder, to which the first had replied that they could always deny having seen him and pretend he had never crossed the Oxus. However, it was concluded – at least for the time being – that it might be wiser not to kill him as the Russians would not give up on finding out what had happened to one of their colonels and the Bokharans would give evidence that they had 'delivered him whole' across the Oxus.

The dislike of the ordinary Afghan for this truculent infidel kept being refuelled by incidents both large and small. When Grodekoff was seen cleaning his teeth in a courtyard,

an inquisitive – or provocative – Afghan asked the interpreter to tell him what the toothbrush was made of. On hearing it was pig's bristles, the Afghans 'fell back in horror and commenced spitting violently, to express their disgust at using the hair of such an unclean animal'. Grodekoff prudently decided to brush his teeth in private in future.

The natives of this part of the country, despite the rule of the Afghans, were predominantly Uzbeks who were far from happy about the Afghan domination. Grodekoff estimated that this was the case throughout most of Afghan Turkestan. He noted that the Afghans treated the Uzbeks as inferiors to be bullied and whipped when they got out of line. The Uzbeks, he commented, looked to Russia to release them from this tyranny – an enticing conviction for a militant tsarist officer who managed to persuade himself that 'the Uzbeks do not manifest any fear towards us, but desire our presence'. He recorded that, when the Afghans were not looking, Uzbeks would approach him and ask wistfully when the Russians were coming, adding 'would God that the time could be hastened for our deliverance'. This was heady stuff and would form an important plank in his final report to St Petersburg.

The next incident appeared a comical one at the time, but was to have sinister repercussions. The Afghan governor of Mazar-i-Sharif asked Grodekoff if he could borrow his uniform to have it copied, as he thought it was very handsome and would look becoming on himself. The Russian agreed and got his uniform back the next day after a tailor had measured and studied it. Grodekoff wryly noted that 'when the English entered Kabul [the following year – in July 1879] they found among other things a Russian uniform, which occasioned immense sensation and alarm throughout India and England'. It is quite as likely as not that this uniform was no other than the copy the governor had made for himself.

Despite these friendly exchanges with the governor, Grodekoff felt he was being treated more as a prisoner than a guest at Mazar-i-Sharif. Guards prevented him from roaming round the streets at night (perhaps because the Afghans were aware of his subversive influence on the Uzbek population) and they refused to convey letters from him back to General Kaufman in Russia. They even tried to seduce his interpreter away from him with offers of a better job. At last, just when he was on the point of escaping in desperation back to Bokhara, a message arrived from the emir in Kabul to say that he ought to be treated as a distinguished guest and assisted in going on his way. The cavalry escort were converted overnight from being custodians to being a guard of honour.

As he progressed onwards with his 40-troop escort on the 18-day ride towards Herat, Grodekoff deliberately set himself up as a champion of the downtrodden Uzbeks. He berated his Afghan escort for their bullying practices. At the settlement of Saripool the locals gave him an ovation and at Maimene, which had once been the flourishing capital of an independent Uzbek state with a population of 25,000, he found the town in ruins and noted that the population had been reduced to less than 3,000 – mostly as a result of Afghan massacres and forced expulsions. The last leg of the journey from Maimene to Herat was through country where the Afghan control was less effective and where Turkoman gangs waylaid travellers. Grodekoff's cavalry escort was increased from 40 to 300. Not surprisingly, he found that no non-Russian European had passed this way for some 15 years. Although Grodekoff did not explicitly say so in his subsequent report, it emerges fairly clearly from this that the Russians were using the unruly nature of the tribes and the unsafe state of the tracks as an excuse for taking an ever tighter control of the whole area leading to Herat, 'the key to India'.

Grodekoff's exploits and views were revealed to British readers very shortly after the events described. He had made his journey in 1878 and by 1880 Charles Marvin had published a book in London about the adventure and its implications. Marvin was a figure of some interest himself, being at one time the St Petersburg correspondent of the *Globe* (where he perfected his Russian and became acquainted with many of the Russian participants in the Great Game). He was later employed in the British Foreign Office, where he was accused but not convicted of leaking secret information about Anglo-Russian relations. Highly critical of British lethargy about reacting to the Russian advances in Central Asia, he pointed out in his book *Reconnoitring Central Asia* (1886) that the Russians regularly made a point of not allowing wild tribes to disturb their southern frontiers; they often moved in, ostensibly to restore law and order, but in practice to occupy the disturbed territory. The process repeated itself as Russia's frontiers advanced into Central Asia. It was this process that Grodekoff was encouraging with his report of his ride through the lawless Turkoman hinterland of Herat. In Marvin's words, 'it must lead in due course to the advance of the avenging Cossacks to the principal bulwark of India'.

When he eventually reached Herat, Grodekoff was welcomed by the governor-general; he was given luxurious accommodation and 15 servants were allocated to look after him. He felt that the profligacy with which manpower was deployed (he saw four sentries doing a job fit for one) was a measure of the cheapness with which life was regarded there.

Well aware of the fact that for the previous five years no

European had had a chance to make a thorough survey of Herat (it was more than half a century since the British Elliot D'Arcy Todd had been stationed there), Grodekoff made full and careful notes about the defences of the town and concluded 'in its present condition Herat is not in a position to defend itself against a European army'. However, he acknowledged that the town possessed immense strategic importance.

This was the end of Grodekoff's self-imposed task for his leave. Now he struck out for home, across the Khorassan mountains to the Caspian coast at Astrabad which he reached in early December. From there he proceeded overland through Russia to St Petersburg, where he was received and congratulated by Tsar Alexander II.

Grodekoff's ride was, in its length and strategic importance, as considerable and significant as most of those adventures recorded earlier in this book. In terms of danger it was less dramatic, but not without risks. By choosing to go overtly as a Russian officer, an obvious European and an avowed Christian, and not in disguise as a Muslim civilian, he to some extent acted as a lightning conductor inviting a strike by militant Islamists. The threats he heard uttered against him when he first crossed the Oxus were real enough. However, he was at all times under at least the ostensible protection of the Afghan governors and administrators who respected – and possibly feared – Russia, even if they harboured no friendly feelings towards her. He never ran the risk of exposure as a spy in the way Pottinger had done, and when he ventured into the more lawless parts of Turkestan he had an escort of much greater strength and reliability than Abbott had had. His journey can fairly be compared to Captain Fred Burnaby's ride through Russian-controlled parts of Central Asia to Khiva two years earlier.

Grodekoff was a colonel behaving like a subaltern on leave, but his status kept breaking through: he was no anonymous agent, but a Russian bear who was recognized for what he was.

# Chapter 13

## Charles Stewart: The Spy Turned Spymaster

*'Other nations use "force"; we Britons alone use "Might".'*
— Evelyn Waugh (1903–66), in *Scoop*

Charles Stewart had the East in his blood. He had been born in 1836 in Ceylon (Sri Lanka) where there was a military tradition in the family. At nine years old he was sent home to England, while his parents remained in Ceylon, and was put in the care of his grandmother – Lady Katharine Stewart. He was sent to boarding school at Marlborough College and learnt the art of surveying on school trips. By the age of 18 he was commissioned as an ensign in the Inniskilling Dragoons and three years later transferred to the Punjab Infantry. By the time he was in his early thirties he had seen active service with the Sikh Irregular Cavalry (later the Bengal Lancers) in the Indian Mutiny and later on the northwest frontier. He distinguished himself in both campaigns and was mentioned in dispatches by his commanding generals as 'earning the confidence of all ranks by the coolness and skill he invariably displayed'. However, by 1880 he was preparing to put regimental soldiering behind him and turn his attention and ambition to more political and sensitive work.

In January 1880, Stewart, who was home on furlough, happened to be staying with Sir Henry Acland, a Fellow of All

Souls College, Oxford, and physician to the Prince of Wales. Even in the tranquil halls of academia, it was a time of general anxiety about what the Russians were plotting in Turkestan. General Skobelev (known as 'old bloody eyes' to the Turkomans) was believed to be poised with a large Russian force at Krasnovodsk on the eastern shores of the Caspian. The Russian's immediate target appeared to be the independent Turkoman stronghold of Geok Tepe, 300 miles east of him in the Karakum Desert, but it was feared that once there he would press on to Merv – 'the Queen of the World' – and so increase the perceived threat to India, where Stewart had spent his earlier military life. While Stewart was staying at Oxford, among the dreaming spires and over the port in the senior common room, 'the project of living in disguise on the Turkoman frontier was broached'. A listening post was necessary if anyone in Britain was to know what the Russians were up to before the British embassy in St Petersburg read about a *fait accompli* in the local press.

If anyone was going to undertake this task, it was Stewart. He had already travelled across Persia in 1866 and had not only mastered the language to an impressive degree, but 'having worked in Persia when on leave from his regiment, had in some measure prepared himself as regards knowledge of the country'.

There was, however, one serious obstacle. While the government of India and the Indian army were alert to the Russian threat and prepared to take whatever measures were necessary to thwart or at least to monitor it, the Foreign Office in London was less concerned about the khanates and emirates of Central Asia than about overall relations with St Petersburg. Whitehall did not want a repeat of the Crimean War and royal circles in London were anxious to preserve good relations with Tsar Alexander II (shortly, as it happened, to be assassinated by a nihilist throwing a bomb beneath his carriage). So while it was to be no problem for Stewart to travel across Turkey and Persia quite openly, and indeed enjoy the hospitality of British legations and consulates, when he approached the troubled region bordering the disputed khanates his own government was likely to become nervous about the possibly provocative presence of an English officer. As Stewart was later to point out in his own words:

> I had only worn disguise because I could travel about more con-
> veniently as an Armenian than as an Englishman. Also I felt
> certain that if Sir Ronald Thomson, the English minister at Tehran,
> had heard of my wandering about the Persian border near the
> Turkoman country, he would have ordered me back, and even if
> he did not, the Russian minister at Tehran would have asked him
> to do it, and I had no doubt he would have acquiesced.

It was just two months after the conversation in All Souls College that this veteran of the Indian Mutiny set out on his prolonged 'shooting leave' to the Turkoman border. He went by the leisurely rhythm of nineteenth-century travel: by train to Paris, overland via Turin and Venice to Trieste, by steamer via Corfu and Syria to Constantinople, then by another steamer to Trebizond on the southern Black Sea coast where his Asian adventure started. From now on everything he saw of military or strategic interest, or of relevance to the approaches to India, was to be assiduously noted down. For instance, before he even starts he wryly comments that the church of St Sophia outside Trebizond was 'full of gunpowder, and was guarded by soldiers so as to prevent anyone entering for fear of an explosion – which must rather interfere with its use as a place of worship'.

Stewart travelled light. He had a pair of small saddle-bags and a valise strapped behind: 'my whole kit was thus in a very convenient form and as I was to be away at least a year, I think I managed with very little'. He did, however, always find room for a Bible in his luggage, which prompted one of his hosts in Persia to remark: 'You English are extraordinary, you always carry a Bible in your pocket.'

Going over one of the snowbound passes on the way to Erzroum in eastern Turkey he found it 'rather unpleasant riding . . . with one foot hanging over a precipice, but we soon got accustomed to it'. Although he carried a sporting gun with him, he complained that he saw very little game after leaving Trebizond. The local pashas and others entertained this travelling Englishman, which was just as well as he found the local caravanserais 'so very extra dirty that I could not stand them . . . and cows and buffaloes in one's bedroom I cannot bear, as they are very restless, and in their company there is a most horrid smell'.

The district around Erzroum had been much fought over. Stewart recorded that while both Turkish and Russian armies had devoured 'every grain of corn that was not concealed', the Russians had paid and the Turks had not. Even where the Turks – often Kurdish irregulars – had given receipts to Armenian Christians, these were never validated. Bands of such Kurdish marauders were still a hazard while Stewart rode through and he was glad to be provided with an armed escort for sections of his route. When he approached the Persian frontier everyone was 'in a desperate state of alarm about robbers'. The four footmen, supplied by a local chief to escort him, refused to go further. One Kurdish traveller they encountered told Stewart it was impossible to cross the frontier without a strong escort 'as twenty mounted robbers were plundering everybody'; but the local pasha provided three mounted police and six infantry soldiers so 'I felt pretty safe that no robbers would attack me'. This turned out to be the case as they had no sooner crossed the frontier than a bunch of Kurdish ruffians 'pretending to be grazing some sheep', clearly abandoned their intention of attacking them as soon as they saw the soldiers.

It did not get any better inside Persia: as Stewart approached Tabriz he was again warned that he should never travel without an armed escort, which was just as well as they immediately encountered 'five men sitting with their rifles ready . . . who I believe really were robbers'. He was not imagining the danger: at the top of one of the next passes that he crossed he 'found a party of travellers in great distress, having just been beaten and robbed of almost all they possessed'. The robbers had even managed to make off with two loaded guns. Stewart felt that this showed a certain lack of determination on the part of the travellers and he told them roundly: 'It is hardly worth while carrying guns to present to the robbers, if that is the only use you can make of them.' A British officer would have made a rather different use of his loaded gun. The fate of any robbers apprehended was not pleasant: Stewart relates that among the 'violent measures which had to be resorted to in order to render the roads safe' was the practice of burying the robbers in holes in the ground; when death occurred 'the body was left with its head exposed as a warning to his comrades'.

At Khvoy, Stewart called on the charming Persian prince-governor and then set about discreetly surveying the fort where the governor lived and which was the most strategically important feature of the Turko-Persian frontier. He found that although it was 'partially constructed according to modern ideas, which would render it very difficult for anyone to take without modern artillery', the fort's own defences were old-fashioned brass guns and there appeared to be no horses or other means of moving them. The sentries had allowed their rifles to get 'fearfully dirty and neglected'.

Stewart needed to change his horse from time to time as each mount in turn became exhausted. At one post-station where he had hoped to do this, he found that a Tartar carrying the Russian post for the Russian consulate at Tabriz and another Tartar carrying the Persian post were given priority, and no fresh mount was available for him. Stewart had inadvertently been the victim of a tradition which dated back to the time of Tamerlane in the fifteenth century, when the conqueror's messengers enjoyed the right to requisition horses at any time to keep the royal mail moving. Later Stewart changed to travelling in a small horse-drawn wagon 'shaped like a canoe' and driven by a Russian Tartar. He commented on the disinclination of the Russians (which he observed during his much later sojourn in Odessa) ever to ride – unless of course they were Tartars or Cossacks. A solitary horseman in Russia – particularly in the Ukraine – would be greeted by cries of 'Tartar boy! Tartar boy!'. The former Sikh cavalry officer was shocked by this lack of equestrian enthusiasm.

Stewart's military interests extended beyond the observation of forts and guns. As he travelled through Persia he became aware that the Austrians were providing officers to train the Shah's army, and much regretted that the British government in India had a few years previously declined to help in this way: 'the pay of twelve English officers would not have come to much, and the influence that England would have gained in Persia would have been considerable'. He knew that the Russians had previously offered their own officers, and thought they might well do so again – a bad omen for Britain.

Stewart's route took him from Tabriz on to Tehran. For large parts of the way, the track was 'by apology called a carriage road'. His wagon took a terrible jolting, and he had to set his teeth to stop him from biting his tongue; but what he really minded was that 'my eye-glass, which was hanging by a cord round my neck, was broken by the shaking'. A cavalry officer without his monocle felt badly disadvantaged.

At Tehran Stewart showed up at the British legation which was at its summer residence at Gulahek, where he was entertained in 'a magnificent drawing-room and dining-room tent pitched by a group of fir trees'. Sir Ronald Thomson, the minister, was 'a most hospitable and pleasant host' and Stewart spent several weeks in Tehran. However, he was careful not to give away his intention of spying out the goings-on on the Turkoman frontier, as he knew that this would be considered unduly provocative by Sir Ronald.[1]

From Tehran, Stewart went on through the holy city of Kum (Qum) across the desert to Isfahan. From here on he was on the more secret part of his mission and covering his tracks;

---

1. Such attitudes do not change much over the centuries. When the author made an overland trip – with the encouragement of the Foreign Office and the British embassy in Moscow – through the (Soviet) Caucasus and into Iran at Jolfa in 1959, he went on to stay at the British embassy in Tehran. There, although the ambassador and his staff were hospitable, he encountered a marked lack of enthusiasm for a British diplomat travelling on a quest for hard information around the Soviet-Iranian frontier, in case this should upset the susceptibilities of the Shah's regime. This lack of appreciation seemed all the harsher at the time since he had been forced to spend an uncomfortable few hours on a bridge over the border river between the Soviet Union and Iran – having been locked out of the former and not yet admitted to the latter.

he chose a devious route because he 'did not wish the people [of Isfahan] to know where he was going'. In a remote desert location, he changed his European dress to an Armenian or Persian one: 'I put on a knitted silk skull-cap, and over it a black lambskin hat. I also donned a long tight-fitting coat of blue-glazed chintz, and over that a loose Persian plum-coloured cloth overcoat. I had white shoes, and ordinary Persian trousers.' (There is an illustration in his book *Through Persia in Disguise* of him in this attire, looking convincingly like a well-off and corpulent Armenian trader.) He was afraid that if his pith helmet were discovered it would cause suspicion, so he threw it down a disused well, but then found that he much missed the protection from the sun it had provided. All the other garments of his Persian garb he found much more comfortable than his European attire and – more importantly – it did not attract 'so much observation and enquiry in out-of-the-way places'.

He took considerable trouble to cover his tracks in other ways, too. The small town of Nain was on his direct route, but he decided to give it a wide berth because there was a telegraph office there and he knew that 'a weekly dispatch is sent from all telegraph stations to the Ministry of Telegraphs for the information of the Shah, describing any remarkable person who may have passed through during the week'. Stewart did not want to risk an interview with the clerk as he had not yet got properly accustomed to his disguise and lacked the confidence to carry it off.

Although he could speak Persian, he realized that he would nevertheless be detected as an outsider, so he described himself as a Calcutta Armenian trader: 'if I wanted to say anything to my companion [who was in on the subterfuge] which I did not wish to be understood, I spoke in Hindustani, which the hearer would assume was Armenian'.[2]

Stewart was well and truly launched on a secret intelligence mission, but that did not mean he was not also conscious of being on shooting leave: he stopped to purchase a fine pair of ibex horns, so that he would have trophies to show on his return – even if he had not shot the ibex himself.

As he got nearer to the frontier region, so the landscape became more bizarre. The salt desert was covered with a glazed coating of clay through which the horses' hooves sunk. Disconcertingly, damp patches appeared as if moisture had oozed out from beneath. Crossing one of these stretches by moonlight 'a strange weird feeling comes over one, as if the ground was the wrinkled skin of some loathsome giant reptile like the fabled dragons of old, and the shiny moisture was its noisome sweat'. Stewart was a traveller with a vivid imagination as well as a practical military approach.

Whereas previously he had been understandably concerned about Kurdish raiders, now it was the Baluchis who were the threat. The border region was 'looked upon by ordinary Persians as a foreign country' and Stewart's guide was 'in a violent state of alarm' at the prospect of a Baluchi attack. After crossing a sandy desert where 'anyone getting lost would perish in a few hours', they came across an old tower and a ruined fort. On the face of it, this seemed a good place to halt and protect

---

2. When the author was travelling as a Russian-speaking British diplomat in the Caucasus and Central Asia in the late 1950s, his command of the language was never good enough to be mistaken for a Russian, but it was generally assumed he was East German. When he declared he was British he was often greeted with disbelief as there had been virtually no British visitors there since the Russian revolution – in fact, far fewer than in the Great Game period of the nineteenth century.

themselves, but it was said to be a favourite haunt of Baluchi raiders, so they went on and hid in a ravine. Once again, the threat was not imaginary: they 'met two men and their wives who had been carried off by Baluchi marauders and stripped of everything they possessed'. One of their party who had offended the Baluchis had been hacked to pieces with swords. The raiders had been 37 in number and mounted on quick-riding camels that could go three or four days without water. Unpleasant as it was, the Baluchis were not feared as much as the Turkomans since they only plundered travellers rather than carrying them off for ransom or enslavement.

When one of Stewart's servants was 'beaten in a most unprovoked manner' at a local caravanserai, and 'the people believing me to be an Armenian merchant, rushed up to my quarters evidently intending to do the same to me', Stewart produced his revolver and they rapidly retreated, apologizing and offering a

sheep in recompense. The disadvantage of being in disguise was that an Armenian was not treated with the awe and respect that an Englishman would be – at least until the Armenian produced his revolver.

In such troubled lands, it seemed safer to join a larger party. Stewart joined up with 'a very civil camel man' who was on his way with a caravan of sugar, and going in the same direction. They set out after dark and did not tell the local villagers which way they were going in case the latter were in league with the robber bands. The camel bells were also taken off and strict silence imposed. The camel man refused to let any pilgrims join them because 'they were such helpless people if attacked'. When they reached the next village everyone went around fully armed which, Stewart observed, was unusual in Persia except on the Turkoman frontier. Part of the trouble was that the local khan had pocketed for his own purposes the allowance the Shah had paid to him for recruiting a home guard: 'he was a woman and no man (they said) and allowed his subjects to be plundered'. The best that could be done was for sentries to be posted as look-outs on top of the village tower.

On the next leg of the journey, Stewart had his first hard intelligence about Russian troop movements. He had met a Russian Muslim who had been sent by the Russian consular agent in Meshed to purchase grain for the Russian army under General Skobelev, which was bogged down and hungry as it settled into its long siege at Geok Tepe. Stewart was to make it his business to learn more about how this siege was going.

It was also at this juncture that he almost had his disguise exposed. He was approached by two Afghan merchants, one of whom denounced him as being an Englishman: 'I have known the English too well while trading in the Punjab to be taken in,'

he said. He then asked Stewart for a letter of introduction to
'St John Sahib' (Sir Oliver St John) in Kandahar. The obvious
reaction would have been to deny any knowledge of St John,
but Stewart was too bright for that. Instead, he confessed to
knowing who St John was and offered to give his Afghan acquaintance a letter to him but protested that 'I don't think my letter
will do you much good . . . I will say that so-and-so, an Afghan
merchant of whom I know nothing, asked me for a letter . . .
and that I, the merchant Kwajah Ibrahim, whom St John Sahib
knew at Shiraz many years ago, gave him the letter.' This was
not at all the reaction the Afghan had expected; he conferred
with his friend, and they revised their views, 'finally agreeing I
was not an Englishman'. It had been a close call.

Just as Stewart had avoided the telegraph office at Nain for
fear of his whereabouts being reported to the Shah, so now he
avoided entering the town of Meshed 'because there were several
people I did not wish to meet'. One of these was the British
consular agent, whom he feared might report his activities to
the British minister at Tehran who would have immediately
ordered him back. 'In fact,' he wrote, 'I was in disguise more to
hide myself from British and Russian Ministers than from anybody
else.'

When Stewart called on the Persian governor at Mohammadabad, he also told him he was Kwajah Ibrahim of Calcutta
and that he had come to buy horses for the Bombay market.
The governor questioned him closely about conditions in Calcutta
and whether the British were oppressive masters. Stewart does
not record his answer: perhaps he felt that his cover required
him to say that they were.

Much to Stewart's astonishment he now learnt that there was
'another Englishman' at Mohammadabad – a Mr Edmund

O'Donovan (more accurately an Irishman than an Englishman) who was a correspondent of the *Daily News*. Stewart decided he would have more to learn than to lose by meeting O'Donovan and duly called on him a few days later. However, he took the precaution of presenting himself as Kwajah Ibrahim. By then he must have adopted his disguise very convincingly, because O'Donovan accepted him without question as a Calcutta Armenian and congratulated him on his excellent English. 'Calcutta Armenians receive a very fair education,' was the glib reply. (Possibly not since Captain Christie and Lieutenant Pottinger had failed to recognize each other in Isfahan in 1810 had an Englishman concealed his nationality from a compatriot so successfully.)

Stewart now made a practice of meeting O'Donovan regularly to exchange news and bazaar gossip about Russian movements and activities around Geok Tepe during the siege. He had other sources of intelligence, too: the locally engaged British agent at Meshed (whom Stewart had so assiduously avoided) managed to send a weekly runner to General Skobelev's camp, and Stewart managed to debrief him over a leisurely hookah smoke on his way through – probably gaining more hard information than the local agent at Meshed. He also had sources in the governor's circle and to exploit the use of these he had to lend credence to his role as a horse-dealer by actually buying occasional horses from the governor; he was somewhat overcharged, but reckoned it was worth the money to avert suspicion and keep his channels open.

Quite apart from the additional hazards of being a foreigner in disguise and collecting illicit intelligence, just the process of living in such close proximity to the Turkoman tribesmen had its own hazards. The whole countryside was covered in small towers which were built as refuges for the inhabitants when they came under attack by Turkomans. The towers had tiny holes into which refugees could crawl for shelter; 'when a Turkoman comes in pursuit and attempts to wriggle himself through the hole, he generally receives a sword-cut or bullet wound in his skull'. Piles of stones would be kept in the towers to rain down on assailants. But while Persian villages were always at risk, the Turkomans seldom attacked Afghan settlements: like most sensible people, the Turkomans had a healthy respect for Afghan fighting qualities.

It was during his time at Mohammadabad that Stewart's dislike of the Persians was consolidated. He visited a prison where various Turkoman raiders were being held; one of them was dying of his wounds and his jailors decided to slit his throat and scalp him so that they could send the scalp to the Shah as phoney evidence of their having killed him in battle, and thus be granted a monetary award for their valour. They made another prisoner do the horrid deed. When Stewart 'felt so disgusted that he called on the governor and remonstrated' (albeit still in his Armenian persona) the governor just laughed in his face: this was 'the most ordinary thing'.

Although details in the India Office records and elsewhere are scant about the specifics of the intelligence Stewart collected, one advantage of his stay in Mohammadabad on the frontier was that he got early news of the fall of Geok Tepe to General Skobelev's Russian army on 24 January 1881. O'Donovan – ever the eager correspondent – had actually witnessed the final assault, and the subsequent massacre of the fleeing Tekke, through his binoculars from a nearby mountain range. He was able to give Stewart a graphic account.

No doubt partly in gratitude for this, Stewart decided he

ought to reveal his true identity to O'Donovan, particularly as he intended to shed his disguise when he reached Meshed on his return journey – having accomplished his clandestine mission – and he did not want O'Donovan to hear about his subterfuge from others. It was a measure of Stewart's success in passing himself off as an Armenian that O'Donovan did not believe him when told that he was an Englishman, and was only persuaded of the truth when shown Stewart's British passport.

On reaching Meshed, Stewart again dressed in the European clothes he had concealed in his saddle-bags (no doubt still lamenting the loss of his pith helmet) and presented himself to the British consular agent whose runners he had been interrogating at Mohammadabad. He had survived from September 1880 until February 1881 without anyone rumbling his disguise, but he subsequently learnt from the governor-general of Khorassan that he had escaped by a narrower squeak than he had realized. When he had approached Meshed some months earlier, one of the governor-general's staff had reported seeing an Armenian engaged in surveying and had reckoned he must be a European 'but could hear nothing further of him'. Stewart recalled that on one occasion a man had accosted him when he was using his prismatic compass and asked him the time, apparently mistaking his compass for a watch. Stewart had told him it was twelve o'clock and had thought that he had got away with it. Be that as it may, Stewart was undoubtedly a master of deception and an agent who would have much skill and wisdom to impart to others.

In Meshed Stewart also met up with a Captain Gill of the Royal Engineers – the same officer who, as a lieutenant six years earlier, had accompanied Valentine Baker in this part of the world. He had developed a penchant for adventurous travel which was to remain with him until he was eventually murdered by the Bedouin. As soon as Sir Ronald Thomson in Tehran heard that Stewart and Gill were on the loose in Meshed, he ordered them back to Tehran – exactly as Stewart had earlier feared he would do.

Travelling back across Persia, Stewart heard a sad tale from a carpet merchant. A Russian private soldier had been captured by the Turkomans and was foolish enough to claim that he was an officer and a major. He was therefore being held for a much higher ransom than anyone was going to pay for him, and tortured 'by having red-hot coals placed on his naked stomach to induce him to send piteous appeals to the Russians'. Stewart sent the man some money and recorded in his book that he thoroughly sympathized with the efforts of the Russians to put down the appalling trade in hostages and slaves that existed in so many parts of Central Asia. On occasions when not in disguise on his travels in Persia and elsewhere, people mistook Stewart for a Russian and would come out 'blessing me for rescuing them from Turkoman raids'. However much he might spy on them, Stewart – like many participants in the Great Game – preserved an active respect and sympathy for his Russian opponents.

Stewart got back to London in April 1881 and read a discreet paper to the Royal Geographical Society about his travels. He was also debriefed in other less public forums. He was recognized as too useful an agent to be kept idle for long. By August the same year he was back in Persia 'on special duty'. For the next few years he was to undertake a series of such special assignments, very few records of which are available in the India Office archives or elsewhere. Among the places he reached was Herat in Afghanistan, where he was startled to find Afghan troops wearing Mackenzie tartan kilts which had been abandoned by the Seaforth Highlanders two or three years previously in the Second Afghan War of 1878–80: 'the effect of the kilt was, however, decidedly spoilt by the men wearing white trousers' beneath them.

Stewart shared – and indeed contributed to – the accepted belief among the British in India that 'anyone holding Herat would have a most commanding influence in the affairs of Afghanistan and Persia'; it was one of the few places in Central Asia – he concluded – where a large army could find provisions to sustain itself. As a political officer by this stage, he was heavily involved in making arrangements for the defence of Herat.

Later appointments were to include the role of British consul at Resht, Meshed and Tabriz. All these were listening posts for which his previous travels and command of the language had well qualified him. However, it was as consul in Odessa, on the Black Sea coast of Russia, that he was to achieve a long-standing reputation as an expert on how to probe Russian secrets and how to travel convincingly in disguise. Other young officers – notably Lieutenant Percy Sykes of the Queen's Bays – were to be sent to him for briefing before their 'shooting leave' in Samarkand or Persia.

If he had stayed in the army, Stewart might well have become a general like so many of the Great Game's most active participants, or if he had transferred to the Diplomatic Service he might have achieved a knighthood, as did the minister in Tehran. He may not have received these honours, but as a special agent and as a consul with a major intelligence role to play, he did not go unrecognized. He was appointed a Companion of the Order of the Bath, a Companion of the Order of St Michael and St George and a Commander of the Order of the Indian Empire.

The officer known for his travels on shooting leave had become an establishment figure, a guru in the intelligence world, and a spymaster par excellence.

# Chapter 14

## Alikhanoff, Naziroff and Lessar:
## The Russian Bear Cubs

'The infant child is not aware
It has been eaten by the bear.'
– A.E. Housman (1859–1936),
in 'Infant Innocence'

If Colonel Nikolai Grodekoff had been a senior officer taking on a task generally associated with younger officers, it did not imply that there was any shortage of younger talent in the officers' messes of the smarter Russian regiments stationed in the Caucasus and Central Asia. However, just as some of the British subalterns who went on shooting leave were from the wilder and more trouble-prone elements in the army, so some of the more daring Russian blades had track records which did not bear too close scrutiny.

One such officer was Lieutenant Maksud Alikhanoff (also known as Alikhanov-Avarski), a member of an aristocratic Caucasian family who had already established a reputation as a dashing young fighting officer, but who had fallen from grace in a traditionally Russian aristocratic manner: he had fought a duel with a fellow officer. This had been the undoing of the poet and socialite Alexander Pushkin who died of wounds from a duel in 1837, and of the poet and guards officer Mikhail Lermontov who was killed in a duel in 1841. Alikhanoff's fall was all the more dramatic since, as a reward for his earlier gallant services as a captain, he had been prematurely advanced to the rank of major and made an aide-de-camp to the Grand Duke Michael, viceroy of the Caucasus. As a punishment for his duelling, he was reduced to the ranks as a private soldier, but before his special assignment he had already worked his way back to the commissioned rank of lieutenant.

The circumstances of his mission revolved around Russian aspirations to absorb the oasis, caravan junction and thriving desert township of Merv into the tsarist empire, not least as a further stepping stone towards India. There was to be a three-pronged reconnaissance of the routes from Russian-held territory to Merv. The first was to be from Askabad, some 200 miles across the steppe to the west of Merv; this was the route that would be taken by a Russian army advancing from the Caspian Sea and the one which would be recced by Alikhanoff. The second was the route that the army would take from Samarkand and Bokhara to the northeast; this was to be explored in the reverse direction by Lieutenant Naziroff. The third was the route from Khiva, directly to the north, and this was to be undertaken by Engineer Gospodin Lessar. The Askabad venture came first.

Colonel Baron Aminoff, as chief of staff of the Transcaspian military district, was stationed at Askabad from where he habitually gazed across the steppes in the easterly direction of Merv. He was well aware that one day – sooner rather than later – his troops were likely to be ordered forward in this direction and before such orders came he was anxious not only to survey the intervening territory but also to gain a closer estimate of the defences of Merv and the attitude of the population.

In February 1882 his opportunity arose. His commanding officer – General Rohrberg – had been withdrawn for consultation to St Petersburg leaving Aminoff in charge and with a relatively free hand. Even better, a genuine Russian trading caravan was poised at Askabad and determined to find new markets – preferably at the intriguing and allegedly prosperous mercantile centre of Merv. The caravan consisted mostly of Tekkes, a tribe renowned for their weaving and dealing in bold-patterned carpets; Edmund O'Donovan, the British journalist who had penetrated to Merv just three years earlier, had written that 'each girl generally manufactures two extra fine carpets, to form part of her dowry when she marries . . . when this has been done, she devotes herself to producing goods for the markets at Meshed and Bokhara'. It was to tap this market and deliver manufactured Russian goods that the Tekke caravan was setting off to the east. Aminoff was determined to insert his own agents with a different agenda.

Alikhanoff, still under a cloud but with his past reputation for daring deeds still remembered, was the obvious candidate. To accompany him Aminoff allocated an even younger Cossack ensign called Sokoleff. The two of them were disguised as clerks in the service of the Russian trader. (At least this was a change from the near-habitual disguise of being a Tartar horse-dealer.) They would mingle with the half-dozen armed Turkoman horsemen, who were to provide protection against bandits, and with the Tekke camel drivers, who had to be cajoled and threatened before they would agree to continue into such hostile territory. To ease the path of the caravan, and to try to ensure a friendly welcome in Merv, a

'Russianized-Khivan' was sent ahead to make contact and hire local guides.

The journey from Askabad to Merv was reckoned to take six days. The first oasis was Lukfabad and here they were stopped by a Persian official who showed an unhealthy curiosity about what they were up to, until Alikhanoff persuaded him that they were only bound for Meshed. When they crossed the Tejend river they encountered mosquitoes of such poisonous ferocity that they were alleged to sting camels to death. Alikhanoff was impressed with the Tejend oasis, which was a much more fertile source of supply for any army than had previously been reckoned. He also noted that there was considerable respect for the Russians here, since there had earlier been a series of punitive raids by Cossack patrols from Askabad. On the first leg of their journey across a 'briar-covered wilderness' they were fortunate to meet up with the guides sent to lead them in by the Russianized-Khivan who had gone ahead.

The guides had very specific and alarming advice. The Otamish tribe who dwelt on the near side of Merv, through which they must pass to reach the centre of the oasis, were 'so hostile to the Russians they would immediately kill them'. There were two alternative plans: either they could press on and pass through the Otamish quarter under cover of darkness, or they could make a detour of several days' duration and arrive at the opposite side of Merv.

The night ride was decided on as the best option. They entered the Otamish settlements at about 11 p.m. and were disconcerted to find it was a full moon and a clear night. The Otamish tents were all around them like black mushrooms. Dogs began to bark. Alikhanoff recorded that 'our fellow travellers grew silent . . . they hardly allowed themselves to whisper'.

Gradually, the tents gave way to clay buildings with low-walled gardens and melon beds irrigated by canals. At this point the guides insisted on separating the Russians from the rest of the caravan, and leading them on ahead. After some three hours of being urged to hurry, Alikhanoff and Sokoleff were thoroughly confused: the moon had gone behind clouds and they were in total darkness. They had the sensation that they were being taken round in circles, as they kept crossing and recrossing what seemed to be the same canals. The guides were whispering in a sinister way to each other and kept popping into secret conclaves.

One of Alikhanoff's Russian companions drew his revolver at this stage and declared that if they were being led into some trap, he intended to shoot the guides first and himself afterwards. Just when it seemed they would never reach their destination, they came to 'the interminably long and wonderful walls of the fortress of Merv'. At 3.30 a.m. they finally dismounted and met their Russianized-Khivan. Having been assured by him that they were not prisoners, they 'threw themselves down on the soft carpets and fell asleep there and then like dead men'.

The whole operation, it seemed, had been a complicated device to ensure that the arrival of a Russian caravan at the heart of Merv was a *fait accompli* before anyone could prevent it. However, plenty of people objected when they woke up in the morning and found this to be the case. A council of chiefs was called and Alikhanoff – possibly straining his credibility as a clerk – persuaded them, with a mixture of arguments and presents, that the caravan was an innocent commercial venture. The chiefs were not all so easily convinced: one of them, having listened patiently to Alikhanoff rhapsodizing about the blessings of Russian civilization, asked, 'If you are a mere trader, how does it come to pass you know all these things?' Alikhanoff brushed him off with a remark about the breadth of Russian education and how it was open to everyone. He was as fluent as he was fearless.

Alikhanoff and Sokoleff spent two weeks leading a double existence. By day they were pushing their master's Russian wares and trying to persuade the elders of Merv that a regular exchange of caravans would be good for the prosperity of the oasis. However, in the early hours of the morning, before the citizens were awake, the two Russian officers discarded their clerks' dress in favour of disguise as native Tekke tribesmen and carried out surreptitious surveys not only of the fort but of the streets and canals which intersected the whole settlement. They might have been two prospective London taxi drivers setting out to acquire 'the knowledge' of the town.

Possibly, they were spotted doing this more often than they realized. Increasingly, reports began to reach them, and the Russian trader who was the entrepreneur behind the whole caravan project, that the locals were planning to murder them. Their credibility and the tolerance of their hosts were running out. It was all too much for the trader, who left Merv for home in a panic, abandoning his unsold goods. Alikhanoff and Sokoleff were made of sterner stuff: they collected what was left of the caravan and their goods and set off. They chose not to follow the most direct route back to Askabad, but started a two-day march northwards towards Khiva to take in a wider sweep of country for their survey. They returned to wide acclaim.

*

Lieutenant Naziroff – like Alikhanoff – was from a Caucasian background. He was born with the name of Nazir Beg and was educated at Baku, becoming a military cadet in 1873. Realizing that the way ahead lay in consolidating his Russian rather than Caucasian connections, he changed his name to Naziroff and gained a commission in the Russian army in Turkestan. He served in a number of military campaigns and missions, and in 1882 (the same year as Alikhanoff's expedition) he was sent to make an exploratory ride to Tchardjui (now known as Turkmenabad) and then to Bokhara and Samarkand. The important part of this commission was the virtually unknown section between Merv and Tchardjui along which any Russian army from their base in Samarkand would have to advance (albeit in the opposite direction from that to be taken by Naziroff).

As he spoke all the languages and most of the dialects of Central Asia fluently, he (unlike Colonel Grodekoff) had the option of travelling in disguise. He thought this would be safer than going as a uniformed Russian officer, so he grew an appropriate beard. He chose two companions who would also blend in well with the local scene: a fellow Caucasian native of Baku and a Persian. Together they made the ride from Astrabad on the Caspian coast, via Meshed and Merv, and then on over the unknown stretch to Tchardjui on the Oxus and back into the by then more familiar Russian-dominated regions of Bokhara and Samarkand. The only earlier record of the unknown stretch of this journey was one written by Alexander 'Bokhara' Burnes some 50 years earlier. This would have been available to the Russians, but they discounted it, not only because it was out of date but also because they reckoned that Burnes had chosen a bad route and they would find a better one for the line of advance by an army. A new topographical survey was needed. They succeeded in producing this, but – as we shall see – the product of their labours was rendered unnecessary by subsequent developments.

We do not know many details of Naziroff's march because he did not publish anything about it, although the contemporary commentator on these matters – Charles Marvin – said his adventures would have made a very interesting book.

Meanwhile, Gospodin Lessar – a young Russian engineer – was shortly to complete the survey of the third line of approach to Merv: across the steppes northwards to Khiva. So by 1883 all the possible lines of approach had been assessed and action could be expected.

However, when it came to the Russian move on Merv in February 1884, none of these routes was really put to the test. The Tekkes of Merv were not expecting an attack as they had been careful not to provoke the Russians in any way. Then, quite suddenly, the same Alikhanoff, who had charmed the elders as the articulate spokesman for a trading caravan just two years earlier, appeared once more in their midst. This time he was wearing the uniform of the tsarist army and accompanied by not only an escort of armed Cossacks but by a few Tekke chiefs who had already thrown in their lot with the Russians.

He informed the assembly of elders that a Russian force had already occupied Tejend (halfway between Askabad and Merv) and – untruthfully – presented this force as the advance guard of a massive Russian army which would soon descend on them. The elders knew that the report of the occupation of Tejend was true; they were shaken by the defection of some of their number; and they were shocked to see Alikhanoff in his true colours and realize that they had been made fools of earlier. After some nervous debate they conceded: Merv – like so many other Central Asian emirates and khanates – would submit to the overlordship of the Tsar.

When the submission of Merv was reported to St Petersburg, the Tsar Alexander III responded by immediately restoring to Alikhanoff his former rank and decorations. His decisive role in a major step forward for Russia in the Great Game had atoned for his ill-considered duel. He was back on the road to promotion and honour.

Engineer Lessar, the third of the Russia bear cubs who emulated the achievements of their British contemporaries on 'shooting leave', was not only one of those who reconnoitred routes towards Merv; he had already undertaken a much more challenging and significant task.

By 1881 the Russian Transcaspian railway already ran from the eastern shore of the Caspian as far further east as Askabad, which was now an established fortress town. The railway project was seen as the key to moving not only trade goods but also – when the time was ripe – troops across Central Asia towards India. It had high-level backing: the overall controller of the project was Prince Khilkoff and the principal planner was General Mikhail Annenkoff. These powerful figures wanted to know whether it would be possible to extend the line yet further eastwards towards Sarakhs and on to Herat in Afghanistan – the much-vaunted 'key to India'. General Annenkoff decided that a young engineer who was bold, honest and disinclined to play politics would be the best instrument for exploring whether such an extension would be possible.

Lessar was the man he chose. The young officer picked a team to go with him, consisting of two overseers to assist in the topographical work, two interpreters and a guide; he also had an escort of 21 Cossacks. Most of the party had their own horses, but five additional camels, a wagon and a cart were also needed to carry all the surveying appliances on top of the necessary provisions and baggage.

The 185 miles from Askabad to Sarakhs ran through the Karakum Desert along the eastern edge of the Khorassan mountains. The principal danger was the possibility of attacks from the Turkoman tribesmen who frequented the desert, which in itself formed a no-man's-land between Persia and Afghanistan. This stage of the survey passed off fairly quietly.

The next stage from Sarakhs to Herat was likely to be trickier. The Hari Rud river formed the frontier here between Persia and Afghanistan. Almost everything on the Persian side was already known and mapped, but nothing on the Afghan side, as no independent travellers – and certainly no Persians – had ever braved the natural hazards of the mountains and the human hazards of the predatory tribesmen – the Sariks, a particularly viscious variety of Turkoman who had not had any contact with Russians and who were thought 'not to be relied upon to treat an explorer of that nation with respect'. Lessar boldly set off without waiting for a Cossack escort on this leg of his survey and found that his Tekke Turkoman guides were more terrified than he was at the prospect of encountering their Sarik cousins.

Lessar's great discovery was that the region he was exploring turned out to be void. The mountains marked on his map did not exist, or at best were gentle hills. They had been shown on maps as ranging up to 20,000 feet high and constituting a major barrier or line of defence between the Russian-occupied territories and Afghanistan. It seems that their contours had been drawn on these empty spaces, partly to fill them in and partly on the assumption that anywhere inside Afghanistan must be mountainous. The bandits did not exist either: it turned out that the Sariks were as frightened of the Afghans and the Persians as these people were of them. These discoveries were immensely positive for Lessar's masters. It meant that there was no real obstacle to extending the Transcaspian railway all the way to Herat, with all the onward implications that this invited.

As a footnote, Lessar observed that even the Afghan fort at Kusan (on the alternative more southerly route from Persia to Herat) was dilapidated: 'a handful of Cossacks could capture it at ease at any time'.

The results of Lessar's discoveries were soon published and available not only in St Petersburg but also in London. While in St Petersburg his findings were considered as unmitigated good news – revealing the potential for a railway track and an open line of advance towards India – in London there was a very different reception to the findings. It had been assumed by successive British governments and viceroys that any approach to Herat from the northwest (i.e. from Sarakhs) would be impeded and probably terminally frustrated by the mountainous terrain and the supposedly fierce marauding tribes. Now it was clear that the backdoor to India had been wide open – or at least ajar – all along. Mr Gladstone's government was jolted out of its preferred policy of 'masterly inactivity' into a more forward and alert stance.

Lessar had one last quest after his safe return to Askabad. This was a wide sweep northwards and eastwards – through

Merv, Khiva and the Karakum Desert. The eager young engineer had an even more ambitious thought this time: it was not a railway line that he had in mind, but the diverting of no lesser river than the Oxus from its destination in the Aral Sea to a new one in the Caspian Sea. The trade and military implications for Russia of such a fluvial diversion would have been vast indeed. But even the ingenious Lessar – the last and in some ways most ambitious of the three Russian bear cubs – was defeated by the Oxus, and he concluded that the engineering of such a project would be too difficult and expensive to recommend, let alone attempt.

So the last word remained with Matthew Arnold, who had concluded his poem 'Sohrab and Rustum' almost thirty years earlier with the lines:

Oxus, forgetting the bright speed he had
In his high mountain-cradle of Pamere,
A foiled circuitous wanderer – till at last
The longed-for dash of waves is heard, and wide
His luminous home of waters opens, bright
And tranquil, from whose floor the new-bathed stars
Emerge, and shine upon the Aral Sea.

# Chapter 15

## Francis Younghusband: The Mystic Explorer

'The Gatling's jammed and the colonel dead
And the regiment blind with dust and smoke.
The river of death has brimmed his banks,
And England's far, and Honour a name,
But the voice of a schoolboy rallies the ranks,
"Play up! Play up! And play the game!"'
 – Sir Henry Newbolt, in 'Vitai Lampada'

Henry Newbolt, who wrote these famous lines, was a contemporary of Francis Younghusband at Clifton College in the 1870s. Other contemporaries included Field Marshal Earl Haig of Flanders fame and Field Marshal Lord Birdwood of Gallipoli fame. It was a Victorian boys' public school in the tradition of Thomas Arnold's Rugby – intent on training young men to go out and rule the ever-expanding British empire. It was a fiercely patriotic environment, unaffected by any embarrassment at such concepts as class distinction, racial prejudice or self-conscious elitism. When Younghusband, with his family background deeply rooted in the India of the British Raj, went from Clifton to Sandhurst and then to the 1st King's Dragoon Guards it might have been expected that he would be a conventional cavalry officer. Instead, he turned into a uniquely mystical figure whose

Evangelical upbringing did not exclude a lifelong fascination with Buddhism, and whose patriotic Christianity (he was instrumental in turning William Blake's poem 'Jerusalem' into a popular hymn) did not prevent his being a founder of the World Congress of Faiths.

Younghusband had a family reason for his early enthusiasm for the Great Game. His uncle was no less a player than the fabled Robert Shaw, the tea planter turned explorer who, with George Hayward, had been one of the first Europeans to reach Kashgar on the Chinese side of the Pamirs, for which he had been awarded the Royal Geographical Society's gold medal. Shaw was a role model to the youthful Younghusband. So, not unnaturally, his first spell of shooting leave from his regiment was an expedition north from Rawalpindi in 1884. He was to write: 'from this first tour in the Himalayas I came back with the exploring fever thoroughly on me'. Younghusband was hooked on inquiring travel.

His first big adventure was in the direction of Manchuria, Mongolia and north China. Near the Russian frontier, Younghusband had his first encounter with Cossacks. He was impressed and commented that 'a Cossack, wherever one meets him, looks as if he were ready to buckle to and fight there and then'. It was an impression that was to stay with him on further more dramatic encounters. After extensive travels he met up with Colonel Mark Bell VC of the Royal Engineers in Peking; Bell was already a serious intelligence gatherer and was about to set off across Chinese Turkestan to spy out military installations. Younghusband asked if he could go along with him, but instead of accepting the offer Bell suggested an even more exciting alternative to Younghusband. He should follow a separate route through the Gobi Desert, round the edge of the Taklimakan Desert by Turfan to Kashgar, and over the Karakorams into India.

Of course, such a trip required a long further absence from his regiment, and he persuaded the British minister in Peking to send a telegraphic request direct to the viceroy of India requesting him to authorize such an absence; Lord Dufferin – who had progressive views about the need for intelligence beyond the frontiers of India – sent a prompt and positive reply. This was indeed a challenge beyond Younghusband's wildest dreams.

His travelling party was minimal: he took one Chinese interpreter and one servant who acted as cook, groom and general porter. The latter – Liu-san – stayed with him throughout the expedition and showed fidelity and courage, while also taking over the interpreting duties when the interpreter abandoned them due to the rigours of the desert. When they reached the edge of the Gobi, Younghusband also took on eight camels and a desert guide. As well as carrying water, the camels were loaded with bricks of tea 'which are used in place of money'. One of the camels broke loose one night and eluded all subsequent searches; fortunately, it had shed its load.

Having started on 'the great caravan route from Peking to Siberia', Younghusband encountered many different nationalities: as well as Chinese, there were American missionaries (mostly involved in weaning the Chinese off the opium habit) and Russian tea merchants. Just as he had been impressed with the Cossacks, so Younghusband instinctively liked the Russians: 'I believe there are no two nations that would take to each other more than the Russians and ourselves.' He was to spend much of his career frustrating their endeavours, but he never lost this initial regard and respect for them.

Younghusband also fell under the charm of the Mongols and their way of life in their yurts. In his book, *The Heart of a*

*Continent*, he describes showing a Mongol family 'a concave shaving mirror, which magnifies and distorts the face in a marvellous way' and recounts what a joke the young Mongol boys had in making the girls look at themselves and observing their horror at what they saw. Younghusband was good for a bit of fun as well as work.

Not all local contacts were as friendly, including 'some uncanny-looking gentlemen [who] came prowling about the camp one day'. Younghusband kept his revolver to hand because he had a lot of money – mostly in the form of silver – hidden about his person or in the baggage. After some hesitation, he persuaded himself he had to trust his sole permanent retainer and gave Liu-san a loaded revolver too. Sometimes they mistook heaps of stones for brigands and nearly 'wasted a lot of ammunition on them'. At other times they were so apprehensive when approaching pools of water that they 'repeated the stage-conspirator performance, advancing noiselessly with revolvers in hand'.

After nearly 60 days of desert travel, eventually the peaks of the Tien Shan mountains came within range of Younghusband's telescope. With his sporting intentions in mind, he told his guide to look out for Ovis Polo (Marco Polo sheep) and managed to collect a fine specimen with horns measuring 54 inches across and 19 inches ('as thick as my thigh') round the base. He had his souvenir of the bleak Gobi Desert.

After a few days' rest at Hami on the eastern edge of the Tien Shan mountains, Younghusband pressed on to Kashgar, about another 40 days' march away. Here he found a Russian consul with 'a comprehensive knowledge of Indian and Central Asian affairs'. Worrying as this might be, Younghusband – with his affection for Russians – was soon exchanging friendly visits and hospitality with him. Moving on from Kashgar he reached Yarkand.

At Yarkand he found a letter from Colonel Bell sent from the Karakoram Pass. Bell – never one for suggesting soft options – proposed that instead of following 'the well known and uninteresting route by Leh to India', he should 'try the unexplored but direct road by the Mustagh Pass to Baltistan and Kashmir'. This was a tall order indeed. No one had been recorded as going over the Mustagh Pass and its reputation was horrendous. However, Younghusband was delighted: 'it was something quite new, and promised to be difficult enough to be really worth doing'. He set about collecting men, ponies and sheepskin coats.

Once he had embarked into the 'labyrinth of pathless mountains', it was not only the terrain and temperature he had to cope with: 'we also had to be ever-watchful against an attack from the Kanjuti robbers, who had for many years infested these parts'. They tended to attack at night 'and cut the ropes of the tent and let it down on the top of you' (exactly the same technique used by the Turkomans and feared by James Abbott 50 years before). So Younghusband found it necessary to live in the open, even on the glaciers, sheltering behind any friendly rock.

One gorge they had to pass through was 'shut in between cliffs of enormous height and nearly perpendicular'. The river rushed through this with great force, so they unloaded the ponies 'and every man set to work to make a road round the base of the cliff by throwing rocks and boulders into the river'. In this way they made a path just wide enough to lead the ponies over.[1]

---

1. Handling rocks in this way can still be necessary in the Karakorams. When the author was leading a group of ten people over the frozen Kunjarab Pass in early October 1996, landslides in front and behind trapped the party and it was necessary for all hands to heave rocks off the route and into the ravines below before any escape could be made.

When they reached the Aghil Pass in the Karakorams they were
confronted by 'a sheer cliff of a couple of hundred feet or so
in height running far away'. However, Younghusband had noticed
that there were tracks of wild asses and 'knew that these animals
must get down to the river to drink'. So he retraced his steps
until he could follow their tracks and unloaded the ponies,
'putting one man on to lead each in front and two others to
hold onto the tail behind' and so managed to reach the river.
Meanwhile, visions of the enormous K2 mountain inspired the

contemplative Younghusband to reflect on 'the greatness and grandeur of Nature's works'. Younghusband was always aware of a divine hand in all he encountered.

The ultimate test of Younghusband and his companions was to be the Mustagh Pass itself. We have two accounts of this: one is from the letter he wrote to his father immediately after arrival in Kashmir, and the other is a longer account set out in his book. To his father he wrote:

> The pass is over the main axis of the Himalayas, and divides the Chinese dominions from the British dependencies. It is also the watershed between the rivers which flow into the Indian Ocean and those which flow towards Turkestan . . . On reaching the summit we looked around for a way down, but there was nothing but a sheer precipice . . . I, an Englishman, was afraid to go first. Luckily my guides were better plucked than myself . . . Step by step we advanced across it, all the time facing the precipice, and knowing that if we slipped (and the ice was very slippery) we would roll down the icy slope and over the precipice into eternity . . . For six hours we descended the precipice, partly rock and partly ice-slope, and when we reached the bottom and looked back, it seemed utterly impossible that any man could have come down such a place.

In his longer account, Younghusband goes into much greater detail about how he sent the ponies round by a more circuitous and safer route, and how no European had crossed the pass before. He also explains that he had no ice axes (only an ordinary pick axe) or 'other mountaineering appliances' with him. He did not even have proper boots, but soft leather 'native' ones without nails or heels – 'mere leather stockings in fact'. These predictably got shredded by the ice. They made a climbing line out of 'every scrap of rope that could be spared from the ponies' gear, and we tied these and all the men's turbans and waist cloths together into one long rope'. One of the servants was shaking so badly that he had to be sent home before they reached the worst part, but no one was lost on the descent. Despite his self-effacing remarks in his letter to this father, clearly it was Younghusband's leadership and the sense that anything was possible to a determined Englishman which kept the party going.

When this 'last and greatest obstacle of my journey had been surmounted', Younghusband reflected in a contemplative and spiritual manner, with deep gratitude for what he had been enabled to achieve. The intrepid explorer's mystical side was allowed to take over at such moments. But not for long: when he reached Srinagar his first action was 'to go off and purchase a knickerbocker suit such as officers wear out shooting in Kashmir'. He was, after all, on shooting leave.

The overland trip across the Gobi Desert and the Karakorams was carried out strictly at the request of Colonel Bell and with the viceroy's backing; the important thing about this first major journey was that it established Younghusband's reputation as an enterprising explorer and fearless agent of military intelligence. On arrival at Srinagar he received a personal telegram from no less a figure than General 'Bobs' Roberts, the commander-in-chief in India (who knew something about courage – having won a VC in the Indian Mutiny). From now on, he was to be the confidant of viceroys and field marshals and the firm friend of rising politicians such as Lord Curzon of Keddleston. He was not allowed to resume regimental duties for long before another special assignment came his way.

Younghusband's later expeditions were much celebrated both

at the time and subsequently. He was sent to find a hidden pass into the 'kingdom' of Hunza, and to persuade its ruler – the mir – to cease his raiding of the caravan routes and his flirtation with Russian agents. Later, he was sent into the Pamirs to monitor Russian incursions there. On both these expeditions he encountered Russian opposite numbers such as the colonels Grombtchevsky and Yanov, and the encounters provoked international tension between Russia and Britain. His coolness in danger and his solid achievements received wide recognition: here was a man who would enter a robber's fortress or a mad mir's court with equal dignity and nerve. This was the Great Game played in a major key and he was consequently created a commander of the Most Eminent Order of the Indian Empire.

These exploits have been fully and graphically recounted elsewhere (notably in Peter Hopkirk's *The Great Game: On Secret Service in High Asia*, 1990, and in Patrick French's definitive biography, *Younghusband: The Last Great Imperial Adventurer*, 1994) and they went far beyond the range of 'shooting leave'. To omit an account of Younghusband's earlier exploits would have been to leave a gap in the story, but to recount in detail his later forays would be both repetitive and outside the scope of this work.

However, one aspect of his Hunza and Pamir adventures which should rightly be recorded here is his consistent attitude towards his Russian opponents and opposite numbers. When he encountered the likes of Grombtchevsky and Yanov in dramatically confrontational circumstances, he not only exchanged courtesies and hospitality with them but he also established a mutual rapport between like-minded officers and gentlemen. 'We and the Russians are rivals,' he wrote, 'but I am sure that the individual Russian and English officer like each other a great deal better than they do the individuals of nations with which they are not in rivalry . . . we are both playing a big game.' They were indeed.

Nowadays, Younghusband is best remembered for his leadership of the military campaign into Tibet in 1903–4 and the subsequent occupation of Lhasa. Again, this episode has been very fully and readably recorded (not only in Patrick French's biography, but also in Peter Fleming's *Bayonets to Lhasa*, 1961, and Charles Allen's *Duel in the Snow*, 2003) and is far removed from the concept of shooting leave. After this campaign he was promoted to a knighthood in the Order of the Indian Empire, although King Edward VIII thought he should have been given a knighthood in a more prestigious order; he had to wait more than another decade before he received the more exalted knighthood of the Star of India (both orders are now defunct).

Younghusband was a much more complex figure than most of the young officers deployed in the Great Game. In some ways he was a militant Christian, within whom faith and patriotism for England were firmly bonded. He was also an imperialist in the best – and occasionally the worst – senses of the word. On the positive side, he never doubted the need to strengthen the defences of India by a forward policy, whether it be in the mountain passes of Hunza and the Pamirs or on the frontiers of that unknown and mysterious neighbour Tibet. This was one of the characteristics that endeared him to empire builders like Lord Roberts of Kandahar and Lord Curzon. He also had a genuine and deep-felt consideration for those Asians working with him; he was a natural leader whom people trusted because they knew he would never let them down.

On the more negative side, he occasionally allowed his imperial pride in British values and standards to lead him into regrettably racist comments and remarks: when summing up the performance of his loyal companion and guide Liu-san, he wrote 'he was a Chinaman, and therefore not a perfect animal'. Then, when exasperated by the indiscretions of one of his escorts in Hunza, he wrote 'Gurkhas are brave, cheery little men, but they have not the wits of a hog.'

His religious views were also far more complex than those of such straightforward Anglicans as James Abbott, who invoked a very British deity in all moments of danger. Although he saw religion and patriotism as unified, increasingly he subscribed to the idea of a universal spirit in which Christianity is not 'so far superior to the Buddhist or Mohammedan religions'. He had moments on the Mustagh Pass and on leaving Tibet when he felt a strong spiritual upsurge in his whole being, a communion with a higher – but not specifically Christian – deity. After his withdrawal from Tibet he had carried with him a small bronze statue of Buddha which he prized and displayed for the rest of his life. In old age he became a founder of the World Congress of Faiths and developed strong relationships with people – usually attractive women – who he felt were on the same spiritual wavelength.

When Francis Younghusband set out on his military career on the northwest frontier, the bold and energetic Clifton boy from the King's Hussars must have appeared a normal and promising candidate for extended shooting leave. By the end of his career it was clear that this was someone who – in his own way – was just as far from the stereotype of the eager, uncomplicated young cavalry officer as was Masson or Wood, Baker or Lessar.

# Chapter 16

## Percy Sykes: The Daring Bounder

'I've never any pity for conceited people, because I think they
carry their own comfort about with them.'

      – George Eliot (1819–80), in *The Mill on the Floss*

Most young officers who took shooting leave to explore the
passes of the Pamirs or make tentative contact with the emirs
and khans of Central Asia made one or two memorable trips
and then settled into a more conventional life of soldiering or
political work. Percy Sykes was the exception: he devoted the
first ten years of his career to a whole succession of remarkable journeys in the less well-known parts of Central Asia and
Persia.

He was an exception in other ways, too. On the face of it,
he was the prototype of the dashing young officer who made
an early reputation for himself by his adventurous undertakings
in the best tradition of the Raj. He came from the most acceptable background: educated at Rugby and Sandhurst he joined
the 16th Lancers in India and quickly transferred to the equally
smart 2nd Dragoon Guards – known as the Queen's Bays – in
which his father had been the regimental chaplain and a respected
figure. He was a good shot and an enthusiastic polo player who
took to pig-sticking. He travelled fearlessly, sometimes in disguise,

and learnt the native languages. He quickly came to the notice of Lord Curzon, and corresponded directly about his travels with Lord Salisbury, who was then both prime minister and foreign secretary. He appeared to be the very model of a latter-day Great Game hero.

However, he was never quite accepted at his own valuation. The turn of the nineteenth and twentieth centuries was an era when officers and gentlemen tended to be (at least superficially) self-deprecating in their accounts of their achievements and modest in their professed ambitions: Sykes stood out as vain-glorious and pushy. For every patron whose support he won, he antagonized an equal number of his own contemporaries. (Antony Wynn has well summarized this antagonism in his admirable 2006 biography of Sykes entitled *Persia in the Great Game: Sir Percy Sykes – Explorer, Consul, Soldier, Spy*). Charles Hardinge (later to become viceroy of India), who worked alongside Sykes at the British legation in Tehran in 1896, found him 'a queer fellow . . . the cause of a good deal of friction with the staff . . . [whose] aspirations amuse me'; in short he was 'a terrible bounder'. Horace Rumbold (later to become ambassador to Constantinople and Berlin), who also worked with him in Persia, found he was 'too self-assertive . . . we none of us liked him'. And even Lord Curzon, who had early spotted Sykes's potential and talent for projecting himself, later referred to his 'somewhat truculent manner and appearance' and finally was instrumental in terminating his career.

Lieutenant Sykes's first special mission was possibly his most dramatic. In 1892 he had applied for a spell of classic shooting leave in Afghanistan: Marco Polo sheep were the big draw and there was always the possibility of a snow leopard. But the army intelligence department, who always had a hand in approving such borderland leave plans, decided that there was a more urgent task for an enterprising young officer. As so often, the British were going through a phase of particular anxiety about Russian aspirations towards India. They thought the best way of determining whether these anxieties were well-founded was to send an undercover agent behind the Russian front-line in Central Asia to observe troop movements, pick up gossip and provide some material for a dossier about the perceived threat. The best listening post would obviously be one of the Russian front-line garrison towns in Uzbekistan or Turkmenistan, and of these the most rewarding – and certainly the most romantic – was Samarkand.

There was nothing strictly illegal about British officers travelling in Russia and noting down what they saw; Fred Burnaby and Valentine Baker had done just this some 20 years before. However, even though the Great Game was nearing its final phase, in some respects the atmosphere had become tenser. Nicholas II's tsarist secret police and network of informers and agents were ubiquitous, and as soon as unwanted British officers were identified they would be expelled unceremoniously, and if their mission was suspected of being of sinister intent (as it almost certainly would be) an international incident, of the sort that had occurred the previous year, in 1891, when Captain Francis Younghusband encountered a Russian patrol in the Pamirs, might well have ensued. The paradox was that in order to reach Samarkand and spend any time there without detection, the adoption of disguise and devious behaviour were essential, but these measures increased the stakes dramatically – arrest, denunciation and national embarrassment would be all the more likely to follow any revelation of their covert activities.

These were the risks which the Indian army intelligence service deemed worth taking, though it remains in doubt as to whether higher authority was consulted for the 1892 mission. The young officers themselves – Sykes was joined by a Lieutenant Coningham – were also game to take the risk.[1] They were dispatched first to Odessa on the Black Sea to be briefed by the British consul-general there – the same Colonel Charles Stewart whose own adventures are the subject of an earlier chapter. He knew about the hazards of travelling in disguise from first-hand experience.

From Odessa, Sykes and Coningham took a ship across the Black Sea to Trebizond on the north coast of Turkey, and from there – where the adventure really started – they went by rowing boat along the shore northeastwards to a beach near Batumi on the Russian coast. Here, they were quickly picked up by the tsarist police on two counts: they were suspected of being the bearers of cholera from further down the coast and threatened with quarantine, and they were – it seems – simultaneously suspected of being Russian anarchists with terrorist intentions. The irony of their position was that they gained their release by persuading the police that far from being Russian terrorists disguised as Englishmen, they were in fact eccentric Englishmen travelling as Russians. They were allowed to cross the Caucasus from Batumi to Tiflis and on to Baku on the Caspian coast. The Russian authority in the Caucasus – which had been subdued

---

1. It is difficult to gauge what the personal consequences of being unmasked on such a mission might have been. Rudyard Kipling, in his short story 'The Man Who Was' about the White Hussars on the northwest frontier of India, tells of an officer who is captured and held incognito and in dire conditions by the Russians for years on end; and certainly more recently – during the author's time in the Soviet Union – western agents occasionally disappeared or were the victims of 'fatal accidents' when travelling in circumstances that were considered questionable.

some 30 years earlier – was by then sufficiently secure for them to take a fairly relaxed view of English travellers. The same was not the case on the other side of the Caspian in Central Asia.

Indeed, even the rail journey to Baku and the voyage across the Caspian from Baku to the railhead in Russian Turkmenistan were potentially tricky: Sykes and Coningham abandoned their English clothes and bought Russian outfits (long cloaks and flat-topped caps which looked remarkably military) and hired an Armenian dragoman (a guide and interpreter) to accompany them. He would also act as a negotiator – a buffer between them and the suspicious authorities. The crossing of the Caspian turned out to be particularly difficult, as their fellow passengers were a gregarious lot and curious about the strangers on board. In the event, Sykes and Coningham were forced to shut themselves in their cabin to avoid unwelcome conversations and, when they reached the far shore and the railhead, they boarded the train to Samarkand separately and only spoke to each other occasionally in French, since neither of them spoke sufficient Russian to get away with talking it in front of genuine Russians. They wisely resisted the temptation to make a fuss or complain when they were summarily turfed out of their compartment by the train guard to make room for a Russian officer.

Having reached Samarkand unchallenged, they got the dragoman to book them into a modest hotel where they continued to keep as low a profile as possible – only emerging from their room when the streets were relatively empty in the evenings. Their fallback story if pressed was that they were foreign textile dealers who had come to explore possible new markets. On their evening excursions they noted the uniforms of the Russian troops and tried to work out what corps or regiments they came from: were they combat units about to embark on fresh ventures or campaigns, or were they administrators and defensive garrison personnel merely holding the fort? Without risking exposing themselves in bars and restaurants, it was very difficult to pick up any military gossip of the type which they had been sent to collect. Tentatively, they tried to widen their field of contacts and enlisted the help of an Armenian who accepted their story of being French textile traders.

Then they had a breakthrough. Their contact turned out to be in the ideal job as far as they were concerned: he was a steward in the local Russian officers' club. He spoke – and more importantly understood – Russian perfectly, and he was continually circulating in the course of his duties among officers who were talking freely of their deployments (the slogan 'careless talk costs lives' had not yet been coined).

The steward was able to pass on a good deal of relevant intelligence about Russian strengths and intentions. He gave Sykes and Coningham troop numbers and names of units and also told them of the lines of supply, revealing that there were imminent plans to extend the rail-link further eastwards (with all the implications for troop movements that this implied). He referred to the establishment of arms factories and of the unpopular conscription of local labour to man these and was also able to relate that several Indians had been expelled on suspicion of being British agents. Most importantly, he told them that there were indeed Russian plans to lay claim to further tracts of the Pamirs and establish bases there. (This was what Younghusband had been independently discovering on the ground the previous year.) Interspersed with all this, and at even greater length, he passed on gossip which he had obtained from other sources about the textile market and the manufacture of uniforms; to the latter Sykes had to pay exaggerated attention to preserve his cover.

None of the military gossip or news was world shattering, but it was sufficient to have justified the expedition and the risks involved. Sykes and Coningham (much encouraged by their nervous dragoman) decided that they should withdraw before they were rumbled by the authorities. They went back to Odessa the way they had come, not without some further awkward moments, and were duly debriefed by Colonel Stewart who congratulated them on their remarkable achievement. From now on, Sykes was to be licensed to travel far and wide with an intelligence brief. Shooting leave was to be his for the asking.[2]

And ask for it he did. Having completed a short and well-earned home leave in England, instead of rejoining his regiment in Karachi by the usual sea route, he received permission to make the journey overland through Persia in 1893. His plan was to take unfrequented or unknown routes wherever possible in preference to the established ones. In doing this, he had a brief both from the foreign intelligence department of the British army in India and also from the Royal Geographical Society in London.

Sykes already had a good contact to start him on his way: Colonel Stewart, the consul-general in Odessa. Encouraged by

---

2. Sir Patrick Reilly (who was Percy Sykes's son-in-law), when he was British ambassador in Moscow in the late 1950s, told the author (who was then Reilly's diplomatic private secretary) much about this expedition and also about Sykes's uneasy relationship with his colleagues. Reilly did much subsequent research and recording of Sykes's achievements and showed some of his work on this to the author at All Souls College, Oxford. Antony Wynn also drew on Reilly's material for his biography of Sykes.

him, Sykes sailed round the Black Sea to Batumi, across the Caucasus via Tiflis to Baku and over the Caspian Sea to Uzan Ada on the eastern shore. He progressed down the coast, through a series of Russian border garrison towns, all of which he closely observed, and into Persia. Here Sykes's dragoman managed to arrange for him to stay at the telegraph office while waiting for ponies, and Sykes went duck-shooting on the lagoon.

He then set off through the country of the Turkomans who overlapped the Russian-Persian border on both sides. There were immediate difficulties: the Persian governor was reluctant to let him go without a much larger escort than he could afford. So again he spent the time shooting and then decided to slip away quietly at dawn before the governor could prevent him. The same problem recurred two days later when another local khan declined to allow him to go on because 'I was sure to be killed or robbed, in which case he would be held responsible'. However, three days of hard negotiation, a letter absolving the khan of responsibility and the gift of a revolver lifted the embargo. Sykes set off again rapidly before the khan had time to change his mind.

The next stage of the journey was across the 'lifeless steppe' parallel with the Atrak river (which Valentine Baker had traced). He was told he would need to carry five days' provisions, so it was necessary to purchase a camel – which was offered at eight times its true value. Like James Abbott in another Turkoman region only slightly to the north of him some 50 years before, Sykes began to have trouble with his guides and camp-followers: they were indulging in whispered conferences and strange nocturnal prowling. Sykes 'barricaded the tent' and sat up all night. He was mightily relieved to quit Turkoman country.

Everywhere he went, his motivation was called in question: that an officer could be travelling in such dangerous and uncomfortable territory for his own amusement was not believed – 'no Oriental ever travelling except for gain or as a pilgrim'. When he reached Meshed, he was granted a warm welcome by the British consul-general, the celebrated explorer Ney Elias. Sykes was overwhelmed by the beauty of the Imam Reza shrine at Meshed but explicitly warns in his book against defying the embargo on Christians entering it; of one Englishman who did so, he says, 'had he been discovered, not only his own, but perhaps hundreds of other lives would have been sacrificed'. In describing Meshed in his book, Sykes makes one of his many ingratiating remarks about Lord Curzon, whose patronage he was actively courting: no other books, he says, 'neither for accuracy nor for recent information . . . compare with the monumental work of the present Viceroy of India'. (Curzon was later to claim that Sykes for his part had 'made a clean sweep of all my most cherished quotations'.)

After a week Sykes pressed on across the Lut Desert to Kerman – 'one of the most unsafe stages on the road' – but experienced no trouble except getting some mules stuck in a snowdrift on one of the passes. Sykes made the significant observation that crossing the Lut was not a problem while there were villages as they had wells, but if the villagers were chased off the water supply would dry up too. Although there had been a trickle of Persian travellers across this desert, Sykes reckoned he was the first European – with the possible exception of Marco Polo – to cross this part of the Lut. He was not one to understate his achievements.

As the villages and wells got scarcer, they hired three mules to carry essential water with them. Occasional fortresses reminded the travellers that – having quit the territory of the Turkomans – they were now entering the equally dangerous terrain of the Baluchi tribesmen whose penchant for raiding was scarcely less. At one caravanserai a gang of robbers threatened Sykes's party with knives, but were repulsed by the 'sight of two revolvers'. At some places the defiles through the mountains were so narrow that the mules had to be unloaded in order to pass, but Sykes concluded that 'a little dynamite would remedy the evil' and there were no serious impediments to military advances. When not grappling with supply, security or physical problems, Sykes was quietly mapping areas which were hitherto 'quite blank' for the Royal Geographical Society.

Sykes's record of this journey shows that, even at this early stage of his career, he was as interested in political as geographical features. He notes that the local levies of cavalry and infantry do police work but are armed with very obsolete weapons, whereas 'brigands generally possess sporting Martini rifles'.

After a week resting at Kerman, Sykes set off – 'delighted to see the map full of blanks' – towards Persepolis. However, empty spaces on the map did not imply the absence of robber bands. Soon after he left Kerman Sykes's muleteers deserted out of fright and were only persuaded with great difficulty and the help of the local governor to continue. A little later, Sykes and his party were shadowed by a sinister band of seven armed horsemen; Sykes pitched his tent for the night, and then 'watched some distance from it, hoping thereby to surprise any raiders'.

However, life was about to get much easier and more sociable. The governor-general of the province – His Highness Prince

Farman Farma – had heard that an Englishman was riding through his domain and sent an invitation to him. Sykes and the prince, who was in his early thirties and only about five years older than Sykes, got on well together from the start. Sykes was impressed by the grandeur of his new acquaintance, who was waited on at table by generals and senior officers in the manner in which medieval monarchs had been by noblemen, and he was also impressed by his sporting zest. The prince would gallop off at full speed, firing off right and left at gazelle and other game. Sykes made a huge effort to keep up with him and succeeded in establishing that he was a true sportsman and worthy to be a friend. It was a relationship that was to help Sykes considerably in his later consular career, and he was not one to let such an opportunity go by default. He ended up being warmly invited by the prince to join him on a shooting trip in Baluchistan during the winter.

Sykes's first long ride across Persia ended dramatically. When he reached Persepolis he heard that there were riots nearby, and at Shiraz he witnessed a skirmish in which several men were wounded and one hacked to death. The unpopular governor of Shiraz was summoned by the Shah to Tehran to answer for what was going on, while those seeing him off on the journey wished him the same fate as his great-grandfather 'who had been boiled to death' by an earlier Shah. As he rode on to Bushire to embark for India and rejoin his regiment, Sykes reflected that a career in Persia was no soft option.

Yet this was the direction in which the die was to be cast for him. By the age of 26, Sykes had already proved himself a daring spy in Russia, a competent explorer and surveyor of the uncharted hinterland of British India and a thrusting envoy capable of making useful political contacts. The authorities in

London and Simla may not have shared his own overweaning estimate of his abilities (it was not only his contemporaries in Tehran who sourly referred to him as 'Napoleon-Attila-Sykes'), but they found him much too valuable to be left playing polo and perfecting his dressage with the Queen's Bays in Rawalpindi. He had barely rejoined his regiment before he was again summoned to Simla to receive instructions from the foreign affairs department of the Indian government for his next major journey. He was spending far more time on 'shooting leave' than he was on regimental soldiering.

The next assignment was, in effect, extremely similar to that on which Charles Christie and Henry Pottinger had been sent just over 80 years before. Back then, in 1810, the Raj had feared an advance through Persia and Baluchistan of a joint French and Russian invasion force. Now, in 1893, it was purely a Russian advance that was feared, but the fear was enhanced by memories of the Indian Mutiny of 1857 and the periodical rumblings of internal discontent that were to remain a feature of British rule in India. It was still the case that the Persian part of Baluchistan (the other part was now absorbed into Sindh and British India) presented one of the most tempting approach roads to India, and it still had a maverick population – unstable and unpredictable. Sykes was asked to update Pottinger's work: to survey possible lines of military advance, locate defensive positions, assess the attitude of local tribes and report on sources of supply – water, crops and horses.

Sykes, though still only a second lieutenant, was to lead the party, but he was to be given the support of Surgeon-Major G. W. Brazier-Creagh of the Royal Army Medical Corps as well as a lance-corporal from the Punjab cavalry, two scouts from the famous Corps of Guides and six Indian servants. They had horses and ponies and hired extra camels. Again like Pottinger, they embarked on the west coast of India and sailed up past Gujarat to Baluchistan. Disembarking was more difficult, as they were moored 200 yards offshore and the horses showed a marked reluctance to swim to the beach, preferring to try to scramble back into the boats. They then set off inland towards Kerman, through a countryside where 'Baluchis murdered nearly everyone they captured, no slave market being open to them'. Sykes added that in exceptional cases, when they wanted to hang on to their captives as slaves for their own use, they took the precaution of mutilating them 'in order to lessen their desire of returning to their homes'.

From the beginning, the camels and camel-handlers were a problem. The latter made a practice of complaining that their beasts were overloaded, even when this was palpably not the case. Sykes tried to show them up for the fraudsters they were: 'a box purposely emptied was opened to prove to them the absurdity of their protests'. But – he records – they failed to see the joke and went on complaining and 'snarling like a pack of jackals'. Once under way, water was difficult to find and when at last a stream was found where the horses could slake their thirst, wolves were seen circling the caravan. The local inhabitants – who had not encountered any Europeans before – refused to sell them food until one of Sykes's men, in a fit of exasperation, tossed the 'particularly evil-looking' headman into a stream. The countryside had not become notably friendlier with the passage of 80 years.

Sykes made a point of climbing any peaks to get a long-range view of the terrain he had been sent to chart. On one occasion a local Baluchi who insisted on accompanying him turned out to have a hidden agenda: when they reached the summit he suddenly declared, 'Sahib, we have all heard of

British justice, and I wish to lay a case before you.' He then went on to recount the story of his problems with his fiancée, and when Sykes opined that he should release her from her engagement he readily accepted this as a verdict from on high which relieved him of any responsibility or embarrassment. Sykes saw nothing odd in this: judgment of Solomon came readily to him.

The passage of Sykes and Brazier-Creagh through Baluchistan was considerably eased by the reappearance of his friend Prince Farman Farma, who sent two Baluchi guides to smooth his path. They pressed on through Bampur (which Pottinger had also visited and described as Bunpoor) to Fahraj where the plentiful wild game attracted wolves and jackals from the surrounding hills. When one of Sykes's 'walers' (horses originally imported into India from New South Wales) collapsed through exhaustion and ill-nourishment, Sykes shot it and used the carcass as a lure for jackals: 'we bagged a number over its dead body'. He was not one to be sentimental about a horse.

As the first Europeans anyone had seen in this area, they must have made a curious impression. On the one hand, the locals appreciated it when Sykes organized a shooting match for them, and they appreciated it even more when Brazier-Creagh dispensed medicine to the infirm and undertook minor surgery. On the other hand, they could not fathom why these strange unbelievers were there at all; it was generally assumed they were secretly prospecting for gold or gem stones in the hills. When they disappeared into a cave 'large enough to hold all the horses', it must have confirmed their suspicions. They were even directed towards a 'treasure hill' with a cave alleged to be full of gold, but this was not on their route and seemed an improbable story anyway.

On New Year's Day 1894 they were so short of provisions that they only kept themselves fed by shooting the plentiful hill partridges. Their guide absconded, complaining that the camel-men were threatening to poison him, but in fact probably because he was tired of being hungry. While Sykes went ahead, Brazier-Creagh stayed with the camel-men to prevent them absconding, too. They reached Bazman just in time since – as Sykes remarked – 'hunger is not agreeable'.

But more long-term help was at hand. Prince Farman Farma sent supplies and an invitation to join his party for feasting, shooting and horse-racing. While they were with him, 'every day we enjoyed excellent gazelle shooting, and a hyena, a lynx, and a wild cat were also included in the bag'. They crossed a desert stretch of more than 150 miles with comparative ease as the prince's guests. Most satisfying of all was the fact that the prince allowed Sykes to mingle with his entourage and the local chiefs who had gathered to meet him, and question them about conditions, allegiances and geographical features; 'we gained more information about the province in a week than less favoured travellers would have collected in many months'. Local chiefs repeatedly told Sykes that they thought that on the death of the Shah the Russians would try to take over Persia; if anyone was going to do that, they added, they would much rather it were the British. Both London and Simla noted such comments with interest. In fact, this was shooting leave being spent in the best tradition of the phrase.

Sykes reached Kerman for the second time exactly a year after his first visit. He had his eye on Kerman; he argued that it needed the presence of a British consul and tried to persuade Prince Farman Farma that this would be in Persian interests too, because he saw himself as a suitable candidate for the post. But he did not hover there long. From Kerman it was a relatively straightforward journey to Tehran where he was welcomed at the British legation. However, he soon managed to put up the backs of his contemporaries by telling them at inordinate length about aspects of the country which – he reminded them – he knew much better than most of them. When presented in audience to His Imperial Majesty the Shah Nasir-ud-Din of Persia, Sykes – never lacking in self-confidence – proceeded to pontificate to the Shah about the country which his family had been ruling for over a hundred years.

Sykes moved on, via the Valley of the Assassins, the Caspian coast and the Caucasus, where he mounted a train for Moscow, St Petersburg, Berlin and finally home. He had 'completed nine months of constant travel and unfailing enjoyment'.

Although Sykes was to continue to make remarkable off-the-beaten-track journeys through Persia (his 1902 book is called *Ten Thousand Miles in Persia or Eight Years in Iran*) these first three trips – the one to Samarkand and the two in Persia – were the only ones that strictly qualified as shooting leave. Thereafter, he was part of a wider political deployment. He managed to persuade the powers that be in Simla that a consulate really was needed in Kerman and that he was the right person for the post. When he took up the appointment in 1894 he travelled out by the route he had taken before via the Caspian and the long ride overland; but this time his sister Ella accompanied him and that intrepid lady was to become his hostess and housekeeper. Later he was seconded to try to establish a defined frontier through Baluchistan between Persia and Sindh.

He got married on home leave and his adventurous and long-suffering wife also travelled to remote parts of Asia on horseback with him (although she tended to be airbrushed out of his subsequent accounts to the Royal Geographical Society).[3] In 1905, after various periods in Kerman and brief military service in the Boer War in South Africa, he was to be promoted to be consul-general in the northeastern Persia city of Meshed. His involvement in the First World War was considerable, first in Britain and France, then in Kashgar (another Great Game centre) in Western China, and finally in 1916 raising the South Persia Rifles as a pro-British force in a part of the world that he probably knew better than any other Englishman. He attained the rank

---

3. He and his wife hired a Scottish nanny for their children who thought she was going to Perthshire, only to find when they embarked that they were bound for Persia instead.

of brigadier-general and a knighthood in the Order of the Indian Empire. He had earned every step of his promotion and recognition by courage, dogged hard work and unremitting self-promotion.

Sykes was indeed a Great Game hero but, as his contemporaries soon discovered, as Lord Curzon eventually concluded and as even his diffident and distinguished son-in-law Sir Patrick Reilly admitted, he was also 'a terrible bounder'.

# Epilogue: All Leave Cancelled

'Everlasting peace is a dream, and not even a pleasant one; and
war is a necessary part of God's arrangement of the world.'
– Helmuth von Moltke (1800–91), from a letter to J. K. Bluntschli

'Russia and England are natural enemies,' Valentine Baker had
been told by one of the Russian hostesses encountered on his
provocative travels. Indeed, so it seemed through most of the
nineteenth century (apart from a short alliance against Napoleon)
and the twentieth century (apart from short alliances against the
Kaiser and Hitler). The Great Game contest between the powers
– with its Central Asian playing fields for young officers pursuing
their euphemistic shooting leave – had perhaps reached its peak
in 1901 with the publication of Rudyard Kipling's *Kim* and with
the activist Lord Curzon established as viceroy of India.

A good barometer of the interest in the Russian threat,
and the northwest frontier in general, was the popular Edinburgh monthly review *Blackwood's Magazine*. Between 1901 and
1910 it carried regular articles and accounts of travels in the
region, many written by young officers, on such themes as 'The
Indian borderland', 'Across the Himalayas in mid-winter', 'Two
years in Afghanistan', 'A day in Chitral', 'Punjab frontier recol-
lections', 'Peshawar and the Khyber Pass' and the memoirs of

'A subaltern in Ladakh'. The list is endless, and the tone of the articles and reminiscences is uniformly imperialist and adventurous; it was no wonder that the youthful John Buchan – who doubtless saw himself in the direct line of descent from such earlier *Blackwood's* writers as Sir Walter Scott and Joseph Conrad – was a frequent contributor in these years.

However, the Game was to stutter to a close with the outbreak of the First World War and the consequent submersion of old rivalries in the face of more pressing danger from German military advances on the western and eastern fronts. Had it not been for the outbreak of war in 1914, there is no reason to think that the Great Game would have faded away. On the contrary, as we have seen the last Tsar – Nicholas II – had been encouraged by Przhevalsky and others to take an active interest in the pursuit of Russian expansion towards the frontiers of India. By the time of his abdication and subsequent murder by the Bolsheviks in 1918, he had already been on the throne for 24 years; his 'forward' ambitions were well established. Britain was not popular in the last years of tsarist Russia: our apparent tardiness in joining the Russian and French confrontation with the Kaiser's Germany caused protests and riots outside the British consulate-general in Moscow. The traditional enmity was slow to be set aside and – as it turned out – quick to revive.

However, the enmity did not revive in its old form in Central Asia. Here the British were preoccupied with containing the marauding activities of the ungovernable Afghan tribesman of the northwest frontier, and equally intent on suppressing what they viewed as premature independence movements within the frontiers of India itself. Meanwhile, the Russians were focused on ensuring that their relatively newly absorbed khanates and emirates were as integrated into the Soviet Union as they had been into tsarist Russia. The Russians wanted to ensure that they did not set themselves up as independent Islamic states or become launching pads for western or bourgeois reactionary intervention against the Bolshevik revolution.

In these circumstances it was ironic that the young British officer who was most closely involved in trying to assess the nature and durability of the Bolshevik regime, and who was to report on the circumstances that finally terminated the Great Game, was himself in many ways not at all dissimilar from the other young officers whose exploits have been recounted above.

Robert Bruce Lockhart was in his mid-twenties when posted as vice-consul to Moscow a few years before the outbreak of the First World War. He was a Scotsman like so many of the self-styled 'Englishmen' who explored the steppes and mountains of Central Asia and who negotiated with the local despots. When all normal diplomatic relations broke down after the Russian Revolution in 1917, he was sent back to Moscow as a personal emissary of David Lloyd George and Arthur Balfour (respectively prime minister and foreign secretary of the British wartime government) with a brief that was as vague as anything provided for James Abbott and as ambiguous as anything supplied to Charles Stewart. He was to find out what was going on, to assess the chances of the Bolsheviks surviving and to try to keep them involved in the ongoing war against Germany.

He did not purport to be on leave – and he would have personally preferred fishing leave to shooting leave – but he was certainly not employed in the hierarchy and structure of the diplomatic service any more than the young officers in the chapters above were employed within the normal military framework. He was an independent spirit serving his country in his own way rather than by any prescribed set of rules. As recounted in his

*Memoirs of a British Agent* (1932), the dangers he ran were as great as those of any of his military predecessors – he was imprisoned in the Lubianka and later in the Kremlin under threat of a death sentence. So it was that the most intimate witness to the end of the Great Game and the practice of shooting leave was an officer in the mould of the earlier practitioners of that peculiar mixture of duty and sport. The spirit of shooting leave – as opposed to the practice of it – had not died in 1914 with the Anglo-Russian alliance, nor in 1918 with the establishment of the Soviet Union.

Nor did the spirit evaporate as a result of the Anglo-Russian alliance of 1941 when Hitler invaded Russia; nor even in 1946 when the Iron Curtain came down across Europe and the Cold War began its 43 years of frigidity. The author's own experiences (referred to in the preface and footnotes of this book) confirmed that the adventures of politically minded young officers prepared to take risks for what they saw as a patriotic objective, which had been established in the nineteenth century, had not altogether expired by the later twentieth century.

Nor had the fascination of Central Asia, and Afghanistan in particular, evaporated for the British. The early years of the twenty-first century found us fighting there again, bravely and at times frustratingly, as so often in the past. Newsreels, novels and films about Kabul and Afghans filled television screens, bookstalls and cinemas. The charm of the Afghans, so mistakenly relied upon by 'Bokhara' Burnes and others, remains as sharply etched as ever, and is still perhaps best described by General John Nicholson (who had served there in the 1840s and was to be killed in the Indian Mutiny): 'the most experienced and astute of our political officers in Afghanistan were deceived by that winning and imposing frankness of manner which it has pleased Providence to give the Afghans, as it did to the first serpent'.

Those on shooting leave in the nineteenth century shot for sport almost every wild creature that moved across the mountain passes and steppes – but not serpents. Serpents are best not provoked.

# Select Bibliography

ABBOTT, James, *Narrative of a Journey from Herat to Khiva*, 2 vols (London 1843)

ALDER, G.J., *British India's Northern Frontier* (London 1963)

ALLEN, Charles, *Soldier Sahibs* (London 2000)

BAKER, Valentine, *Clouds in the East: Travels and Adventures on the Persian-Turkoman Frontier* (London 1876)

BIDDULPH, John, *The Tribes of the Hindu Kush* (Calcutta 1890)

BLACK, C.E.D., *Memoir of the Indian Surveys 1875–90* (London 1891)

*BLACKWOOD'S MAGAZINE* (Edinburgh 1901–10)

BONVALOT, Gabriel, *Through the Heart of Asia: Over the Pamirs to India*, 2 vols (London 1889)

BUCHAN, John, *The Half-Hearted* (London 1900)

BURNABY, Frederick, *A Ride to Khiva: Travels and Adventures in Central Asia* (London 1876)

BURNES, Alexander, *Travels into Bokhara*, 3 vols (London 1834); *Cabool – Being a Personal Narrative of a Journey To, and Residence In, That City in the Years 1836, 7 & 8* (London 1842)

CONOLLY, Lieutenant Arthur, *Journey to the North of India, Overland from England, Through Russia, Persia and Affghaunistaun* [sic], 2 vols (London 1834)

DUBROVIN, N.F. *N.M. Przheval'ski* (St Petersburg 1890)

EDWARDES, Major Herbert, *A Year on the Punjab Frontier, in 1848–9*, 2 vols (London 1851)

EDWARDES, Michael, *Playing the Great Game: A Victorian Cold War* (London 1975)

FRENCH, Patrick, *Francis Younghusband* (London 1994)

GRANT, Captain N.P., *Transactions of the Royal Geographical Society*, vol. 5

HOLDICH, T.H., *The Indian Borderland 1880–1900* (London 1901)

HOLMES, Richard, *Sahib: The British Soldier in India 1750–1914* (London 2005)

HOPKIRK, Peter, *The Great Game: On Secret Service in High Asia* (London 1990)

INDIA OFFICE RECORDS, Political and secret letters from India, vols 14, 18, 21, 23, 25, 26

JOHNSON, Robert, *Spying for Empire: The Great Game in Central and South Asia 1757–1947* (London 2006)

KAYE, Sir John, *Lives of Indian Officers* (London 1904)

KEAY, John, *When Men and Mountains Meet* (London 1977); *The Gilgit Game* (London 1979)

LOCKHART, R.H., *Memoirs of a British Agent* (London 1932)

LUNT, James, *Bokhara Burnes* (London 1969)

MACGREGOR, Colonel C.M., *Narrative of a Journey Through the Province of Khorassan and on the North-west Frontier of Afghanistan in 1875* (London 1879)

MACLEAN, Fitzroy, *Eastern Approaches* (London 1949); *A Person from England* (London 1956); *To Caucasus* (London 1976)

MARSH, Captain, *A Ride Through Islam: Being a Journey Through Persia and Afghanistan to India via Meshed, Herat and Candehar* (London 1877)

MARVIN, Charles, *Colonel Grodekoff's Ride from Samarkand to Herat, Through Balkh and the Uzbek States of Afghan Turkestan* (London

1880); *The Russian Advance Towards India: Conversations with Russian Statesmen and Generals on the Central Asian Question* (London 1882); *The Russians at Merv and Herat, and the Power of Invading India* (London 1883); *Reconnoitring Central Asia* (London 1884)

MASON, Philip, *The Men Who Ruled India* (London 1985)

MASSON, Charles, *Narrative of Various Journeys in Balochistan, Afghanistan and the Punjab, Including a Residence in those Countries*, 3 vols (London 1842); *Narrative of a Journey to Kalat* (London 1843)

MEYER, K.E. and BRYSAC, S.B., *Tournament of Shadows: The Great Game and the Race for Empire in Asia* (Washington 2001)

MORGAN, Gerald, *Ney Elias, Explorer and Envoy Extraordinary in High Asia* (London 1971)

POTTINGER, Lieutenant Henry, *Travels in Beloochistan and Sinde* (London 1816)

RAYFIELD, Donald, *The Dream of Lhasa* (London 1976)

STEWART, Charles, *Through Persia in Disguise* (London 1911)

SYKES, P.M., *Ten Thousand Miles in Persia* (London 1901)

SYKES, P.M. and SYKES, Ella, *Through Deserts and Oases of Central Asia* (London 1920)

VAMBERY, Arminius, *Travels in Central Asia* (London 1864)

VIBART, H.M., *Addiscombe and its Heroes and Men of War* (1894)

WHITTERIDGE, Sir Gordon, *Charles Masson of Afghanistan* (London 1986)

WINTERBOTTOM, Derek, *Henry Newbolt and the Spirit of Clifton* (Bristol 1986)

WOOD, Lieutenant John, *Journey to the Source of the Oxus* (London 1841)

WYNN, Antony, *Persia in the Great Game: Sir Percy Sykes, Explorer, Consul, Soldier, Spy* (London 2003)

YOUNGHUSBAND, Francis, *The Heart of a Continent* (London 1896); *Wonders of the Himalaya* (London 1924)